# ABOUT A BODY

The body can inform the work we do in mental health. This unique collection invites the reader to consider the way we think about the embodied mind, and how it can inform both our lives and our work in psychotherapy and counselling.

The body is viewed as integral to the mind in this book and in the approaches illustrated in it. Instead of splitting off the body and treating the patient as a body with a mind, contributors from a variety of approaches ask the reader to consider how we might be with, and work with, 'bodymind' as an interrelated whole. Subjects covered include:

- The application of affective neuroscience to life as well as to clinical issues.
- The body in psychotherapy with a person who is facing death
- The history, significance and scope of body psychotherapy today
- Psychoanalytic approaches to working with the embodied mind
- Authentic Movement groups in the development of wellbeing in our bodymindspirit
- The body and spirituality

This book is unique in its pluralism: it includes a wide range of differing views of the importance of the body in psychotherapy, both in theory and in practice, and it relates these to the latest discussions in affective neuroscience. It will be invaluable for those working in, or studying, psychotherapy and counselling, and will also interest those working generally in the mental health field.

**Jenny Corrigall** is a research psychologist and a psychoanalytic psychotherapist, working in Cambridge.

**Helen Payne** is Reader in Counselling and Psychotherapy at the University of Hertfordshire and a senior registered dance movement therapist. She is editor for the *International Journal for Body, Movement and Dance in Psychotherapy*.

**Heward Wilkinson** is co-founder of the Scarborough Psychotherapy Training Institute, until recently was Chair of the Humanistic and Integrative Section of the United Kingdom Council for Psychotherapy, and was editor of the *International Journal of Psychotherapy* 1996–2004.

**Contributors:** Gerda Boyesen, Roz Carroll, Claudia Herbert, Phil Mollon, Susie Orbach, Jaak Panksepp, Helen Payne, Joy Schaverien, Maura Sills, Michael Soth, Heward Wilkinson, Courtenay Young, Beverley Zabriskie.

# ABOUT A BODY

## Working with the embodied mind in psychotherapy

*Edited by Jenny Corrigall,
Helen Payne and Heward Wilkinson*

Routledge
Taylor & Francis Group

LONDON AND NEW YORK

First published 2006 by Routledge
27 Church Road, Hove, East Sussex, BN3 2FA

Simultaneously published in the USA and Canada
by Routledge
270 Madison Avenue, New York, NY 10016

*Routledge is an imprint of the Taylor and Francis Group, an informa business*

© 2006 selection and editorial matter, Jenny Corrigall, Helen Payne and
Heward Wilkinson; individual chapters, the contributors

Typeset in Times by Regent Typesetting, London
Printed and bound in Great Britain by TJ International Ltd, Padstow, Cornwall
Paperback cover design by Sandra Heath

*British Library Cataloguing in Publication Data*
A catalogue record for this book is available from the British Library

*Library of Congress Cataloging in Publication Data*
About a body : working with the embodied mind in psychotherapy / edited
by Jenny Corrigall, Helen Payne, and Heward Wilkinson.
    p. ; cm.
    Includes bibliographical references and index.
    ISBN-13: 978-0-415-40071-8 (hbk.)
    ISBN-10: 0-415-40071-6 (hbk.)
    ISBN-13: 978-0-415-40072-5 (pbk.)
    ISBN-10: 0-415-40072-4 (pbk.)
    1. Mind and body therapies. 2. Mind and body. 3. Psychotherapy.
I. Corrigall, Jenny. II. Payne, Helen, 1951- III. Wilkinson, Heward.
    [DNLM: 1. Psychotherapy--methods. 2. Mind-Body Relations
(Metaphysics)    WM 420 A156 2006]
    RC489.M53A255 2006
    616.89'14--dc22
                                                                            2006021362

ISBN13: 978-0-415-40071-8 (hbk)
ISBN13: 978-0-415-40072-5 (pbk)

ISBN10: 0-415-40071-6 (hbk)
ISBN10: 0-415-40072-4 (pbk)

# CONTENTS

CONTENTS

# ILLUSTRATIONS

**Figures**

**Tables**

# NOTES ON CONTRIBUTORS

**Gerda Boyesen,** who died on 29 December 2005, was the founder of biodynamic psychotherapy, which incorporates many of the ideas of Reich and Freud and works with the libidinous energy of the body. She trained originally as a clinical psychologist, a Reichian psychotherapist and a physiotherapist. Through the observation of her clients she developed a connection between the body and the psyche. Many strands of contemporary body psychotherapy have been influenced by her work.

**Roz Carroll** is a body psychotherapist, a trainer at the Chiron Centre for Body Psychotherapy and at the Minster Centre, and a lecturer and author on the implications of neuroscience for psychotherapy. Her publications can be accessed on her website www.thinkbody.co.uk

**Jenny Corrigall** trained with the Cambridge Society for Psychotherapy as a psychoanalytic psychotherapist and works in Cambridge. She helps to organize professional conferences for the UK Council for Psychotherapy and has co-edited a book from a previous conference *Revolutionary Connections: Psychotherapy and Neuroscience* (Karnac 2003).

**Claudia Herbert** is the founder director of the Oxford Development Centre, which incorporates Psychology for Business, Oxfordshire's Independent Psychology Service, the Oxford Stress and Trauma Centre and Blue Stallion Publications. She is a specialist in the field of post-trauma reactions, for both single and complex client problems

**Phil Mollon** is a psychoanalyst within the Independent Group of the British Psychoanalytical Society. He has written a number of books in the areas of trauma, shame and self psychology, including *EMDR and the Energy Therapies: Psychoanalytic Perspectives* (Karnac 2004). He works in the National Health Service (NHS) at the Lister Hospital in Stevenage.

**Susie Orbach** co-founded the Women's Therapy Centre (WTC) in London in 1976 and the WTC in New York in 1981. A visiting professor at London School of Economics, convenor of the relational psychoanalysis grouping in London, a co-founder of Psychotherapists and Counsellors for Social Responsibility, of ANTIDOTE and ANYBody, she has written widely both in her column in the *Guardian* and in books and technical papers on psychoanalysis, women's psychological development, the process of therapy, politics and therapy, and eating problems. She has a long-standing interest in the body, has been studying body countertransferences since the mid 1980s and is theorizing our almost infinite capacity to transform our bodies.

**Jaak Panksepp** is Professor at Washington State University, and was until recently Distinguished Research Professor of Psychobiology, Emeritus, at Bowling Green State University, Ohio; Adjunct Professor of Psychiatry at the Medical College of Ohio at Toledo; and Head of Affective Neuroscience Research, Falk Center for Molecular Therapeutics, Northwestern University. He is the author of *Affective Neuroscience: The Foundations of Human and Animal Emotions* (1998) and editor of *Textbook of Biological Psychiatry* (2004).

**Helen Payne** is a senior registered dance movement psychotherapist and Fellow of ADMT.UK, a UKCP accredited psychotherapist and researcher. Trained in Authentic Movement, Laban dance, person centred counselling and group analysis, her publications include *Creative Movement and Dance in Groupwork*, (1990) *Handbook of Inquiry in the Arts Therapies* (1993), *Dance Movement Therapy: Theory, Research and Practice* (1992) and *Body, Movement and Dance in Psychotherapy* (a Taylor and Francis journal).

**Joy Schaverien** is a professional member of the Society of Analytical Psychology and a Training Analyst and Supervisor for the British Association of Psychotherapists. She is Visiting Professor in Art Psychotherapy at the University of Sheffield. She teaches regularly at the C.G. Jung Institute of Copenhagen and was co-coordinator of the International Association for Analytical Psychology (IAAP) Supervision programme in Moscow

**Maura Sills** is the co-founder of the Karuna institute. The institute offers training in core process psychotherapy, which has its origins in Buddhist philosophy, psychology practice, and ethics. This is supported by Western developmental psychology.

**Michael Soth** is a psychotherapist, trainer and supervisor, who has been working as training director at the Chiron Centre for Body Psychotherapy (www.chiron. org) since 1990. As Chiron will now be concentrating on advanced training for counsellors and psychotherapists rather than professional training, he has recently helped found the Centre for Integral-Relational Learning (www.cirl. co.uk), which will continue the development of body psychotherapy as well as group facilitation.

**Heward Wilkinson** is an integrative psychotherapist, chair of the UKCP Humanistic and Integrative Psychotherapy Section (till 2005) and senior editor of the *International Journal of Psychotherapy*, EAP Journal (1996–2004), author of many papers on the philosophical aspects of psychotherapy, pluralism in psychotherapy, and the integration of psychoanalysis and existential approaches. He is chair of the UKCP Professional Conference Committee.

**Courtenay Young,** an accredited humanistic, transpersonal and body-oriented psychotherapist, is currently president of the European Association for Body-Psychotherapy and was a founder member of the US Association for Body Psychotherapy. He is a board member of the European Association for Psychotherapy (EAP), and compiles the EABP *Bibliography of Body-Psychotherapy* (on CD-ROM). He works as a psychotherapist and NHS counsellor in Edinburgh, Scotland.

**Beverley Zabriskie** is a Jungian analyst in private practice in New York City, where she is a founder and faculty member of the Jungian Psychology Association. She is on the editorial board of the *Journal of Analytical Psychology* and was programme chair of the Sixteenth International Association for Analytical Psychology Congress of 2004 in Barcelona. Publications include 'A meeting of rare minds' (the preface to *Atom and Archetype: the Pauli–Jung Correspondence*, 2001 and 'Transference and dream in illness: waxing psyche, waning body', *Journal of Analytical Psychology*, 45 (2000). She is a past president of the National Association for the Advancement of Psychoanalysis.

# FOREWORD

The United Kingdom Council for Psychotherapy (UKCP) as an umbrella body for psychotherapy organizations in the United Kingdom has, throughout its history, continued to represent and encourage diversity of approaches.

The body of UKCP is made up of more than eighty member organizations, all of whom are committed to representing and supporting their own particular modality base. Within this we see the coming together of these organizations into section groupings that continue to represent modalities at a wider systemic level.

The UKCP's Professional Conference (2004) demonstrated this appreciation and respect for diversity with its intriguing title 'About a Body'.

The intimate and, for some, inseparable links between the Mind and Body were apparent throughout the conference, now represented in this volume, bringing together and debating conceptual frameworks in a healthy and enlivened way.

Sincere acknowledgements are due to the contributors in this book, to the speakers at the conference and to Jenny Corrigall, Helen Payne and Heward Wilkinson, along with members of the Professional Conference Committee, for all their hard work in bringing together this Body of work.

Lisa Wake
Chair of the United Kingdom Council for Psychotherapy
December 2005.

# ACKNOWLEDGEMENTS

Chapter 2: Figure 2.1 is from Panksepp, J. (1998) *Affective Neuroscience: The Foundations of Human and Animal Emotions*, and is reproduced with permission from Oxford University Press.

Chapter 3: Figure 3.1 is from Panksepp, J. (1998) *Affective Neuroscience: The Foundations of Human and Animal Emotions*, and is reproduced with permission from Oxford University Press.

Chapter 8: 'One hundred and fifty years on: the history, significance and scope of body psychotherapy today' by Courtenay Young, first published in the *International Journal of Body, Movement and Dance in Psychotherapy* 1(1) (2006), is reprinted with permission.

Chapter 14: 'When psyche meets soma: the question of incarnation' by Beverley Zabriskie, first published in the *International Journal of Body, Movement and Dance in Psychotherapy* 1(1) (2006), is reprinted with permission.

# 1

# TOUCHING EACH OTHER
# YET BEING OTHER

*Heward Wilkinson*

## 'In this body, a fathom long . . .'

There is a famous teaching of the Buddha, quoted in the title of her contribution by Maura Sills (Chapter 13):

> In this body, a fathom long, with its thoughts and emotions, I declare are the world, the origins of the world, the cessation of the world and the path leading to the cessation of the world.
>
> (Anguttara Nikaya, IV, 45)

This sentence encapsulates some of both the richness, and the dilemmas, of the issues around the body which we explored in the conference 'About a Body' and which are reflected in this book.

This body, of which the Buddha is speaking and which he says encompasses everything pertaining to our life and to our salvation or liberation, is the experienced body, the phenomenal body, the phenomenological body. Some would say there is no other body. They would say that the physical world itself is analysable in terms simply of actual and possible experience (Berkeley 1710; Ayer 1940).

But not the realist materialists (Dennett 1991). For the materialists the experienced body either is identical with, or is causally completely dependent upon, the physical body – that body whose remains poignantly persist after our experiencing self has died.

These initial formulations of mine are oversimplified, but indicate in a preliminary way some of the creative tensions this book carries within it. For instance, some of the contributors at any rate *start* from a Darwinian materialist position. This is true of Jaak Panksepp in his chapters, even though he subscribes to what he calls 'double aspect monism', and is clear that 'science has no mind-scope' (which unequivocally implicates the phenomenal aspect). These contributors will differ substantially in their metaphysical emphasis from those who *start* from a substantially, or primarily, spirit-centred position (such as most of those from humanistic, transpersonal, Jungian, and body psychotherapy based positions). On the face of it, the former would be fairly chary of such claims as Maura Sills makes about Emoto Masaru's work, that he has demonstrated that 'water that has been exposed to different kinds of thoughts and emotions will form different types of crystalline structures when it is frozen' (p. 199).

Most of the contributors from humanistic, transpersonal, Jungian and body psychotherapy based positions would likewise be sympathetic to, or endorse, talk about 'subtle energy', and would balance Western with Eastern medicine approaches. They in their turn would be wary of such remarks of Panksepp's, with its ostensible reductionism, as:

> A guiding premise of the affective neuroscience approach is that various emotional feelings and other affective states reflect primitive states of consciousness that emerge substantially from the neurodynamics of brain circuits that control instinctual emotional behaviours in animal brains.
>
> (p. 14)

Some of our contributors actively pursue dialogue over such controversies, in an academic way; others creatively present their positions; the book as a whole, in its overall pluralistic implication, balances these differing viewpoints on theory and practice. This introductory chapter will seek to fluidly reflect the variety within the contributions, evoking the issues which arise without too slavish an attempt merely to summarize, though it is hoped the central ideas will be touched on clearly enough.

Several of the dichotomies explored, explicitly or implicitly, here include: mind/brain; mind/body; brain/body; emotion/cognition; reptilian/mammalian; monist/dualist; materialist/non-materialist; non-verbal/verbal; body contact in the work/non-body contact based work; environment/genetics. And we could – provocatively – add, even: 'hard science' versus 'alternative science'. Again, I have not yet so much as mentioned 'psychoanalysis / non-psychoanalysis', which was a major tension – but also, to our delight, point of dialogue – of the conference and this book, especially, but not only, in the dialogue between Roz Carroll and Susie Orbach (Chapter 5). In the light of *that* tension, we might express the 'hard science' versus 'alternative science' dilemma as the question put in terms of psychoanalytic assumptions: is countertransference a form of symbolic inference from subtle sensory data present and past, or is it a form of telepathy? Daniel Stern's recent work (Stern 2004), in my view, shows very significant movement in this respect (Wilkinson 2003).

But it is a much richer, more complex, and paradoxical tapestry than this list of dichotomies suggests. The dichotomies, perhaps, frame the unfolding but it transcends them, not in any neat, but in a subtle way. This will emerge more fully as we consider the various specific contributions.

In my overview of the themes of this book, I see the chapters as falling into three groupings: first, those concentrating on affective neuroscience and psychotherapy

(Panksepp, Chapters 2 and 3; Carroll, Chapter 4); second, those primarily concerned with dialogues in relation to psychoanalysis and the body, and the integration of different theories and practice (Orbach and Carroll, Chapter 5; Young, Chapter 6; Mollon, Chapter 7; Soth, Chapter 8; Herbert, Chapter 10); and third, those focusing on the body and spirituality (Boyesen, Chapter 9; Payne, Chapter 11; Schaverien, Chapter 12; Sills, Chapter 13; Zabriskie, Chapter 14). I will follow these groupings in my reflections on the variety and the pluralism of the contributions to this book.

## Back to Freudian primary process via affective neuroscience

This heading is a somewhat impish paraphrase of Jaak Panksepp's position, but it brings out something important about it all the same. He is one of our central contributors, the one who provides the major affective neuroscience underpinning of the book, as already implied, and in his chapters a deeply anti-reductivist trend surprisingly emerges, against the background of his Darwinian starting point.

Panksepp, in line with Damasio (1994), Solms and Turnbull (2002) and others, sets out to offset the undue emphasis on cybernetic models rooted in cognition, linked to behaviour, appealing to feeling instead. Instead, Panksepp appeals to the core early affective neuro-systems which humans share with all mammals:

> The possibility that two very different processes, such as emotional actions and emotional feelings, arise from substantially the same brain mechanisms is a critical aspect of the *dual-aspect monism* strategy that has guided my own strategy for four decades. According to such a view, a close study of the neural substrates of instinctual emotional behaviours of other animals may reveal the neural principles that generate raw emotional feelings in humans.
>
> (pp. 14–15)

On the face of it this expresses the reductive strategy already touched on. But we note that, like Damasio (1994, 1999), Panksepp alludes to Spinoza (1663), and Spinoza is of course the paradigmatic exponent of *dual-aspect monism*. So, if we turn to the experiential, as opposed to the behavioural, dimension of this monism, or to both together, what do we get? If we turn to both together, we get a conception of emotion as inseparably enmeshed with bodily expression, as articulated for instance by William James (1890), but as also taken as bedrock by body psychotherapy. And if we turn primarily to the experiential dimension of this, we get the anti-Cartesian emphasis, very strong in Panksepp (which leads him to a concerned wrestling with the ethical dilemmas of, and the necessary ethical codes governing, animal research into affective neuroscience), that *animals are every bit as profoundly experiencing subjects, sentient centres, as are humans.*

This leads Panksepp to a conception of the relation of the animal in us to the cognitively and culturally developed human in us, which is profoundly Freudian,

3

and from which, like Freud, he derives our proneness to psychological disorder – and the means of its resolution. As a result he roots it in a modelling of this primal mammalian emotional dimension for which he actually uses the Freudian language of 'primary process'. He quotes (p. 15) Robert Burns' touching poem about his overturning the nest of a field mouse, which includes the words:

> Still thou art blest, compar'd wi' me!
> The present only toucheth thee.
> *(To a Mouse,* 1785)

And goes on, with Freudian sombreness and gravitas:

> Because of our vast ability to look far back in memory and to imagine dreadful future problems, we humans are prone to sustain internally generated emotional arousal and disturbances much more than other animals. Through *primary-process,* affectively driven intrapsychic processes – the attributions, judgements, beliefs and construals, driven by the primal emotional 'energies' of anxiety, desire, and grief – humans commonly sustain affective arousal long after the precipitating circumstances have passed.
>
> (p. 16, my italics)

Susie Orbach later (Chapter 5) expresses reservations about a caricature version of this model, in which the body enacts what is denied or repressed by the mind, a caricature she finds both in much psychoanalysis and in much body psychotherapy, but it is clear that this *is* a caricature of a complex double relationship which Panksepp, like Freud, is here invoking.

But what we could easily miss is that, suddenly, as in the Freud of *Interpretation of Dreams* (1900), here we have a profoundly phenomenological conception of human and mammalian primary experiencing, as absolutely non-reducible, and as constituting the field and the background of human existence, which suddenly gives human embodied experience the anti-reductive authority which, for instance, a Martin Buber (1923) – or the Buddha – accord to it. And it is one which leads on to a positively Jungian conception of the archetypal dimension of human experience – one which comes out in Panksepp's postulate of a primal feeling base which is objectless, or rather only *indeterminately* object-tending, which leaves room for the Jungian conception (not a million miles away from Freud's (1905) concept of 'drive' of archetypes as *potentials* for shaping the patterns of experience in interaction with the environment. This subtle conception comes out in such sentences as the following:

> The image that may be most correct is that large-scale emotional-affective attractor landscapes, that are intrinsically (non-reflectively) intentional, pull in relevant cognitive relationships the way strong weather systems embrace and change the landscape, often in a lasting way.
>
> (p. 20)

4

And this is also reminiscent of the 'It', as Groddeck (1977) rather than Freud envisaged it, as a global indeterminate totality of tendencies which encompasses the whole of the self.

Here we suddenly see why there has sprung up the profound, if ambiguous, present day alliance that there is, between affective neuroscience research, and the work, informed by a strong sense of spirituality, of the body psychotherapists, as well as those whose bases are in psychoanalysis, or Jungian analytical psychology.

Panksepp proceeds to map these potentials in detail in seven basic systems he has identified so far, those that mediate Seeking, Fear, Rage, Lust, Care, Panic and Playfulness.

In Chapter 3, he brings out some of the subtle implications of his conception, in two instances. On the one hand he indicates the possibility that the social threshold of autistic children may be significantly increased by the use of opioid antagonists, since excessive opioid blocks the social Seeking system in them. And, on the other, he argues strongly against the use of psycho-stimulants, such as Ritalin, with Attention Deficit Hyperactivity Disorder (ADHD) diagnosed children, on the grounds that they inhibit the impulse to rough-and-tumble play, which is the profoundest need of many of these children. Here his model strongly supports psychotherapeutic commonsense.

Roz Carroll, in Chapter 4, offers us the more detailed application of that model for psychotherapy. She succinctly puts the complexity of Panksepp's position – and its implication for psychotherapy – as follows:

> A surge of oxytocin (such as accompanies orgasm and breastfeeding) is correlated with deep feelings of contentment and love. But it still depends on the actual social environment to make it relevant – putting oxytocin directly into rat brains doesn't make them happier unless there are other rats to play with.
>
> (p. 56)

She gives a mass of detail, in terms of Panksepp's seven systems, of the interrelations of therapeutic work in the light of his work, which it would be redundant to attempt to summarize, and also makes the connections with others working at the same interface, such as the work of Schore (1994) and Trevarthen and Aitken (2001).

Carroll's contribution is a graphic demonstration, at the very least, of the power and life of the use of the neuro-affective *metaphor* in conjunction with other therapeutic metaphors. This is a wonderful demonstration of psychotherapy's omnivorous power of assimilation of the multiplicity of belief frameworks and metaphors to its creative purposes.

5

## The body in therapy and the body in analysis

In Chapter 5, Carroll is the first contributor to the dialogue which continues in the book from this point onwards. The actual dialogue in this chapter has been left in its living form, as it occurred, including the winding up question and answer with the audience, as it is such a graphic demonstration of the subtlety of the dialogue process concerning all these issues. As with Lacan's *Seminar* (1966), some of the background which gives significance to the words of these live discussions is difficult to elicit, from the struggle to put into words, which is going on in these live interchanges. Yet this actually adds to the sense of delicate dialogue which is communicated here.

What a fascinating reversal is glimpsed in this interaction – one which continued to be characteristic of the contributions by the psychoanalytically oriented and the body psychotherapists at the conference, and now in this book. It is not quite that the body psychotherapist emerges as psychoanalytic and that the psychoanalyst emerges as body oriented – but it is not very far from that. Carroll begins with a mapping of the four major elements of her approach: first, basic relatedness; second, the use of self, countertransference; third, interventions to highlight the client's awareness of sensory elements; and fourth, the use of specialized body work skills.

Despite the fact that this work, as Carroll presents it, is more dialogical, and more active in using the therapeutic space, than most psychoanalytic psychotherapists would commonly countenance (though relational psychoanalysis is moving strongly in this direction), yet in terms of process and pattern, psychoanalytic psychotherapists would recognize virtually all of this – and Orbach of course does.

As we have seen already, Orbach, in effect, proceeds to challenge body psychotherapy as being *too psychoanalytic*, as using the body as the repository of repressed material which the mind has disowned. In line with the indeterminacy of primal affective tendencies Panksepp envisages, Orbach, in a way reminiscent of Lacan, treats the body as *constructed* – not as a given, but as co-created in conjunction with the total culture and the environment. This, once again, is reminiscent of Groddeck's (1977) wider concept of the 'It' and also of Loewald's (1980) relational model of the drives discussed in Mitchell (2000). This conception of the body is emergent from, and in holistic interaction with, the whole self, not merely the mind. She encapsulates this as follows:

> If I can encapsulate my position very quickly, I would say that the body is not so much the truth but it's a relational outcome of the intersubjective field of the carer and the baby just as much as the mind is. Winnicott frequently tells us that 'there is no such thing as the baby. Whenever you see a baby you see a mother and baby pair'. . . . I would like to extend this idea to say *there is no such thing as a body. Whenever you see a body, you see a body that has been internalized in the context of a relationship with another body.*
>
> (pp. 68–9, my emphasis)

6

She then illustrates this, profoundly and dialectically, in terms of two very vivid and poignant examples, of the kind of unexpected creative experiences in the embodied countertransference, which make the more cautious reach for extended senses of 'projective identification', and which tempts the bolder to talk of telepathy, psycho-physical fields, or the psychoid. In relation to such material Carroll uses the terminology of countertransference as a perception 'of the other': 'It is fundamentally a powerful perception of the other that then is elaborated and developed'(pp. 74–5).

In the discussion, both Orbach and Carroll wrestle with normative issues in terms of a reformulation of Winnicott (1958) in terms of what Orbach calls an adaptive self (responsive to impingements) and an undeveloped (and potentially spontaneous) self. The final interchanges convey a graphic sense of the mixture of profound agreement, and the sense, variously expressed, of starting from different points and then converging. Something very deep and mysterious was expressed as an interchange in this dialogue, and it remains alive in these pages.

## The split between psychoanalysis and body psychotherapy

In a way, Courtenay Young (Chapter 6) next presents the other side of the coin. He retells the story, also told in the late 1990s by both David Boadella (1997) and Nick Totton (1998), of the marginalization of the body within psychoanalysis. This is a story which has been exaggerated and oversimplified on both sides (Wilkinson 2000), but which is true, and painfully true enough to warrant not being forgotten (the fate, and the use made, of Wilhelm Reich, in particular, is gruesome indeed). The importance of Pierre Janet in the history of body psychotherapy is re-emphasized again. Young indicates the convergence in recent times, mentioning in particular the conference, from which this book came, as a watershed. He places the whole split in the context of that wider split within the whole of Western culture which is postulated by many within the humanistic movement (with a small 'h'), and which is indexed often (perhaps simplistically, see Wilkinson 2000) by the name of Descartes.

## Recent non-verbal therapies for trauma

In the context of all these complex dialogues and differences, the role of Eye Movement Desensitization and Reprocessing; (EMDR, Shapiro 2001) and approaches, such as Emotional Freedom Techniques, derived from Thought Field Therapy as developed by Roger Callahan (2001), offer something refreshingly simple and undialectical, by contrast.

Phil Mollon (Chapter 7), coming from his psychoanalyst's background, is able to recommend these approaches, which may otherwise gain (like Neurolinguistic Programming for instance, in some unguarded contexts) the reputation of overslick attempts at short-cutting. Mollon, however, writes with an undogmatic authority, which neither rejects these approaches, nor treats them as panaceas which will wholly replace longer-term narrative and relationally based types of work. In so doing, he refreshingly restores to psychoanalysis some of the vigour and freedom it had in the days of its youth and of the younger Freud (1900). He also gives many examples of pragmatic forms of interweaving of psychoanalytic approaches with the free and comfortable use of these forms of intervention. He combines these with down to earth suggestions about how these interventions may interweave with neuro-affective, neurobiological processes, such as Rapid Eye Movement (REM) sleep in connection with dreaming, and alpha rhythms, relating these to Eastern 'mindfulness' strategies, and so on. Many of the strategies have elements akin to cognitive therapy. He explores all these with a comfortable fluency and freedom which makes him a pleasure to read. He remarks, perhaps over self-deprecatingly (from the point of view of those of us who are not purists about what constitutes psychoanalysis): 'Obviously, the work is not psychoanalysis – but I doubt that I could do it if I were not a psychoanalyst' (p. 109).

Such strategies will become ever more pervasive in the coming years: they are a *different* dimension of body work, whose relation to other dimensions, such as those explored by Roz Carroll, is a most interesting challenge.

## Does the split in the work reflect the split in theory?

In Chapter 8, Michael Soth describes the context of an account of a therapeutic relationship which was for a long time a failure, because of a therapeutic agenda which re-enacted in the countertransference the very split which was the client's predicament. In so doing, Soth pursues a narrative as a kind of parable. The parable he is telling is that of convergence – convergence of the whole multiplicity of aspects of the self, in the context of the relational experience of re-enactment. Thus he pursues, through a psychoanalytic relational strategy, a trans-psychoanalytic conception of integration. Is it psychoanalytic? Yes. Is it integrative? Yes. Are these in conflict? Soth does not think so, but it is the question which, once again, this contribution leaves us to contemplate. Does it envisage a convergence which is beyond conceptualization, or at any rate requires multiple conceptualization? Again, this is what Soth believes. It is the question we can rest with as we engage with this rich and subtle contribution.

## Transcending single approaches in trauma treatment

In Chapter 10, Claudia Herbert illustrates the convergent and multi-approach to all this from yet another route; perhaps most predominantly her point of departure is from cognitive approaches, but she widens it out dramatically in a way which connects with the recognitions we have already been following.

Herbert holds that in order to address the complex nature of trauma, a complex integrated approach is likewise necessary; and the integration she offers is one which is by now readily intelligible to us from the affective neuro-science perspective offered, for instance, by Panksepp:

8

for clients to function as an integrated whole they need to be able to feel and experience a balanced flow of communication between all three systems of the brain, namely the cognitive, rational (involving neocortical brain functioning), the emotional (limbic system) and the bodily, sensory (reptilian brain) systems.

(p. 152)

As with Phil Mollon, she is able to envisage a very free integration of many approaches, body based or verbally based, which would belong within that framework.

## An approach brought to life

Poignantly, with the death on 29 December 2005 of Gerda Boyesen, our publishing of Chapter 9, derived from her presentation at the conference, takes on a valedictory character. Her talk has been skilfully supplemented and elucidated by Clover South-well, and is a presentation which has a delicious personal spontaneity, congruent with the vision of body psychotherapy she developed, yet is grounded also in remarkable insight and search for balance; as such it becomes the more poignant.

Her chapter conveys, in the most spontaneous way, the emergence of the teaching of a master. This is an oral teaching and not an academic exposition, yet if one tracks Boyesen's story carefully, in its deceptively simple anecdotes, one gains a strong sense of how subtle and many-layered her conceptions are. This is the heart of psychotherapy and is a fine tribute to Gerda's recent passing.

Perhaps we can illustrate with her story, so easy to miss or leave unappreciated, of 'the Aunt Lilian effect' (which all of us who have ended up listening to strangers' stories on trains, long before we became psychotherapists, will recognize):

> Aunt Lilian was in my husband's family. I did not know her well, but often met her at the many big family parties. Once Aunt Lilian said to me, 'Gerda, I do not understand why everyone tells me their life stories, when I only want to say "How are you?"'
>
> I did not understand it either, but some hours later I realized I had suddenly told her my life story! I had told her, 'I have to divorce my husband, I cannot live with him'. I hadn't told this to anyone, nobody else, and she was my husband's aunt! So, what was happening? Well, when she meant just to say 'How are you, Gerda?' she said, 'Ge-e-erda, how ARE you?' And as I answered, it all poured out!

(p. 134)

How much there is in that story. Unobtrusively, body suddenly becomes spirit, in this dimension of her work. And we all understand it. Yet here it is untheorized – here is another question for us to ponder.

## Dancing spirit into embodied pattern

Helen Payne gives an account of Authentic Movement work (in Chapter 11) as a form of dancing spirit into embodied pattern. This is not specifically a form of dance movement therapy (though it can be an aspect of it) and my heading is simply a metaphor. But this heading expresses and indicates the way in which a flow, revealing a spiritual or human meaning, is expressed in spontaneous movement. Authentic Movement is a form of enacted free association in a group, in front of specific witnesses who remain in stillness, and who express their spontaneous responses in words as witness at request. So it is a kind of *joint* active free association.

> The witness endeavours to be present in the mover's movement and, while attending to her own thoughts, sensations, feelings, images and impulses, to allow these to be influenced by what she sees in the presence of the mover. She is in a state of being rather than doing although still active in tracking her inner attitude. This inner embodied tracking is similar to the phenomenon of the therapist's countertransference found in psychodynamic psychotherapy. The inner tracking, akin to mindfulness, is a state of acceptance . . .
>
> (p. 166)

> AM is a completely self-directed approach in which participants may discover a movement pathway that offers a bridge between the conscious and the unconscious and between the group, the individual and the universal. It can be called the movement form of 'active imagination.
>
> (p. 174)

Thus, it does indeed dance spirit into embodied pattern.

Authentic Movement was developed by Mary Starkes Whitehouse (1958), who was a dancer, teacher, early movement therapist, had a Jungian analysis and studied at the Jung Institute, Zurich. Her papers explore the role and experience of spontaneous and creative movement. Payne's development of this approach offers further integration with significant elements of the humanistic and transpersonal traditions, especially developing elements of communal witness.

It has, to my eyes, striking affinities with the theory of psychodrama. I am thinking of Moreno's (1937: 213) concept of 'tele', as that which is manifest in the affinities which emerge in psychodrama groups. In the light of this, it is not surprising that transpersonal, archetypal and Shamanic elements readily emerge in the field which is evoked in such work as envisaged within this approach.

Thus, this is one of the approaches which is, implicitly, and at points explicitly, at the psycho-spiritual end of the spectrum whose range is indicated in this book. No other approach in the book so fully evokes the power of movement as a means of archetypal expression within the public imaginal realm.

## Embodied countertransference without touch

Joy Schaverien, in Chapter 12, puts most acutely and vividly a point which other contributors make, but which in her hands takes on, poignantly, a paradoxical edge which explodes many of the antitheses which we have touched upon and which beset this field. She puts it as follows:

> There may be extreme pressure to collapse the boundaries with regard to physical and external contact. It will be argued that the most profound form of touch may emerge only when physical contact and meetings outside therapy are resisted. It is this abstinence that paradoxically facilitates the individuation process to the end of life.
>
> (p. 180)

Once we grasp that we do touch each other where there is no physical contact, then the 'body psychotherapy' versus 'verbal psychotherapy' antithesis is transformed. Of course, this abstention does not need to be expounded as a dogma; all we need for this recognition is the *possibility* of body psychotherapy which is conducted without physical contact.

In fact, in this light, we are *all* body psychotherapists. For example, when Schaverien describes herself as moved to tears by the client whose work she is narrating in this contribution, we consider this as a form of visual touching. The metaphor of being 'touched' by someone becomes more than a metaphor; it becomes a form of energetic and affective contact and communion. Communion, after all, means 'one together'. In this case story a profound evolution of communion and of touch and meeting is being evoked. Once more many common antitheses (between transference and real relationship, for instance) crumble in the face of this exposition.

## The subtle dimension

In Chapter 13, Maura Sills effortlessly integrates the insights of body psychotherapy with the understandings derived from Buddhism, especially, and from other spiritual traditions. Or rather, she points out in depth that Buddhism has *already* integrated them: 'In Buddhism, the mind is more like a field that includes the entire body. Furthermore, it expands, flows and interpenetrates the mindbodies of others' (p. 200).

In this contribution, Sills draws in depth from Eugene Gendlin's work and alternative scientific investigators such as Mosaru Emoto and Ruppert Sheldrake. This is an important element of the tapestry in this book, since it is the most thoroughgoing of all of the contributions in its integration of the spiritual into the human whole.

Buddhism appears as the 'state of the art', the most complete and comprehensive phenomenological approach available, in which everything available in other traditions can be assimilated.

> A body is the holding field of a variety of processes – mental, psychological, physiological, emotional and spiritual. These processes can be accessed through awareness. It is the inner practices of awareness that in and of themselves can open the possibility for an unfolding process of transformation to take place.
>
> (p. 209)

## Body as narrated

In Chapter 14, Beverley Zabriskie, appropriately, ends our story by telling story and envisaging body archetypally as story, which links with themes we have seen in the contributions of both Panksepp and Orbach. She appeals to Jung's bridging concept of the psychoid, but her profoundest impulse is to express this in the story which lies behind that of Oedipus – that of the Sphinx (obliquely this is another delicate visiting of the Freud/Jung argument of course).

> In the imaginal language and metaphor of embodied mind, we are summoning the Sphinx.
>
> (p. 213)

> From archaic ritual to the most current neurosciences, the lifespan of the body has occupied the human mind.
>
> (p. 214)

The narrated body links to the completeness of the body's role envisaged in the teaching from the Buddha with which we began.

The book ends with Zabriskie's profound summary, which set a seal on this deep and richly tapestried conference:

> Our bodies link us to all other sentient beings in our own time and era, and to all who have ever been embodied. They provide us with the vehicle through which the psyche expresses itself as we crawl, walk, and limp through the many phases of our incarnated lives, and give voice to the experience of being human.
>
> (p. 221).

## References

Anguttara Nikaya, IV, 45, Rohitassa Sutta, Pali Canon, trans. 1975, Kandy, Sri Lanka: Buddhist Publication Society.

Ayer, A.J. (1940) *The Foundations of Empirical Knowledge*, London: Macmillan.

Berkeley, G. (1710) *Treatise Concerning the Principles of Human Knowledge*, reprinted 1998, Oxford: Oxford University Press.

Boadella, D. (1997) 'Awakening sensibility, recovering motility: psycho-physical synthesis at the foundations of body-psychotherapy: the 100-year legacy of Pierre Janet (1859–1947), *International Journal of Psychotherapy* 2(1): 45–57.

Buber, M. (1923 / 1970) *I and Thou*, Edinburgh: Clark.

Callahan, R.J. (2001) *Tapping the Healer Within*, New York: Contemporary Books.

Damasio, A. (1994) *Descartes' Error: Emotion, Reason, and the Human Brain*, London: Putnam.

——(1999) *The Feeling of What Happens: Body, Emotion and the Making of Consciousness*, London: Heinemann.

Dennett, D. (1991) *Consciousness Explained*, Boston, MA: Little, Brown.

Freud, S. (1900) *Interpretation of Dreams, Standard Edition*, ed. J. Strachey, Vol. 5, London: Hogarth Press.

——(1905) *Three Essays on the Theory of Sexuality, Standard Edition*, ed. J. Strachey, Vol. 7, London: Hogarth Press.

Groddeck, G. (1977) *The Meaning of Illness: Selected Psychoanalytic Writings*, London: Hogarth Press.

James, W. (1890) *The Principles of Psychology*, New York: Henry Holt.

Lacan, J. (1966) *The Four Fundamental Concepts of Psychoanalysis: The Seminar of Jacques Lacan Book XI* (ed.) J. Miller, trans. H. Sheridan, New York and London: Norton.

Loewald, H.W. (1980) *Papers on Psychoanalysis*, New Haven, CT: Yale University Press.

Mitchell, J. (2000) *Mad Men and Medusas: Reclaiming Hysteria and the Effects of Sibling Relations on the Human Condition*, London: Allen Lane and Penguin.

Moreno, J.L. (1937) 'Sociometry in relation to other social sciences', *Sociometry* 1: 206–19.

Schore, A.N. (1994) *Affect Regulation and the Origin of the Self*, Hove: Lawrence Erlbaum.

Shapiro, F. (2001) *Eye Movement Desensitization and Reprocessing*, 2nd edition, New York: Guilford Press.

Solms, M. and Turnbull, O. (2002) *The Brain and the Inner World: An Introduction to the Neuroscience of Subjective Experience*, New York: Other Books.

Spinoza, B. de (1663) *Principles of Cartesian Philosophy*, reprinted in *Complete Works* trans. S. Shirley, New York: Hackett.

Stern, D. (2004) *The Present Moment: In Psychotherapy and Everyday Life*, New York: Norton.

Totton, N. (1998) *The Water in the Glass: Body and Mind in Psychoanalysis*, London: Rebus Press.

Trevarthen, C. and Aitken, K.J. (2001) 'Infant inter-subjectivity: research, theory and clinical application', *Journal of Child Psychology and Psychiatry* 42 (1): 3–48.

Whitehouse, M.S. (1958) 'The Tao of the body', reprinted in D.H. Johnson (ed.) (1995) *Bone, Breath and Gesture: Practices of Embodiment*, Berkeley, CA: North Atlantic Books.

Wilkinson, H. (2000) 'An inspired resurrection of Freudian drive theory, but does Nick Totton's Reichian "bodymind" concept supersede Cartesian dualism?', *International Journal of Psychotherapy* 5 (2): 153–66.

——(2003) 'The shadow of Freud: is Daniel Stern still a psycho-analyst?', *International Journal of Psychotherapy* 8 (3): 235–54.

Winnicott, D.W. (1958) 'Mind and its relation to the psyche-soma', in *Through Paediatrics to Psychoanalysis*, London: Hogarth Press; reprinted 1992, London: Karnac.

# 2

# THE CORE EMOTIONAL SYSTEMS OF THE MAMMALIAN BRAIN

## The fundamental substrates of human emotions

*Jaak Panksepp*

If we take a neuro-evolutionarily informed approach to the mental apparatus, we must recognize that our minds contain the rudiments of many fundamental psychological processes that emerged long before humans walked the face of the earth. Among the most important for understanding psychiatric disorders are the basic emotional tendencies of the brain: fear, anger, sexual urges, maternal devotion, separation distress and social bonding, playfulness, and a general desire-SEEKING system for seeking all life-sustaining objects of the world.[1] All non-human mammals exhibit all of these basic emotional tendencies, and to the best of our knowledge, they also experience the associated affective feelings. Although we humans can cognitively reflect on these feelings and can even make art out of our emotions, using our higher symbolic capacities, the raw affects that lie at the foundation of our mental life reflect ancient brain/mind value-encoding process that are shared remarkably homologously by all living mammals and many other vertebrates. Because of advances in neuroscience, we finally have credible scientific approaches to understand the neurobiological nature of core affective processes in humans by studying the brains and behaviours of these kindred animals (Panksepp 1998a, 2005b). Since the core emotional mechanisms are concentrated in deep and ancient regions of the brain, they cannot be studied in any detail in our own species, despite recent advances in human brain imaging. Thus, animal brain research is essential to make progress on the details of these poorly understood brain functions.

A guiding premise of the affective neuroscience approach is that various emotional feelings and other affective states reflect primitive states of consciousness that emerge substantially from the neurodynamics of brain circuits that control instinctual emotional behaviours in animal brains. The possibility that two very different processes, such as emotional actions and emotional feelings, arise from substantially the same brain mechanisms is a critical aspect of the *dual-aspect monism* strategy that has guided my own research for four decades. According to such a view, a close study of the neural substrates of instinctual emotional behaviours of other animals may reveal the neural principles that generate raw emotional feelings in humans. However, there are many other affective feelings beside emotional ones, including a large array of sensory affects (i.e., the pleasures and displeasures of sensations) and various bodily feelings, including the hungers and thirsts that reflect the bodily balances that are critical for life. To understand them, we also need animal brain research, but here I will largely focus on the emotional affects that are most readily studied in animal models. Such action tendencies are commonly inhibited by higher cerebral processes in humans, leading to various methodological difficulties for studying primary-process mentation, as well as heightened prevalence of psychiatric and psychosomatic disorders from repressed bodily urges. Animal brain research provides the clearest entry point into the nature of such systems.

This approach is finally allowing us some detailed access to the brain mechanisms of affect. Of course, the vast cognitive abilities of humans add special dimensions to how emotional feelings are elaborated within the human mental apparatus. Although free-running and excessive affect is a common aspect of psychiatrically significant mental distress, certain combinations of cognitive and affective capacities, especially the memory aspects, allow humans to become especially susceptible to psychiatric disorders. It is our unique human tendency to dwell on, and hence to sustain, our emotional disturbances that casts a longer shadow on our mental life than is common in animals. It is from our highly interwoven affective and cognitive nature that so much sustained emotional turmoil arises. With intense emotional arousal, our obsessive ruminative tendencies are massively amplified. Thus, our emotions can disrupt and narrow the breadth of our thinking patterns when they are intense, just as they can intensify and energize our cognitive concerns at milder levels of arousal.

To highlight these points, let me share two verses from Robert Burns' 'To a Mouse'. While ploughing a field in November of 1785, Burns overturned the nest of a field mouse. In eight poignant verses he meditates upon human and animal conditions. The second verse laments:

> I'm truly sorry man's dominion
> Has broken Nature's social union
> An' justifies that ill opinion
> Which makes thee startle
> At me, thy poor, earth-born companion
> An' fellow mortal!

In the final verse Burns concludes

> Still thou art blest, compar'd wi' me!
> The present only toucheth thee
> But och! I backward cast my e'e
> On prospects drear
> An' forward, tho' I canna see
> I guess an' fear.
>
> (To a Mouse, 1785)

This is the human dilemma: through our remarkable cognitive abilities, we create complex mental lives, with unique intrapsychic tensions that often require the help of friendly and supportive others to facilitate more productive and happy outcomes. Because of our vast ability to look far back in memory and to imagine dreadful future problems, we humans are prone to sustain internally generated emotional arousal and disturbances much more than other animals. Through primary-process, affectively driven intrapsychic processes – the attributions, judgements, beliefs and construals, driven by the primal emotional 'energies' of anxiety, anger, desire and grief – humans commonly sustain affective arousal long after the precipitating circumstances have passed. Thereby our expansive cognitive nature becomes a critical agent in creating our own emotional problems. Such cognitive aspects of the emotional equations may never be as well modelled in other animals as the unconditional nature of the core affects. Since the neural mechanisms of experienced thoughts are more difficult to fathom than affective processes, we may never know to what extent other mammals are able to approximate levels of internally self-generated distressing thoughts that are common features of human life. However, a study of animal brains can tell us much about the nature of our raw emotional feelings. Although science has no mind-scopes, animal brain research finally informs us, perhaps for the first time in human intellectual history, of the nature of those deep evolutionary emotional processes without which psychiatric disorders could not exist (Panksepp 2004). My aim here is briefly to summarize the emotional affective aspects of various neuropsychological equations that can lead to psychiatric disturbances.

Sustained emotional arousal can also lead to sustained turmoil in our bodies, yielding various psychosomatic disorders and disturbances in our everyday quality of life. Similar effects can also be observed in animal models. In the midst of emotional disequilibrium it is often difficult, for both animals and humans, to find the affective comfort zones that are essential for mental equilibrium. At least half of the scientific problem for understanding mental disorders is a clarification of the neural nature of affective processes in the brain. It is this part of the overall equation that animal brain research can finally clarify. In doing so, it opens up the possibility of discoveries of new affective chemistries within the mammalian brain, for instance emotion specific neuropeptides that are excellent targets for new drug development (Panksepp and Harro 2004).

At risk of overemphasis, the animal work provides little insight into the cognitive interventions and restructurings that are essential for effective psychotherapies. Although the cognitive aspects of emotional disorders must be studied through human first-person self-reports, a knowledge of cross-species emotional systems provides coherent systemic views about the nature of core affective states, including the social nature of placebo effects that are so useful in most effective psychotherapeutic interventions. It is often a relief for clients to learn that they have fundamental affect generating and mood regulating systems in the brain that can become overwhelmed. By blending the neuroscientific affective and psychological cognitive knowledge, we can achieve more robust understanding than by either alone, leading to blended disciplines such as the robust emerging synthesis known as neuropsychoanalysis (Solms and Turnbull 2002).

In sum, since various affective feelings encourage individuals to obtain and retain resources, they may hold the keys to how we prioritize actions, as well as the associated cognitive plans. Although adult human intellectual structures may seem totally intertwined with emotional feelings, affects need to be distinguished as distinct brain processes that have profound developmental consequences for the emergence of cognitive structures. For instance, when we engage positive emotional feeling in children, so their intellectual passions are aroused, we open up robust possibilities for the construction of new cognitive terrain. Persistent negative feelings, many emerging from ambivalent love relations, can promote the emergence of distinct cognitive structures that can have lifelong implications for attitudes and behavioural strategies (Schore 2001). The core emotions of animals (just like those of young children) are not hidden under layers of neocortical inhibitions – of symbolic repressions and other defences – so their feelings are expressed more directly and more intensely, which makes their affective attitudes especially informative through careful neurobehavioural inquiries.

## On the neglect of affect in neuroscience

It is remarkable that, through most of the twentieth century, brain science has had so little to say about how affective experience is created in the brain. Indeed, most brain researchers and philosophers still believe that the existence of subjective experience remains an impenetrable mystery to science. Of course, how mind emerges from the physiochemical processes of the brain remains a major challenge for modern neuroscience, but the neural nature of many basic emotional experiences in humans are now penetrable because all mammals share the foundational processes for affective consciousness. As already noted, emotional feelings are only one of several distinct types of affects. There are also the various pleasures and pains of sensation (sensory affects). Another major category may be the many homeostatic arousals and moods (hungers, thirsts, etc.) and post-consummatory satisfactions, as well as various general bodily feelings of exhilaration and tiredness (interoceptive affects). My focus here will be on the emotional affects which seem to be organized around instinctual action coordinates in the brain. I follow the view of William James that

> Instinct is usually defined as the faculty of acting in such a way as to produce certain ends, without foresight of the ends, and without previous education in the performance.

> (James 1890: 383).

I make/accept the additional assumption that most affective processes are also instinctual, and emerge largely from the underlying neural substrates that generate the corresponding instinctual-emotional actions. These underlying affects are, I believe, the main sources of what behaviourists typically call rewards, punishments and reinforcements.

*Table 2.1* Distinct attributes types of cognitive and affective consciousness (see Panksepp 2003)

| Affective | Cognitive |
|---|---|
| **State functions** | **Channel functions** |
| Less computational | More computational |
| More analogue | More digital |
| Intentions-in-action | Intentions-to-act |
| Action-to-perception | Perceptions-to-action |
| Neuromodulator codes | No neurotransmitter codes |
| (e.g. neuropeptides) | (e.g. heavily glutamatergic) |
| More sub-neocortical | More neocortical |

How the multidimensional nature of affective consciousness is integrated with various forms of cognitive consciousness within the human mind remains largely unexplored territory in neuroscience, although there is currently much excitement about such topics. By contrast, such issues are well developed in the clinical psychological/psychiatric approaches to mental disturbances. However, despite the profound interpenetrance of affective and cognitive dimensions of mental life, it is important to envision the many differences between these types of mentation (see Table 2.1). Briefly, cognitive aspects of mind are those that arise from the harvesting and processing of information from the exteroceptive senses, while affective aspects of mind are intrapsychic processes that are more closely linked to interoreceptive processes and evolved brain states.

Such distinctions between cognitive and affective aspects of mind (Table 2.1) allow us to restore 'energetic' concepts to the intellectual agenda in the mind sciences. With modern affective neuroscience research strategies, we can now envision how affect is actually generated within the brain (Panksepp 2003, 2005b). For instance affective consciousness is reflected in various intentions that are part and parcel of instinctual actions, while cognitive consciousness is more involved in intentions *to* act. Further, during emotional arousal, actions guide perceptions, while during cognitive mentation, perceptions guide actions. While affective consciousness is more closely affiliated with concepts such as 'energetic field dynamics' in the brain (whereby enormous neural ensembles work together to establish characteristic tensions and movements in the body), cognitive consciousness is based more on 'information processing' principles. For effective higher cognitive activities, the lower emotional substrates are often kept under tonic regulatory inhibition. Presumably one major goal of psychotherapy is to promote cognitive regulation of affective processes, in the many ways that may happen, without losing touch with one's feelings.

One of the most important distinctions between emotional feelings and thoughts is that the primary locus of control for affective consciousness is sub-neocortical, while that of cognitive consciousness is neocortical. It is important to note that when the primary-process affective zones are damaged, the whole mental apparatus tends to collapse. In contrast, damage to neocortical zones tends to impair more specific tools of cognitive consciousness, while basic capacity for affective living-ness is retained (Shewmon et al. 1999). This distinction lies, I believe, at the root of one of William James's classic assertions about consciousness:

> The traditional psychology talks like one who should say a river consists of nothing but pailful, spoonful, quartpotsful, barrelsful,and other moulded forms of water. Even where the pails and the pots are actually standing in the stream, still between them the free water would continue to flow. It is just this free water of consciousness that psychologists resolutely overlook. Every definite image in the mind is steeped and dyed in the free water that flows around it. With it goes the sense of its relations, near and remote, the dying echo of whence it came to us, the dawning sense of whither it is to lead. The significance, the value, of the image is all in this halo or penumbra that surrounds and escorts it, – or rather that is fused into one with it and has become bone of its bone and flesh of its flesh.
>
> (James 1890: 255)

If the 'free-water' of affect has embedded within it a vast number of 'pailfuls' and 'spoonfuls' of cognitions (most of them epigenetically created), we can better appre-ciate why we need special research strategies to clarify the affective flow of mind.

Although cognitions and affects obviously merge in phenomenological experi-ence, currently there is an all too common imperialistic tendency among cognitive neuroscientists to conflate emotions and cognitions to an extent that may hinder our capacity to focus scientifically on the distinct neural aspects of the core affects. It is a great flaw, I believe, not to recognize the distinct neuro-evolutionary nature of affect, a form of primary process phenomenal experience that is more ancient than most of our cognitive capacities to think, reflect and exhibit reasoned judge-ment. If we just consider the evolutionary layering of the brain (MacLean 1990), the raw affective substrates of mind have a more ancient evolutionary history than our sense of cognitive awareness (Panksepp 1998b). Of course they eventually co-evolved in higher limbic regions of the brain, but not to recognize their independent interoceptive and exteroceptive sources may be as scientifically muddled as not to recognize the distinct, albeit functionally integrated, functions of liver and the kidney within medical science. By making disciplined distinctions between affective and cognitive forms of consciousness, one can better study and integrate neurobiological and psychological approaches to psychiatric imbalances, without neglecting the obvious, that these two mental abilities are thoroughly blended in our mature cognitive experiences.

I suspect that the desire to conflate emotions and cognitions has three sources. *The first* is the obvious fact that so much of our cognitive life revolves around our feelings, and in adult mental experience, certain types of cognitive and emotional arousals tend to go together. Obviously, during the first years of human life, children can have intense affects that are not accompanied by rich cognitive reflections. *The second* may be related to the fact that it is much easier to conceptualize the

19

affective-cognitive interactions in human mental life than to implement scientific strategies which can get at the neuro-causal underpinnings of the ancient pre-propositional (objectless) affective states. This requires animal brain research and, it is to be hoped, conducted with an emotional sensitivity that has not always been a characteristic of animal research. *The third* may be the power of constructivist perspectives in human affect science and cultural studies: everything in our minds seems to be largely constructed by our experiences in the world. It is hard for many to imagine that affect can exist independently of thoughts – that in their initial developmental form they are largely objectless states of mind which, through various types of learning, come to imbue the material-cognitive world with values (leading to fully blended object-relations processes during development). From practical clinical perspectives, if we do not fully consider both the cognitive dispositions of our clients and the affective tools they possess as gifts of nature, we cannot work optimally with the many ways emotional energies are skewing their lives. By recognizing affective, energetic states of mind as distinct entities, we can bring a large number of novel neurological insights to bear on psychiatric problems (Panksepp 2004).

It is largely through our search for the neuro-causal mechanisms of the various affects in animal models that we can aspire to study emotional-affective mechanisms independently of the infinitude of possible associated cognitions that clinicians need to consider. For instance, we can instigate affective states simply by electrically and chemically stimulating specific areas of the brain, with no intervening cognitions. Regrettably, there are only a handful of investigators who pursue such neuro-evolutionary psychobiological inquiries. Hence most still find it hard to conceive that evolution could have constructed any mental contents in brain dynamics that are independent of environmentally driven cognitions. However, raw affects, as primary-process value systems, may be initially objectless in newborn mental lives. We can experience fear without having an object of fear, which may lead to free-floating anxieties. Certain states of the nervous system may have affectively experienced contents without any objects in the world to which they are *intrinsically* attached. In other words we can feel exhilarated desires without knowing what in the world has aroused them. Our instinctual feelings are neither initially nor intrinsically linked to many distinct object and events in the world. However, such linkages, often perceived as causal, are rapidly created within the mental apparatus. We then readily project such states onto stimuli that then become cognitively fear-filled. We can feel both sad and joyous without those feelings being associated with distinct states of the world, even though those feelings readily get linked to a variety of world events. Although classical conditioning is a useful technique for studying some of these learned linkages, we remain far from understanding how higher cognitive affective-perceptual merging transpires in the brain. The image that may be most correct is that large-scale emotional-affective attractor landscapes, that are intrinsically (non-reflectively) intentional, pull in relevant cognitive relationships the way strong weather systems embrace and change the landscape, often in a lasting way.

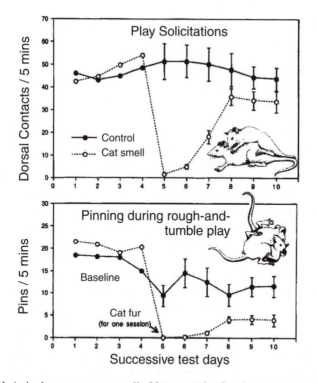

*Figure 2.1* A single exposure to a small ~20 mg sample of cat hair on the fifth day of testing (which was the first time the animals ever smelled a cat) inhibited rat rough-and-tumble play completely, and this contextual fear response continued for up to five subsequent test days, at higher levels with the measure of pinning (bottom) and less with the dorsal contact measure of play solicitation (top). Reprinted from Figure 1.1 of *Affective Neuroscience* (Panksepp 1998a) with permission of Oxford University Press.

The basic emotional systems, at the outset of infant psychological development, are only weakly linked to the objects of the world, and often in surprising ways. For instance, rats are not intrinsically afraid of the sight of cats. However, states of fearful trepidation are aroused by the mere smell of predators such as cats and ferrets (Figure 2.1), and only when such fearful smells are associated with predatory intent, do rats gradually become afraid of the sight of cats. However, such intrinsic olfactory fears are not evident in primates. For them, sudden looming objects are fearful. There are also other universal cross-species 'objects' of fearfulness. For instance, pain can arouse fearfulness in all mammals. However, there are few intrinsic object-related fears; most are learned. The FEAR system can be linked, through associative learning, to a large variety of external stimuli (some being prepared for ultra fast learning, such as snakes and spiders for humans, while other stimuli are difficult to link up, such as the taste of sweetness).

It is an open question how many intrinsic 'objects' the other basic emotional systems have. Surely, bodily restraint may be a common primal source of anger.

Gentle touch may activate nurturance. Whether sexual lust has intrinsic links to any distance receptors in human, such as the perceptual features of a nubile, symmetrical and healthy body, seems likely but unproved. On the other hand moths and many other animals are aroused and attracted intrinsically by sexual pheromones. Human eroticism is probably robustly linked to certain kinds of somatosensory inputs, but most linkages are learned, leading to possibilities for a variety of sexual preferences and fetishes.

The concept that raw affects are initially objectless in the brain, allows a fruitful rapprochement between basic emotion theory and constructivist views of emotions. The basic affective tools that evolution has provided – the ancestral voices of the genes to use one provocative phrase – emerge in brain development without initial strong intrinsic connections to world events. It is through life experiences, both individual and cultural, that such linkages are forged. Constructivist theories of emotions obviously need some basic tools for anything useful to be constructed. The intrinsic, evolutionarily provided emotional abilities revealed by affective neuroscience are such tools. Even though such emotionally valenced systems cluster into constellations of positive and negative affects, it seems unlikely that only two primal types of affective feelings are the raw materials from which all other affects are created within mammalian brains. Indeed, affect has to be grounded in action tendencies, and cannot be an independent sensory function of the brain.

In psychoanalytic terms, each individual's experiences cathect the important objects in their world. Through learning, as well as through the guiding role of initial genetic variability in emotional systems, each person becomes a unique affective being through their individual genetic inheritance and epigenetic experiences in the world. In behavioural terms, fluctuating affective processes serve as reinforcements for learned behavioural change. However, to conceptualize 'reinforcement' without any affective content, as is still popular in neurobehaviourism, reflects, I believe, a flawed materialistic ontology. It leads to the arrogance of a ruthless, fine-scale neuronal reductionism, that does not adequately reflect the large-scale neural network dynamics of the brain.

As William James almost surmised in Chapter 24 of his *Principles*, raw affective experiences reflect an instinctual form of consciousness (James 1890). Also, as Freud once noted:

> No knowledge would be more valuable as a foundation for true psychological science than an approximate grasp of the common characteristics and possible distinctive features of the instincts, but in no region of psychology were we groping more in the dark.
>
> (Freud 1920: 31–2)

Unfortunately, such concepts were largely discarded at the beginning of the cognitive revolution when computer-computational based information-processing became the prevailing metaphor for mind. Instinctual responses, which could have encouraged development of energetic concepts were neglected, partly because there was no efficient way to study them in the human laboratory and partly because adult humans are adept at developmentally emergent, culturally promoted inhibitions over instinctual displays. With the victories of first the behaviourist and then the cognitivist revolutions in twentieth century psychology, it was gradually forgotten that such instinctual displays reflect ancient mechanisms of mind that we still share with other animals. However, now that the affective neuroscience revolution is ripening, a careful analysis of emotional-instinctual behaviours in animal models may finally garner insights into the nature of the energetic instincts from which raw emotional-affective experiences emerge. And in using the concept of 'instinct' I am not arguing that they simply reflect genetic programmes of the brain, but rather, the genetic heritage interacting with early environments that construct categorically distinct developmental neural landscapes in the brain-mind.

In sum, the guiding premise of the ethology-inspired affective neuroscience approach, inspired by a *dual-aspect monism* ontology and epistemology, is that emotional instinctual behaviour generating systems in mammals are the fundamental substrates of emotional feelings. Thereby, we can use instinctual emotional behaviours as reasonably veridical measures of certain basic affective feelings. In other words, angry behaviours reflect angry feelings; fearful behaviours reflect certain anxieties; separation distress systems may help create sadness. According to this view, all basic emotions in the brain have dedicated, evolutionarily derived, circuits for the mediation of certain core psychobehavioural states. Indeed, since Walter Hess's classic work (Hess 1957), we have known that one can evoke angry behaviour in all mammals during localized electrical stimulation of the brain (ESB) from electrode sites situated in essentially identical subcortical neural regions. He found that complex behaviour patterns, responsive to the environment, as well as a symphony of physiological changes to support such emotional states went together as a unified package.

Many other emotional states can be evoked in this way, and when we ask animals whether they like or dislike such brain stimulation, they are rarely neutral about such states. Such states are also accompanied by sudden affective shifts in humans (Panksepp 1985; Heath 1996), and one can obtain antidepressant effects from certain brain areas (Mayberg et al. 2005). It is through a study of such ESB-evoked emotional states that a lasting understanding of the basic emotions can be achieved. We can be certain that these emotions are organized by intrinsic genetically dictated systems of the brain, since we can activate them by placing electrical 'noise' with no intrinsic informational content, and obtain coherent emotional responses in all mammals that have been studied. If these regions of the brain are damaged, consciousness is seriously impaired. A great deal has already been learned about the complex anatomies and neurochemistries of these circuits (Panksepp 1982, 1985, 1998a, 2005b), but a great deal more needs to be learned. An overview, constructed with synoptic inspiration from Doug Watt (1999), is available in Table 2.2.

*Table 2.2* Summary of the key neuroanatomical and neurochemical factors that contribute to the construction of basic emotions within the mammalian brain

| Basic emotional systems | Key brain areas | Key neuromodulators |
|---|---|---|
| General positive motivation **SEEKING**/expectancy system | Nucleus accumbens – **VTA** Mesolimbic and mesocortical outputs Lateral hypothalamus – **PAG** | Dopamine (+), glutamate (+) Opioids (+), **neurotensin** (+), many other neuropeptides |
| **RAGE**/anger | Medial amygdala to **BNST**, medial and perifornical hypothalamic to **PAG** | **Substance P** (+), ACh (+), glutamate (+) |
| **FEAR**/anxiety | Central and lateral amygdala to medial hypothalamus and dorsal **PAG** | Glutamate (+), **CRH, CCK, DBI**, alpha-**MSH, NPY** |
| **LUST**/sexuality | Cortico-medial amygdala, BNST, preoptic hypothalamus, VMH, **PAG** | Steroids (+), **vasopressin, oxytocin, LH-RH, CCK.** |
| **CARE**/nurturance | Anterior cingulate, BNST Preoptic area, VTA, **PAG** | **Oxytocin** (+), **prolactin** (+) Dopamine (+), **opioids** (+/-) |
| **PANIC**/separation/distress | Anterior cingulate, BNST and preoptic area Dorsomedial thalamus, **PAG** | **Opioids**(-), **oxytocin** (-) **Prolactin** (-), **CRF** (+), Glutamate (+) |
| **PLAY**/joy | Dorso-medial diencephalon Parafascicular area, **PAG** | **Opioids** (+/-), glutamate (+) ACh (+), **TRH**? |

Some terms are presented in bold (a) if there is massive anatomical convergence of emotional primes (i.e. **PAG** in the second column) or (b) if they are neuropeptide regulators that may be targets for new medicinal development (i.e. those in the third column).

The monoamines serotonin, NE (norepinephrine) and DA (dopamine) are typically not indicated as they participate to some extent in all emotions. Also, the higher cortical zones devoted to emotionality, for which there is modest preclinical data (albeit considerable human data), mostly in frontal, temporal and insular cortices are not indicated.

Index:

**ACh** acetylcholine
**BNST** bed nucleus of the stria terminalis
**CCK** cholecystokinin
**CRH** corticotrophin releasing hormone,
**DBI** diazepam-binding inhibitor
**LH-RH** lutenizing hormone-releasing hormone

alpha-**MSH** alpha melanocyte stimulating hormone
**NPY** neuropeptide Y
**PAG**, periaqueductal grey
**VMH** ventromedial hypothalamus
**VTA** ventral tegmental area

Minus signs indicate inhibition of an emotional process, and plus signs activations

*Source*: Data derived largely from Panksepp (1998a), as first abstracted by Watt (1999)

## Brief functions summaries of basic emotional systems

Considerable evidence from animal brain research suggests that at least seven basic emotional systems are concentrated in subcortical regions of the brain and are situated in essentially the same brain regions in all mammals (Panksepp 1998a). This knowledge has been derived by the powerful causal technique of electrically and chemically stimulating specific regions of the brain. The seven basic systems identified so far are those that mediate SEEKING, FEAR, RAGE, LUST, CARE, PANIC and PLAYfulness. Modern neuroscience is providing a detailed understanding of many critical parts of integrated brain systems but should have no pretence at having clarified the psychological whole. As already indicated, the many interactions with cognitive processes remain largely unstudied at basic neuroscience levels, and indeed such psychological questions are easier to pursue in humans, where introspective reports are more readily harvested. Indeed, cognition–emotion interactions may need to be studied on a species by species basis. However, since the general principles of core emotional systems are evolutionarily conserved across mammalian species, as well as some other vertebrates, we can finally understand the rudiments of our nature by understanding the emotional neurology of our fellow creatures. These psychobehavioural 'endophenotypes' can provide a new foundation for biological psychiatry (Panksepp 2004, 2006).

Let me focus on the Big Seven by starting with the most intriguing and highly generalized emotional system and one that has not been well recognized in most psychological theories. This system helps mediate the exhilaration and euphoria that is often characteristic of intense goal-seeking behaviours. In behavioural terminology, it would be considered the 'appetitive motivational system' that mediates the exploration, search and foraging for resources, with many neural subcomponents (Ikemoto and Panksepp 1999). In more psychological terms, it energizes desire and the many rich and energetic engagements with the world, as individuals seek goods from the environment as well as meaning from the everyday occurrences of life.

First, a remarkable system that has emerged from brain research is that which mediates the appetitive desire to find and harvest the fruits of the world, a state perhaps similar to the psychoanalytic concept of libido. I originally called this the EXPECTANCY desire system, but when that did not attract as much attention, as did a subsequently advanced 'wanting' conceptualization of this system (Berridge and Robinson 2003), I have relabelled it the SEEKING system to sustain the ethological-behavioural focus that every emotional system deserves. To my relief, this has now proved to be a more attractive label, even though the core concept has not changed. We can now also recognize this system as a major foundational substrate for Spinoza's concept of *conatus* (Spinoza 1985). Animals 'love' to self-activate – to self-stimulate – this system in addictive ways. This system should be conceptualized as a basic, positively motivated action system that helps mediate our desires, our foraging and our many positive expectancies about the world, rather than the behaviouristic concept of 'reinforcement' (Panksepp and Moskal

2006). Although highly resolved cognitive information descends into this system, the output is much less resolved, coaxing the animal to behave in libidinal, appetitively aroused, goal-directed ways. The many interactions of this system with higher brain regions help highlight the degree to which basic emotive state control systems can link up with cognitive systems that mediate secondary-process awareness and appraisals. This system operates in both positive and negative emotional situations (e.g., seeking safety) and helps maintain fluidity in behaviour as well as learning and other cognitive activities (Ikemoto and Panksepp 1999). This system can help generate various energetic mental states and delusional behaviours that are characteristic of acute-florid psychotic breaks, where one's imagination, and ability to make causal inferences from correlated events, can become excessive. Indeed, all basic emotional systems help mediate learning. Within the normative range of activities, such learning is clearly adaptive, but with over or under arousal, delusional claims become amplified, yielding various mental health consequences.

Second, the core structure of one of our major FEAR systems, very similar across all mammalian species, courses from central amygdaloid regions down to the periaqueductal grey (PAG). This system seems to generate a pure form of trepidation and flight through various types of learning from simple associative to conceptual. This energetic state, of uptight trepidation, can become associated with many events. Our worlds have abundant dangers, many of which we need to learn about, and others which we intrinsically fear. For instance, most young humans do not enjoy either unprotected heights or strange dark places where one's mind is readily captivated by fear. Rats, on the other hand, enjoy darkness more than light; as already noted, they become extremely timid in the presence of small samples of cat fur. That emotional response has been wired in by evolution to help rats avoid places where predators hang around. Neuroscientists have unravelled the details of classical conditioning that regulate fear. They have tended to focus on information that enters the FEAR system via so-called 'high-roads' (more cognitive-perceptual inputs), and via 'low-roads' (the more primitive sensory inputs). Regrettably most have ignored the 'Royal Road' – the evolved FEAR system itself, which governs the instinctual action apparatus that intrinsically helps animals avoid danger (Panksepp 2004). There are other distinct anxiety systems in the brain, for instance those that mediate separation anxiety, and there may be others that have yet to be clearly conceptualized. In any event, the arousal of these systems evokes or leads to mental tensions that characterize various anxiety disorders (Panksepp 1990). Most of the many chemistries of this system (Table 2.1) remain undeveloped in human biological psychiatry. One can anticipate that future medicines that regulate these systems will be most effective when applied in psycho-supporting therapeutic contexts.

Third, animals need to protect life-sustaining resources, and a major emotional response to achieve that emerges from the RAGE system. This system can also be aroused by restraint and frustration, and at times, even fear. If we do not get what we want, it is likely that there will be more activity in our RAGE system than there would be otherwise. This system has been intensively studied under the rubric of the defence motivation system (Siegel 2005). As with every other subcortically concentrated emotional system, higher cortico-cognitive processes can provide inhibition, guidance and other forms of higher regulation over such emotional impulses, more effectively in adults than children. We presently have no psychotropic medications that can specifically control pathological anger, but the chemistries that are concentrated along this circuit (e.g., Substance P to activate and opioids to inhibit) may eventually yield such neurochemical tools to facilitate emotional self-regulation in conjunction with the education of higher cognitive processes (Panksepp and Zellner 2004). The neuroscientific analysis of RAGE circuitry will yield other new medicines, even though the critical importance of work on this system for understanding aggressive urges is not as well recognized as it should be.

Fourth, sexual courtship and orientations are strongly built into the brain LUST circuits of all mammals. Only humans can exercise extensive cognitive choice in such matters, because of the richness of their higher cerebral mechanisms. In any event, male and female sexual systems are laid down early in development, while babies are still gestating, but they are not brought fully into action until puberty, when maturing gonadal hormone secretions begin to spawn male and female sexual desires. However, because of the way the brain and body get organized, female-type desires can flower in male brains, and male-type desires can thrive in female brains. However, like all emotional systems, especially through reciprocal controls with cognitive processes, there is abundant plasticity to allow learning and culture to promote a complexity that cannot be disentangled in animal-based neuroscience. Still, it is noteworthy that orgasmic feelings in humans arise from the deep subcortical brain systems that mediate animal sexuality (Holstege et al. 2003).

Fifth, after reproductively successful sexual congress, the next generation could not thrive if it were not for CARE systems that encourage parents, especially mothers, obsessively and pleasurably to care for their offspring. The maternal instinct, so rich in every species of mammal (and bird too), allows young organisms to prosper. The more devoted the care, such as abundant ano-genital licking in rats, the stronger psychobehavioural resilience and competitiveness of the next generation (Meaney 2001). How does the female brain change from a non-maternal to a maternal state? The changing tides of peripheral oestrogen, progesterone, prolactin and brain oxytocin figure heavily in such neural transformations, but the sustained exposure of both females and male rats can also sensitize the CAREgiving circuitry. Perhaps humans could simply sustain maternal care with their higher cognitive-conceptual abilities, but that is an assumption rather than a demonstrated fact. Because males and females have such large differences in these brain and body systems, males require more emotional education to become fully nurturant, engaged caretakers. Only in species where paternal participation in infant care is critical for the proper nutrition of the lactating mother, as in Titi monkeys and penguins, is paternal nurturance as natural as the maternal variety. To have left the CARE urge to chance, or the vagaries of individual learning, would

27

have probably assured the extinction of those species. Although there are many details to be clarified, hormonally promoted sensitization of CARE circuitry, probably by genetic activations that remain to be documented, encourages all mammals to respond supportively to their newborn babies – those squiggly infant lives that carry our hopes and our recombined packages of genes into the future.

Sixth, when young children get lost, they are thrown into a PANIC. They cry out for care, and their feelings of sudden aloneness and distress probably reflect the same ancestral neural codes from which adult sadness and grief are built. A critical brain system for the feeling of social loss is that which yields separation distress calls (crying) in all mammalian species. Brain chemistries that exacerbate feelings of distress (e.g., Corticotrophin Releasing Factor) and those that powerfully alleviate distress (e.g., brain opioids, oxytocin and prolactin) are the ones that figure heavily in the genesis of social attachments and probably the regulation of depressive affect (Nelson and Panksepp 1998). These are the chemistries that can assist or defeat us in our desire to create intersubjective spaces with others, where we can learn the emotional ways of our kind. Many social chemistries remain to be found, but when they are, we will eventually have new ways to help those whose social emotional 'energies' are more or less than they desire (Panksepp 2003). Precipitous arousal of this system may be one of the underlying causes for panic attacks. This knowledge may also link up with a better understanding of childhood disorders such as autism, since some children with this condition may be socially aloof if they are addicted to their own self-released opioids as opposed to those activated by significant others (Panksepp et al. 1991).

Seventh, young animals PLAY with each other, in order to navigate social possibilities in joyous ways. The urge to play was also not left to chance by evolution, but is built into the instinctual action apparatus of the mammalian brain. It could be argued that PLAY is that experience expectant process which brings young animals to the perimeter of their social knowledge, to psychic places where one must pause to contemplate what one can or cannot do to others. Play allows animals to be woven into their social structures in effective ways. It may achieve this by utilizing the many plasticities of the brain to create social brains that will work optimally in the environments in which young animals find themselves. Perhaps social brains are created as much by a few basic social-emotional tools as any type of refined evolutionary moulding of higher cognitive-type brain 'modules'. We know less about this emotional system than any other, partly because so few are willing to recognize that such gifts could be derived as much from mother nature as our kindest nurture. We have challenged our colleagues to consider that joyous 'laughter', so common in human play, also exists in other species (Panksepp and Burgdorf 2003), and that if we do not build social structures that promote real childhood play, we may be promoting cultures that have more problems such as Attention Deficit Hyperactivity Disorders. Human children, just like rats that are not allowed safe places to exercise their ludic energies – their urges for rough-and-tumble engagement – may release such energies more readily in classroom situations. To be too playfully impulsive within the classroom is to increase the likelihood that one will be labelled as an ADHD-type troublemaker, destined to be quietened with play urge reducing amphetamine and cocaine-like psycho-stimulant drugs. The animal model work already indicates that ADHD-type organisms can benefit from extra rations of rough-and-tumble activities each and every day (Panksepp et al. 2003). Early play may be essential for emergence of well-modulated social abilities, perhaps partly by activating many genetically controlled pro-social brain plasticites that are finally being clarified.

The above is not necessarily an inclusive list of basic emotions, but it is one that can be rigorously and well defended on the basis of neuro-psychobehavioural facts – a full triangulation among the essential research strategies. One can easily suggest the existence of other basic emotional systems, from disgust to dominance, but there is presently not yet enough compelling data to include them as fundamental *emotional* systems. Obviously, *disgust* is a basic sensory affect, but it might be a mistake to consider the neural substrates as constituting a blue-ribbon, grade-A emotional system. On the other hand, even though it is easy to generate an evolutionary scenario for the emergence of *dominance* as a basic system, its aspirations would by necessity be defeated in many members of each species. It is as likely that dominance emerges from the interactive confluence of many brain basic emotional systems – of PLAY, RAGE, FEAR, SEEKING and LUST, or some permutation of them.

Likewise, there are many socially constructed emotions, from pride to shame, that may arise from our ability to experience second-order awareness in various socio-cognitive contexts that arouse patterned symphonic activities in several basic emotional systems. However, no one has yet generated a scientific strategy to identify how, precisely, they may emerge. Human brain imaging is really not of much use in adjudicating such issues, since it is not well suited to clearly visualizing densely packed opponent-process systems in subcortical regions of the brain, where energetic states are created as much by the power of molecules as by the abundance of action potentials. Still, it is easy to envision how cold non-emotional cognitions could be transformed into hot affect-drenched appraisals through the widespread influence of a few emotional primes and the various attentional state control systems of the brain. Most of that remains uncharted research territory, but the basic emotional systems may be essential tools for the construction of many unique mental complexities in our species.

My short list of seven basic emotional systems is not meant to suggest that there are no other affects. For instance, the pleasures and displeasures of sensation are numerous, but they are not appropriately placed in the *emotion* category, for they are not dependent on 'moving out' dynamically to engage the environment in emotion characteristic ways. There are also a large variety of bodily states, from many hungers to fatigued states of the flesh, that need to be considered in any comprehensive affect science. My focus here has been only on the basic emotional systems shared by all mammals, systems that are not yet widely accepted, or even acknowledged, by neurobehaviouristically focused investigators who would deny mentality to the other animals, as if all of that was created through the special creation of the human neocortex.

We remain at the tail end of an era ruled by rather stark behavioural biases – that mental complexities are created by learning through systematic correspondences of certain behaviours with unified reward and punishment processes (Rolls 1999), which create generalized approach and avoidance tendencies. My reading of the evidence is that there are many distinct rewards and punishments in the brain, and only some should be deemed emotional. On the positive emotional reward side, we have the euphoria of SEEKING, the appetitive eroticism and orgasmic pleasures of LUST, the maternal devotions of CARE, and the exhilarating joy of PLAY. Among the distinct punishments we have the trepidation of FEAR, the pain of grief-ridden PANIC, and the powerful intensity of RAGE. In addition there are a large number of sensory rewards and punishments, and bodily homeostatic states that feel good and bad. For their fulfillment, via learning, all need the SEEKING system.

Thus, the positive emotion of SEEKING serves a super-ordinate function, as an essential infrastructure and scaffolding for all of the other basic emotions. It facilitates the goal-directedness of all the positive affects, and may promote the seeking of safety (exhilarated flight when FEAR is too intense) or the seeking of victory (when RAGE has promoted intra-specific combat over resources). Thus, even intense negative emotions are tinged with the support of a goal-directed SEEKING urge.

It is one of the tragedies of academic psychology that so few experimentalists are willing to discuss the full complexities of affective life and the indirect cross-species empirical strategies we must pursue to understand them. This is largely because the affective aspects of mind can never be directly observed, only through the neurally controlled actions of organisms. Most experimentalists believe that one can simply discard the affective aspects of the neural network functions, and simply talk about neural control of behaviour. This type of ruthless reductionism is fundamentally flawed if the affective aspects of these circuits are fully considered. Instead of proceeding with gentle reductionistic strategies that do not marginalize the mentality of other animals, there is all too abundant and often simple-minded academic jousting over the priority of perspectives handed down to us from the pre-neuroscientific behaviourist and cognitive eras (Davidson 2003).

The neglect of affect in neuroscience and psychology may also be partly due to the fact that scientists are often in denial about their own emotional feelings, partly because of temperamental factors and perhaps even due to their abundant cortically based rational intelligence, which tends to inhibit primary process emotionality (Panksepp 2004). Evolution built more complexity into the mammalian nervous system than has yet been widely recognized by academic psychology, but clinicians cannot ignore this if they desire to help people. By working out the neurodynamic and neurochemical details of core emotional circuits in animal models, we can generate robust new knowledge to facilitate the psychotherapeutic enterprise.

## Notes

1 Capitalizations (such as 'SEEKING') are used not only to emphasize that these words are not used in their everyday sense but refer to systems based on a brain analysis, but also to minimize mereological fallacies, or part–whole confusions, which are so prevalent in modern cognitive neuroscience.

## References

Berridge, K.C. and Robinson, T.E. (2003) 'Parsing reward', *Trends in Neurosciences* 9: 507–13.

Burns, R. (1785) '*To a Mouse*'. Online. Available http://www.readytogoebooks.com/RB79.html (accessed 4 January 2006).

Davidson, R.J. (2003) 'Seven sins in the study of emotion: correctives from affective neuroscience', *Brain and Cognition* 52: 129–32.

Freud, S. (1920) *Beyond the Pleasure Principle, Standard Edition*, ed. J. Strachey, Vol. 18, London: Hogarth Press.

Heath, R.G. (1996) *Exploring the mind–body relationship*, Baton Rouge, LA: Moran Printing.

Hess, W.R. (1957) *The Functional Organization of the Diencephalon*, London and New York: Grune and Stratton.

Holstege, G., Georgiadis, J.R., Paans, A.M., Meiners, L.C., van der Graaf, F.H. and Reinders, A.A. (2003) 'Brain activation during human male ejaculation', *Journal of Neuroscience* 23: 9185–93.

Ikemoto, S. and Panksepp, J. (1999), 'The role of nucleus accumbens DA in motivated behaviour, a unifying interpretation with special reference to reward-seeking', *Brain Research Reviews* 31: 6–41.

James, W. (1890) *The Principles of Psychology*, New York: Henry Holt.

MacLean, P.D. (1990) *The Triune Brain in Evolution*, New York: Plenum

Mayberg, H.S., Lozano, A.M., Voon, V., McNeely, H.E., Seminowicz, D., Hamani, C., Schwalb, J.M. and Kennedy, S.H. (2005) 'Deep brain stimulation for treatment-resistant depression', *Neuron* 45: 651–60.

Meaney, M.J. (2001) 'Maternal care, gene expression, and the transmission of individual differences in stress reactivity across generations', *Annual Review of Neuroscience* 24: 1161–92.

Nelson, E. and Panksepp, J. (1998) 'Brain substrates of infant–mother attachment: contributions of opioids, oxytocin, and norepinepherine', *Neuroscience Biobehavioural Reviews* 22: 437–52.

Panksepp, J. (1982) 'Toward a general psychobiological theory of emotions', *Behavioural and Brain Sciences* 5: 407–67.

——(1985) 'Mood changes', in *Handbook of Clinical Neurology, Vol. 1 (45), Clinical Neuropsychology*, Amsterdam: Elsevier Science.

——(1990) 'The psychoneurology of fear: evolutionary perspectives and the role of animal models in understanding human anxiety', in *Handbook of Anxiety*, Amsterdam: Elsevier/ North-Holland Biomedical Press.

——(1998a) *Affective Neuroscience: The Foundations of Human and Animal Emotions*, New York: Oxford University Press.

——(1998b) 'The periconscious substrates of consciousness: affective states and the evolutionary origins of the SELF', *Journal of Consciousness Studies* 5: 566–82.

—— (2003) 'At the interface of affective, behavioural and cognitive neurosciences: decoding the emotional feelings of the brain', *Brain and Cognition* 52: 4–14.

—— (ed.) (2004) *Textbook of Biological Psychiatry*, New York: Wiley.

—— (2005a) 'Affective consciousness: core emotional feelings in animals and humans', *Consciousness and Cognition* 14: 19–69.

—— (2005b) 'On the embodied neural nature of core emotional affects', *Journal of Consciousness Studies* 12: 161–87.

—— (2006) 'Emotional endophenotypes in evolutionary psychiatry', *Progress in NeuroPsychopharmacology and Biological Psychiatry* in press.

Panksepp, J. and Burgdorf, J. (2003) '"Laughing" rats and the evolutionary antecedents of human joy?', *Physiology and Behaviour* 79: 533–47.

Panksepp, J. and Harro, J. (2004) 'The future of neuropeptides in biological psychiatry and emotional psychopharmacology: goals and strategies', in J. Panksepp (ed.) *Textbook of Biological Psychiatry*, Hoboken, NJ: Wiley.

Panksepp, J. and Moskal, J. (2006) 'Dopamine, pleasure and appetitive eagerness: an emotional systems overview of the trans-hypothalamic "reward" system in the genesis of addictive urges', in S. Barsch, (ed.) *The Cognitive, Behavioural and Affective Neurosciences in Psychiatric Disorders*, New York: OUP.

Panksepp, J. and Zellner, M. (2004) 'Towards a neurobiologically based unified theory of aggression', *Revue Internationale de Psychologie Sociale/International Review of Social Psychology* 17: 37–61.

Panksepp, J., Lensing, P., Leboyer, M. and Bouvard, M.P. (1991) 'Naltrexone and other potential new pharmacological treatments of autism', *Brain Dysfunction* 4: 281–300.

Panksepp, J., Burgdorf, J., Turner, C. and Gordon, N. (2003) 'Modeling ADHD-type arousal with unilateral frontal cortex damage in rats and beneficial effects of play therapy', *Brain and Cognition* 52: 97–105.

Rolls, E.T. (1999) *The Brain and Emotion*, Oxford: Oxford University Press.

Schore, A.N. (ed.) (2001) 'Contributions for the decade of the brain to infant mental health', in special issue of *Infant Mental Health Journal*, 22 (1–2): 1–269.

Shewmon, D.A., Holmes, D.A. and Byrne, P.A. (1999) 'Consciousness in congenitally decorticate children: developmental vegetative state as self-fulfilling prophecy', *Developmental Medicine and Child Neurology* 41: 364–74.

Siegel, A. (2005) *The Neurobiology of Aggression and Rage*, Boca Raton, FL: CRC Press.

Solms, M. and Turnbull, O. (2002) *The Brain and the Inner World*, New York: Other Press.

Spinoza, B. (1985) On the Origins and Nature of Ethics, in E. Curley (ed. and trans.) *The Collected Works of Spinoza*, Princeton, NJ: Princeton University Press.

Watt, D. (1999) 'Consciousness and emotion: review of Jaak Panksepp's "Affective Neuroscience"', *Journal of Consciousness Studies* 6: 191–200.

# 3

# EXAMPLES OF APPLICATION OF THE AFFECTIVE NEUROSCIENCE STRATEGY TO CLINICAL ISSUES

## *Jaak Panksepp*

In the previous chapter, I summarized how the basic pre-clinical affective neuroscience view of emotional organization of the mammalian brain can facilitate our understanding of human emotional feelings. In this chapter, I will look at the clinical implications of this work, which are substantial, both in the arena of new medication development as well as how we conceptualize psychiatric disorders.

In 1972, it was discovered that all opioid addictions are mediated by a single receptor molecule in the brain, the mu-opioid receptor – the first neurotransmitter receptor objectively identified in the mammalian brain. If this receptor is blocked with drugs such as naloxone or naltrexone, then all the pleasurable and pain-alleviating effects of opiates from morphine to heroin are eliminated. Without this receptor, there can be no opiate addiction and the social chaos that results from abuse of powerful opiate drugs that bind to this receptor. Soon after the discovery of this receptor, it was widely recognized how the magic of opiate molecules in controlling pain, coughing and life-threatening diarrhoea was mediated. However, the widespread distribution of mu-opioid receptors throughout the brain meant that they controlled many other processes.

As soon as this receptor was discovered, we wondered whether there were neurophysiological similarities between opioid dependence and social dependence – whether social attractions and attachments were regulated by this addictive sys-tem of the brain. After all, both share a dependence phase – the remarkable affec-tive rush that is evoked in the early phases of relationships, whether with drugs or objects of social desire. However, no matter how positive those initial feelings, they tend to fade, resembling the 'tolerance' phase of drug addiction, where one has to take large and larger doses to sustain the positive affect. As the power of initial social attraction, like morphine, tends to fade away, so one often tends to seek new social objects to restore the initial feelings. But even when the powerful initial affect has faded, a dependence process has set in. One cannot feel emotion-ally normal, or whole, when the drug or subject of dependence is suddenly taken away. Following both opioid withdrawal and the loss of a loved one, a powerful opponent affective response emerges, consisting of similar symptoms of psychic pain, such as crying, lack of appetite, irritability and difficulty sleeping. The distress is alleviated promptly by the object or subject of affection, and a feeling of psychic normality is restored.

To evaluate whether endogenous opioids did control such social affects, we separated young animals from their mothers to see if opiate receptor stimulants would alleviate the resulting separation distress, as monitored by frequency and intensity of crying. In fact, the separation distress of young animals, whether they were puppies, guinea pigs, rats or even baby chicks, was dramatically alleviated by low doses of all the drugs and neuropeptides that stimulated mu-opioid receptors of the brain. In most of these animals, blocking the mu receptors with naloxone or naltrexone often increased separation distress. Subsequently, we evaluated hundreds of psychoactive agents, and only those that stimulated the oxytocin and prolactin receptors of the brain came close to opioids in their capacity to alleviate separation distress. All others had modest effects by comparison. If the instinctual responses of separation distress are indicative of the underlying emotional feelings, we would predict that facilitation of opioid, oxytocin and prolactin activity in the brain would symptomatically alleviate the feelings of human sadness and grief. Although little work has been done to evaluate such possibilites, recent imaging of human brain opioid systems has indicated that activity of such neurochemical systems is low during sadness (Zubieta et al. 2003).

If we consider that one of the most powerful forms of social affect is derived from the emotional power of human touch, we might expect endogenous opioids to be part of that affective equation. Early psychoanalytic work demonstrated that loving human touch was essential for the survival of human infants (Spitz 1965), and the power of social contact had been demonstrated in many other species (Harlow 1971; Panksepp et al. 1991). When we first evaluated this idea in a simple model of contact comfort (Figure 3.1), it was clear such positive social feelings were mediated, in part, by brain opioids (Panksepp et al. 1980). If young animals could not feel their endogenous opioids, because receptors were blocked with naloxone, they would not settle down (with eye closure and head nodding) as they did when administered placebos. Undrugged animals promptly stopped exhibiting distress vocalizations, and they settled down nicely, but they took two to three times as long to settle down following opioid blockade. Subsequently, we demonstrated that the abundant touch and physical activity of rough-and-tumble play also released endogenous opioids (Panksepp and Bishop 1981), and opiate-blocking agents reduced this kind of vigorous social engagement.

These findings were extended by Barry Keverne's group in Cambridge, especially in their demonstration that primates would release each other's endogenous opioids when they groomed each other (Keverne et al. 1989). Presumably we humans also touch each other by the way we talk to each other, and the more care and concern we detect, the more opioid activity is probably engendered in our brains. Indeed, the 'placebo effect' is now known to be substantially medi-

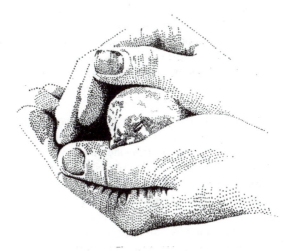

*Figure 3.1* When held gently in human hands, newborn chicks exhibit a comfort response consisting of the cessation of vocalizations and eye closure. These effects are attenuated by opiate receptor blocking agent naloxone, indicating internal opioids help mediate contact comfort responses. Figure is adapted from photograph in Panksepp, Bean, Bishop, Vilberg and Sahley (1980), as reprinted from Figure 14.9 of *Affective Neuroscience* (Panksepp 1998a) with permission of Oxford University Press.

ated, in part, by brain opioids (Petrovic et al. 2002), further highlighting the fact that many of the medical/psychiatric benefits of placebos might be derived from activation of positive social neurochemistries in the brain and body. It is possible that the healing power of religious practices, from prayer to meditation, may have similar underlying causes.

If animals do not receive enough positive social interaction, they tend to become depressed. A simplified model was generated through the study of socially isolated newborn chicks. Housed by themselves, with abundant food and water, young chicks would exhibit a depressive syndrome, capable of being alleviated by antidepressants, that was more intense in females than in males (Panksepp et al. 1991). Indeed, many animals would die from this aloneness, and simply providing a companion animal to these apparently depressed animals was completely thera-peutic. It is noteworthy that human depression afflicts females more readily than males. Might depression be accompanied by low brain opioid activity, resulting from the depletion of positive social neurochemistries?

It has long been know that opioids can exert strong antidepressant effects, and some of the newer variants such as buprenorphine (that are not very addictive since they are only opiate receptor stimulants at low doses) can exert remarkable antide-pressant effects in individuals that have responded to no other medications (Bodkin et al. 1995). It would seem that the use of mixed opioid agonists-antagonists, such as buprenorphine, is much under-utilized in the treatment of human depression, especially suicidal depression. It is possible that low doses of buprenorphine would temporarily restore pleasure chemistries in the brain to such an extent that one can therapeutically work through acute suicidal crises more easily than one could with other sedatives that are more commonly used. Also, considering that oxytocin is as effective in the amelioration of separation distress as opioids, it is worth considering that such medications should be quite effective in alleviating human sadness/ grief, and perhaps the more chronic conditions of melancholia, and the ensuing chronic depression.

In this context it is also worth considering that one major reason young people are attracted to opioid drugs, leading to addiction, is because they feel alienated, with inadequate positive social feelings from their interactions. They discover that opioids can alleviate their chronic distress. Considering that oxytocin tends to maintain opioid sensitivity in the brain (Kovacs et al. 1998), one wonders whether early childhood rearing practices that focus on loving interactions, with abundant physical touch/warmth, would tend to reduce the incidence of opioid addiction. However, once it (an addiction?) has started, it would seem that the utilization of mixed opioid agonists/antagonists, such as buprenorphine, should have a more prominent place in early interventions provided in combination with abundant positive social support, in soothing-calming environments where confidence and desire for living can be restored. Many powerful interventions could emerge from attempts to restore potential imbalances in social neurochemistries in various disorders, especially when provided in life-affirming therapeutic environments.

## Opioid dysregulation in autism

Our emerging understanding of the complex chemistries of social feelings can lead to new interventions with intractable childhood disorders of social motivation such as autism, which is characterized by deficits in socialization, communication and imagination.

It is well recognized that autism has strong biological dispositions, as highlighted by the concordance rate of up to 90 per cent for identical twins (with susceptibility loci now identified in half the chromosomes, suggesting complex epistatic genetic interactions), which is twice the level of concordance seen in schizophrenia. Many brain abnormalities have been identified in autism, including larger cerebral hemispheres and often smaller and poorly organized subcortical limbic areas. For instance, the abundance of small, poorly branching neurons in the temporal lobes (amygdala and hippocampus) suggest that limbic-emotional connectivity with cortico-cognitive areas is impaired, and deficits in genes such as reelin may lead to migrational mistakes in cortical cell layering. Although there is no presently known way to restore such connections, abundant early single-trial learning as well as broad-scale sensory integration interventions are often beneficial, as should eliminating potentially exacerbating toxins in the children's environments.

Although no medications have been specifically approved for autism, the similarity between many of the classic symptoms of autism (e.g., pain insensitivity, lack of crying, social aloofness, various stereotypies) were sufficiently similar to those we had observed in our animals treated with low doses of opioids, that we entertained the idea that at least a subset of autistic children may exhibit autistic aloneness, because of excessive opioid in their systems (Panksepp 1979). This idea was proposed because it had an immediate therapeutic end-point, and could be easily evaluated through the use of opioid antagonists. Of course, we did our best to evaluate the potential efficacy of such a medication first, through pre-clinical testing.

Our most compelling evidence came from analysing the social motivation of dogs given low doses of morphine or naloxone. We systematically evaluated changes in their desire to interact socially by focusing on how intensely the animals wagged their tails and how willing they were to lick our faces. Of course, we did this in a very systematic and replicable way using blind-testing procedures, and we found that low doses of morphine (0.25 and 0.5 mg/kg) made the animals more autistic-like; they would not wag their tails as much in our presence, and it took them longer to come and lick our faces. In contrast opiate receptor blockade with naltrexone led to more tail wagging and faster face licking, the kinds of pro-social effects – increases in social desire – we hoped to obtain in autistic children (Panksepp 1981).

It took an unexpectedly long time to get the clinical trials going, partly because the use of the orally effective opiate receptor antagonist naltrexone was banned from human trials for several years by the Food and Drug Administration in the United States in the mid 1980s. There was some fear that the drug was a potential carcinogen. Indeed, it was subsequently discovered that opioids do regulate tumour growth, but the low doses naltrexone (LDN) that we were hoping to use actually tend to reduce tumour growth, which is currently leading to abundant off-label use of this agent as a cancer treatment (www.lowdosenaltrexone.org).

In any event, when we first evaluated the agent in Linz, Austria, with Patrick Lensing, and in Paris, France, with Marion Leboyer, we obtained positive effects in about half the children. The optimal dosage regimen seemed to be 0.25 mg/kg given orally every other day (masked in a favourite food to hide the very bitter taste). About half the children exhibited increased social motivation, attempts to communicate, and more flexible social interactions and toy play (Panksepp et al. 1991). Often the benefits, which included increased cheerfulness, were most evident on the intervening no-drug days, but there was a lot of variability from child to child.

Our clinical impression was that only those children responded well who exhibited some opioid-withdrawal symptoms soon after the initial administration of the medication – symptoms such as tiredness, negative affect, even crying (sometime for the first time). This suggests that some children may in fact have higher than normal opioid activity in their brains. Of course, since reducing opioid tone can increase social motivation in animals, we need to advise parents of the implications of this for their child. Thus, we routinely advise the parents that this medication is not like aspirin for a fever, where one can simply get a medical response without the parents' participation. If their child turns out to be one of the lucky ones where their social window can be nudged wider open with naltrexone, the parents need to exhibit increased social sensitivity to get the most out of the medication for their child.

Still, the present status of naltrexone in treating autistic symptoms remains ambiguous, largely because the track record of double-blind studies is mixed, with only about half exhibiting statistically significant therapeutic effects (typically studies done on quite young children, with very low doses of the medication), while the reported failures often use older children or young adults, and much higher doses of medication, administered daily. Also, our philosophy was that one should not give medications which increase social motivation, without alerting parents to the need to be attentive to increased levels of social solicitation and responsivity, so we intentionally included such a demand characteristic in our methodology, but most studies that have failed to see effects take no special measures to facilitate increased parental attention and engagement. Of course, it could be that this placebo effect is the main reason for the therapeutic effects seen in about half the children, but that is unlikely in double-blind studies (e.g., Bouvard et al. 1995).

The evidence for abnormalities in circulating opioids has remained mixed. Although Gillberg et al. (1985) originally demonstrated that opioid-like activity was elevated in the brains of about half the children, subsequent studies have failed to find elevated cerebrospinal β-endorphin levels in autistic kids. Of course, there are now many distinct types of opioids in the brain, and no thorough evaluation of all of them has yet been conducted. In studies of plasma opioids, some typical opioids have been normal while certain unusual species have been massively elevated, and normalized in children that are naltrexone responders (Bouvard et al. 1995). Although elevated opioids seems unlikely to be a primary cause of autism, it appears to be an exacerbating factor in about half the children, and a good double-blind study is needed just in those children that exhibited elevated opioid levels and/or initial positive responsivity to naltrexone.

In any event, this agent can provide some relief from some of the troubling symptoms of autism in some of the children, especially if it is used in the context of good social support from parents or caretakers. It is by no means clear that the main therapeutic effect is due directly to the opioid blockade, and it remains possible that the naltrexone makes certain children more socially responsive because their own internal opioid reward systems are responding more appropriately to social stimulation. Indeed, if this is the case, perhaps even lower doses of naltrexone, such as the 4 mg doses that are now common in the LDN therapies of various medical disorders, might be optimal, especially when given just before bedtime (perhaps as a trans-dermal preparation, to avoid the aversive taste). Under those conditions, one's own opioids would be expected to be higher, and perhaps more responsive, when one awakens.

Although many variables remain to be evaluated in LDN therapy, it can be quite a benefit to family life when it works. Responders who have good verbal skills can provide some insight into what is happening psychologically. For instance, I asked a very high-functioning 16-year-old autistic girl, who was very self-centred and obsessive, but had good language skills, what she was experiencing from the benefits that were apparent on the medication. Soon after starting 0.25 mg/kg naltrexone, she started to participate more in family activities, would be more willing to go out shopping with her mother, and would be considerably more social and even talk about what was happening on the TV shows she was now watching with her parents. During a visit, I asked Jennifer, 'You seem so different after the medication. How has the medication changed you?' She looked at me, a bit perplexed and said: 'Medication hasn't changed me. The world has changed!' This is a profound statement about how we project our feelings into the world. When our emotions change, often the world appears very different to all of us.

The larger lesson of the above work is that the study of basic emotions in animal models is a robust strategy for asking important psychological questions that we could ask in no other way. In animals we can

1   evaluate the role of genetic vulnerability in detail (e.g., via the sue of knockout mice)
2   systematically study environmental toxic factors, since they can be directly manipulated
3   study the relevant underlying brain and body systems in detail
4   isolate the developmental processes more rigorously
5   evaluate biological therapies before considering their use in humans.

In any event such a strategy first coaxed us to evaluate the efficacy of naltrexone in the treatment of young autistic children. However, all psychiatric problems are not medical problems, and now I would like to share one childhood problem that may be more of a social-developmental problem than a neurobiological one.

## Play and Attention Deficit Hyperactivity Disorders

We have now been studying the basic mechanisms of rough-and-tumble play in a laboratory rat model for a quarter of a century. This is one of the easiest and most enjoyable emotional processes to study systematically, since all young rats have a strong intrinsic urge to play. Early work has been summarized in Panksepp et al. (1984) and in various more recent reviews (Vanderschuren et al. 1997; Panksepp 1998a; Siviy 1998). This is an important experient-expectant process that has important implications for brain and psychological development (Spinka et al. 2001; Gordon et al. 2003), as well as the understanding of the nature of social-joy within the mammalian brain. Most recently we have been focusing on play vocalizations as a direct measure of this positive emotional experience, and have garnered considerable evidence about the nature of social joy, perhaps even the evolutionary nature of our childhood laughter (Panksepp and Burgdorf 2003).

A fuller understanding of mammalian play systems may offer new and practical therapeutic ideas for various developmental disorders, but most especially for the millions of American children diagnosed with Attention Deficit Hyperactivity

Disorder, who are being treated with potential drugs of abuse, which may have long-term developmental effects on the brain and mind.

Psycho-stimulants like Ritalin (methylphenidate) are among the most powerful play-reducing drugs ever discovered through the use of animal models. Might it be that so many children are given Ritalin these days partly because it reduces disorderly behaviours that arise from poorly regulated playful urges? If so, adequate research should be conducted to determine how play and psycho-stimulants influence long-term brain organization. Troublesome facts have already arisen from animal research. These drugs easily 'sensitize' animal brains making them hyper-responsive to similar drugs throughout the lifespan. Typically young animals do not sensitize as readily as older animals, but some sensitization has been observed in young animals.

Our past work with animal models has demonstrated that play 'therapy' reduces impulsive behaviours resembling ADHD (Panksepp et al. 2003). Might play also be therapeutic for children diagnosed with ADHD? We may shed light on such issues if the deep sources of play in animal brains are, in fact, evolutionarily similar to those that motivate our own children to romp with each other. Using animal models, we have shown that playfulness arises from ancient, subcortical brain systems we probably share with other animals. Play is certainly a fundamental source of joy, but it probably also helps organize the brain/mind in pro-social ways. It may, along with separation-distress and social-bonding systems, be one of the fundamental tools that nature provides for the epigenetic construction of the social brain.

How might play facilitate normal brain development? Our pet hypothesis is that it 'fertilizes' brain functions by promoting genetic activation of neurotrophin-type molecules, such as brain derived neurotrophic factor (BDNF), which help brains mature in beneficial ways. For example, our research group (Gordon et al. 2003) has collected data suggesting that gene-expression of BDNF in the frontal cortex and amygdala is facilitated by playful activities. However, there are many other fertilizers from GDNF to FGT (Glial Derived Neurotrophic Factor and Fibroblast Growth Factors) to be analysed (Riva et al. 2005). If play is an experience-expectant process for the construction of the social brain, there may be serious consequences for brain maturation in children who have little chance to play normally, as happens in many families today. Since the urge to play is a neurological 'drive' or urge, we suspect that if it is left unfulfilled then symptoms of ADHD may readily emerge in social situations where rough-and-tumble activities are restricted, such as classrooms. Surprisingly, the rough-and-tumble play of our species was not formally studied until quite recently (Scott and Panksepp 2003), and we were surprised that boys and girls generally exhibited the same number (frequency) of specific play gestures, even though the roughness of the play, which is difficult to measure objectively, was probably higher in boys, who are generally bigger and stronger. Eric Scott and I have now completed a feasibility study of a play-intervention programme for pre-kindergarten classes within our local public school system and the children liked it very much even if some of the teachers did not. We have not yet been able to pursue such a study with ADHD-type children.

There are a variety of compelling issues to be considered: what if it turned out that a substantial percentage of ADHD kids receiving psycho-stimulants are simply normal kids who have strong, unsatisfied desires to play? What if these medications sensitize their brains? It is disturbing to contemplate these issues, especially since some animal research already suggests that early experiences with such drugs can promote addiction later in life (Panksepp et al. 2002), although there are also other studies that suggest such drugs may reduce addictions (Andersen 2005). For the time being, our research goal is to determine how access to rough-and-tumble play modifies the long-term organization of the mammalian brain (Panksepp et al. 2003), and to see how psycho-stimulants either facilitate or impede such processes in animal models.

We are also already probing the genetic code with micro-array (gene chip) technologies, and wish to determine which genes are tuned up or down in animals permitted to play. We want to evaluate differences between animals that play a lot and those that do not. We are eager to know if differences may exist between boys and girls, by studying male and female rats at various ages. We want to know whether patterns are different between winners and losers, not only as they emerge during joyous playground activities but also on the embittered battlefields of adult life (which should provide data relevant to the types of social loss that often promote depression: Kroes et al. 2006). And, of course, we want to know how psycho-stimulants modify genetic expression profiles in young brains.

Some may believe that it is premature (even presumptuous) to suggest that such animal data may have important implications for human clinical practice. This is bound to remain a controversial issue until robust predictions are generated for humans. For starters, our predictions are that

1    when properly evaluated, we will find that psycho-stimulants reduce the urge of human children to play;
2    a regular diet of physical play, each and every day during childhood, will be able to alleviate ADHD type symptoms in many children that would otherwise be on that 'clinical' track;
3    play will have long-term benefits for children's brains and minds, benefits that are not obtained with psycho-stimulants;
4    under some conditions, psycho-stimulants may sensitize young brains and intensify internally experienced urges that may, if socio-environmental opportunities are available, be manifested as elevated desires to seek drugs;

if and when we finally get to the genetic studies, we anticipate that the profiles of gene-activation resulting from lots of play and lots of psycho-stimulants will be quite different in the brain.

In short, we suspect the data will show that different genetic tunes can be strummed in various regions of the brain by the relevant pharmacological and socio-environmental factors. We anticipate that the bottom line of such research will be in accord with what Plato asserted in *The Republic* (section IV) when he insisted that

> our children from their earliest years must take part in all the more lawful forms of play, for if they are not surrounded with such an atmosphere they can never grow up to be well conducted and virtuous citizens.
>
> (Plato 2000: 573a)

At present we are devoting much research effort to figure out the nature of social joy within the mammalian brain. Our main model, rough-and-tumble play in juvenile rats, has now been refined to one exquisite indicator of the underlying affective processes, a 50 kHz chirpy vocalization that is abundant during play (Knutson et al. 2002). When we discovered that we could obtain this vocalization simply by tickling young rats (Panksepp and Burgdorf 2003), we initiated an intense research programme to characterize this simplified model of joy (Panksepp and Burgdorf 2003), and we are narrowing our search to specific systems of the brain (Burgdorf and Panksepp 2006), which may yield new neurochemical control systems that may help us think about much better medications for social-emotional problems of our own species, especially depression.

## Development of new medications

Once we understand the neurochemical details of the various core emotional systems, we will have the basic knowledge needed to think about how we might best seek to alleviate the affective burdens of people in emotional distress. We can finally be certain that many of our passions and our hungers and all variety of delights and agonies of the soul have chemical codes. Some of the chemical messengers cut across many species of feelings (i.e., the biogenic amines such as norepinephrine and serotonin), while others are unique to one or another motivation.

Many of these *specific* carriers of the affective life will be molecules of the neuropeptide class (short protein sequences), which can control neuronal system sensitivities and responsivities for extended periods of time. This not only helps explain why many feelings linger, but also provides new ways to think about how we might coax them to linger in different ways. I have discussed these possibilities more extensively elsewhere (Panksepp 1993, 1998a; Panksepp and Harro 2004). However, I would reaffirm my belief that the subtle mind medicines that we can create from this knowledge will be best used with a new sensitivity for those who need such help. Many of these molecules will work best when combined with sensitive psychological care offered in environments that support the ability of people to see their lives from different affective perspectives. In this vision, people with deep emotional needs and disturbances, will have to be full participants in professional attempts to restore affective balance (Panksepp 1999). They should not just be given pills and sent on their way.

The battle over whether psychological or biological therapies are better for psychiatric disturbances finally shows signs of abating. Modern brain imaging has demonstrated, time and again, that psychotherapy has demonstrable and beneficial effects on the brain. This is creating a sea-change in our conception of who we are and what we are seeking to accomplish in therapeutic interventions (Cozolino 2002). Dan Siegel said it well in the Foreword to Louis Cozolino's penetrating book: clinicians immerse themselves

> in the stories of individuals who come for help in feeling better. . . . Whatever the approach, lasting change in therapy occurs as a result of changes in the human mind . . . which involve changes in the functions of the brain. Exactly how the mind changes during the therapeutic process is the fundamental puzzle that the synthesis of neuroscience and psychotherapy seeks to solve.

## The all pervasive cognitive-emotion interactions

Since emotional states are so effective in channelling perceptual and cognitive processes, an increasing number of investigators seem eager to conflate cognitive and affective processes during the current 'emotion revolution' that is captivating cognitive science (e.g., Lane and Nadel 2000). Although it is essential eventually to understand how emotional and cognitive processes interact at the neuronal level, for their interchange is intimate at the psychological level, little progress, aside from some coarse localized brain regions of interest, little deep understanding can be achieved until we better understand the basic core emotions. I suspect the current attempt to see both affect and thought as two sides of the same cognitive coin hinders a solid scientific confrontation with one of the most important and most neglected issues of mind/brain science – the fundamental nature of affect. As already noted, it is possible that the many socially constructed emotions rely on the more basic ones for their affective impact, and their cognitive distinctiveness to the core relational themes they represent. Hence, emotions such as abhorrence, contempt, empathy, loathing, scorn, smugness, even disgust, guilt and shame, may require certain types of cognitive framings in order for several concurrently aroused basic affects to coalesce into a new emotional entity. To understand these emotions, we must truly consider cognitive and affective processes conjointly.

The fact that most everyday cognitions are deeply embedded in affective structures (yielding an abundance of socially constructed emotions) should not lead us to neglect the even deeper evolutionary nature of affective experience. For instance, human infants come into the world as profoundly affective creatures. Their initial cognitive limitations are erased gradually by experiences in loving intersubjective spaces where they can be potent actors on the world stage that now envelops them. Their first explorations are not devoted to the inanimate world, but the eyes, the voice, the touch of the caregiver – who is, we hope, a mother whose brain affective systems have been well prepared not only by culture but also by the loving touch of neurochemical systems that can make engagement with an infant a special delight. It is from the rich intersubjective dance of mother and child from which future possibilities are woven, in both humans (Trevarthen 2001; Reddy 2003) and other mammals (Meaney 2001). To believe that these infants, in their first engagements with life, are unconscious packages of reflexes as opposed to affectively engaged human beings is an intellectual travesty that is not yet erased from the sad ongoing history of the behavioural sciences. It has been even worse when scientists have considered the lives of other animals (Panksepp 2005a).

It is of the utmost importance for our society to promote a new and deeper level of emotional education – an affective intelligence that can abort the emotional neglectful 'sins' of parents being passed on to children in cycles of child abuse that are more commonly mental than physical. Every emotional system that has been studied exhibits use-dependent plasticity. This means that if one has been exposed to too many horrible experiences, then the brain systems that mediate the resulting feelings will have been strengthened. Infants that have lived at the centre of caregivers' positive emotional engagements, and have been offered manageable life challenges with which they become engaged, have been given a precious gift of life. When we begin to understand how the solidification of emotional habits occurs at the neuronal level, which is much deeper than simple learning of phobias, then we may also learn how to partly disentangle the damage that has been wrought by emotional misfortunes (Panksepp 2001; Sunderland 2006). We remain far from such knowledge at the present time, largely because of a lack of will in our culture to pursue such questions in our fellow animals. Without emotionally informed animal brain research, it is to be hoped done with utmost inter-species sensitivity, that kind of knowledge will never be ours.

## In sum

The understanding of the foundations of human and animal nature, and the recognition that we are inheritors of core emotional-affective systems that are remarkably similar to those of other mammals, will, we hope, eventually penetrate our culture. If that is achieved, without marginalizing the best of our cultural achievements, it can be a very beneficial cultural achievement for the human race. There is a primitive affective consciousness built into the infrastructure of our brains that is the birthright of every mammal, bird and perhaps some other animals as well. Considering the fact that emotional feelings are so important in guiding cognitive and social decision-making (Damasio 1994; Adolphs et al. 2003), we must certainly wonder whether the existence of cool rationality in the human mind has been overrated.

The acceptance of this possibility – that the lower sub-neocortical region of our brain may have a consciousness of its own, has yet to be accepted by the neuroscience community. Most scholars of emotions are still committed to the view that affective feelings, to be experienced, need to be 'read-out' into the higher regions of the brain. Some would place the read-out in the somatosensory regions of the neocortex (Damasio 1994, 2003). Some would place the read-out in the working memory regions of the dorsolateral frontal cortex (LeDoux 1996). Yet others suggest that all forms of consciousness are critically dependent on our linguistic abilities, and hence mostly on the language regions of our left hemispheres (Rolls 1999). How this magical 'read-out' might occur has not been clarified by anyone. I personally do not believe it exists, even though those higher areas are very important in regulating emotions by generating attributions and all the cultural dimensions of emotional life. Abundant evidence already shows that the sub-neocortical regions have the neural sophistication to construct certain emotional aspects of our mental lives, the parts we share with many other animals – raw affective experiences. The key areas which are critical for this achievement may be very deep and ancient brainstem structures such as the PAG and surrounding tectal areas, which help elaborate a core self (Panksepp 1998a, 1998b; Damasio 1999).

None of us really needs higher order thoughts to achieve a coarse affective level of awareness (pain is an excellent example). Yes, our cognitive apparatus is remarkably important in resolving our affective experience into all manner of subtle nuances. Crucial as those attributional contents are for our mental life, the energetic engines to achieve the intensity of felt emotions are sub-neocortically situated. Infants emerge into our cognitive worlds by seeing how their feelings relate to the world into which they were born. And, of course, our understanding of the world is critically dependent on the emergence of those cortico-cognitive abilities. This gradually emerging cognitive apparatus adds an enormous cognitive richness to our lives, but without our inborn, fully embodied, neuronally energized capacity to feel good and bad about the world – those basic tools for living that we inherit – we and the other animals would be zombies.

A major challenge of twenty-first century neuroscience is to confront the deep evolutionary nature of human emotional response systems and the affective feelings they help create. Most psychiatric problems ultimately reflect difficulties individuals encounter in regulating their feelings, whether precipitated by environmental and organic problems or, most commonly, by interactions of the two.

Most of my own scientific career has been devoted to deciphering the fundamental sources of emotions in human and animal brains. This project is based on the recognition that the foundations of our emotions are shared, in principle, with other mammals. Through animal brain research, we may shed more light on the neuro-evolutionary sources of our human emotions than by studying members of our own species. Obviously, we cannot evaluate deep neuroscience issues in humans the way that we can in other animals, just as we cannot easily evaluate cognitive contents in animals with anything like the efficiency we can in humans. On the other hand, a mountain of evidence suggests that the essential neural substrates for a multitude of emotional-affective processes are concentrated in those sub-neocortical regions of the brain, commonly known as the limbic system (MacLean 1990), that we share homologously with other mammals.

The overriding premise of my work has been that if we study the shared neural foundations of human and animal nature, especially through a study of the various

evolved *state-functions* of the mammalian nervous system, we will gradually reveal
one of the great mysteries of life – the fundamental neuro-evolutionary sources of
affective experiences in all mammals. Again, this is not to suggest that the *channel-
functions*, which reflect specific types of information processing (e.g. cognitions),
can yield any comparably robust cross-species knowledge. However, if we pursue
the neuro-emotional work well, we may gain a profound understanding of the
nature of affective life in all mammals, which may even promote a new, and deeply
appropriate and needed, sensitivity toward both wild and domestic animals.

Because obvious ethical concerns forbid such research on humans, only animal
brain research can reveal how the specific circuits and molecules of the brain
generate the miracle of affective consciousness. A careful reading of the evidence
garnered from other animals demonstrates that our basic emotional feelings may
arise substantially from evolutionary processes that evolved to generate 'instinctual'
emotional behaviours. In other words, affective feelings appear to be closely linked
to the 'action neurodynamics' that generate instinctual emotional displays within
the animal brain. Whether this requires read-out by higher neocortical systems is
unresolved, but it does not appear to be essential from what we presently know
about these systems. If anything, emotional behaviour in animals is increased by
removal of neocortical tissues, and these behaviours do not appear to be affectively
vacuous. One of the most dramatic and intriguing positive emotional urges is that
for rough-and-tumble play in young animals. The joyous feelings underlying such
action patterns do not have to be learned, even though they probably guide both
behavioural choices and a great deal of subsequent learning. Indeed, the instinctual
nature of affects within human brains makes them one of the major factors upon
which all of us base our life decisions.

To derive useful knowledge from such animal studies (e.g., novel therapeutic
agents as well as novel non-organic approaches), we will have to understand the
molecular underpinnings and psychobehavioural consequences of these systems
better than we presently do. Fortunately, the neuroscience and molecular biology
revolutions have now provided the essential tools for a penetrating pursuit of such
questions. The work has already yielded potential neurochemical codes for various
emotions, drives and appetites – the many state-control systems of the deeply
SELF-referential brain – that may be the primal sources of our biological values
and possibly a major source process for consciousness itself.

My own long-term aim is to take the type of analysis described in this chapter
to a genetic level. New genetic methods are capable of probing how the DNA
'orchestra' plays its tunes under different environmental circumstances. 'Gene
chip' technologies, which monitor the changing activities of tens of thousands of
genes simultaneously, are among the most promising ways to clarify such issues.
However, utilization of such difficult techniques requires communication and
collaboration among scientific subcultures not well acquainted with each other's
views. My short-term hope is to characterize, with the help of skilled colleagues,
the molecular-genetic consequences of playfulness (Panksepp et al. 2002).

In concluding this chapter, I want to add a few comments about an issue that may be of considerable concern – the ethical issues associated with the study of affect in animal models. Many will justifiably feel both emotional discomfort and cognitive concern about such work on which our neural knowledge of emotions is based. These are appropriate and difficult issues: as soon as we accept that other animals have emotional lives, the ethics of such research must become a key issue. This is one reason I dealt with such issues at the very outset of my text on *Affective Neuroscience* (Panksepp 1998a). Since we have no reasonable alternative way to obtain this knowledge, ethical compromises may need to be made by investigators willing to seek this knowledge. The pursuit of such investigations puts special responsibilities upon investigators to pursue their inquiries with the least amount of stress to their animal subjects. Indeed, many of the issues I have described can be pursued in such a way that critical studies concerning emotional circuits can be conducted under full anaesthesia.

Such concerns have convinced me to pursue positive emotions more than aversive ones. Still, the bottom line is that we will never obtain this important knowledge unless we are willing to pursue certain lines of experimental inquiry, without denying that there are ethical sacrifices that must be made in order to obtain this knowledge. There is also the likelihood that most laboratory animals do not have the cognitive depths to consider such issues from human perspectives, and that if we take special additional efforts to assure that our experimental animals are allowed to live within their 'comfort zones' that perhaps we have not offended them as much as we would have if they had had the capacity cognitively to conceptualize their place in the living order. Obviously, if we do not pursue detailed animal brain research on such issues, we will forever remain ignorant of the deep neurobiological nature of those affective processes that guide human and animal lives. If we do not pursue this kind of work, we will never understand the biological nature of 'the soul' (Panksepp 1998b).

# References

Adolphs, R., Tranel, D. and Damasio, A.R. (2003) 'Dissociable neural systems for recognizing emotions', *Brain and Cognition* 52: 61–9.

Andersen, S.L. (2005) 'Stimulants and the developing brain', *Trends in Pharmacological Sciences* 26: 237–43.

Bodkin, J.L., Zornberg, G.L., Lucas, S.E. and Cole, J.O. (1995) 'Buprenorphine treatment of refractory depression', *Journal of Clinical Psychopharmacology* 16: 49–57.

Bouvard, M.P., Leboyer, M., Launay, J.-M., Recasens, C., Plumet, M.-H., Waller-Perotte, D., Tabuteau, F., Bondoux, D., Dugas, M., Lensing, P. and Panksepp, J. (1995) 'Low-dose naltrexone effects on plasma chemistries and clinical symptoms in autism: a double-blind, placebo-controlled study', *Psychiatry Research* 58: 191–201.

Burgdorf, J. and Panksepp, J. (2006) 'The neurobiology of positive emotions', *Neuroscience and Biobehavioral Reviews* 3(2): 173–87.

Cozolino, L.L. (2002) *The Neuroscience of Psychotherapy*, foreword by D. Siegel, New York: Norton.

Damasio, A.R. (1994) *Descartes' Error*, New York: Avon.

Damasio, A.R. (1999) *The Feeling of What Happens*, Orlando, FL: Harcourt.

——(2003) *Looking for Spinoza*, Orlando, FL: Harcourt.

Gillberg, C., Terenius, L. and Lonnerholm, G. (1985) 'Endorphin activity in childhood psychosis', *Archives of General Psychiatry* 42: 780–3.

Gordon, N.S., Burke, S., Akil, H., Watson, J. and Panksepp, J. (2003) 'Socially induced brain fertilization: play promotes brain derived neurotrophic factor expression', *Neuroscience Letters* 341: 17–20.

Harlow, H.F. (1971) *Learning to Love*, San Francisco, CA: Albion.

Keverne, E.B., Martensz, N. and Tuite, B. (1989) 'B-endorphhin concentrations in CSF of monkeys are influenced by grooming relationships', *Psychoneuroendocrinology* 14: 155–61.

Knutson, B., Burgdorf, J. and Panksepp, J. (2002) 'Ultrasonic vocalizations as indices of affective states in rats', *Psychological Bulletin* 128: 961–77.

Kovacs, G.L., Arnyai, Z. and Szabo, G. (1998) 'Oxytocin and addiction: a review', *Psychoneuroendocrinology* 23: 945–62.

Kroes, R.A., Panksepp, J., Burgdorf, J., Otto, N.J. and Moskal, J.R. (2006) 'Social dominance-submission gene expression patterns in rat neocortex', *Neuroscience* 137(1): 37–49.

Lane, R.D. and Nadel, L. (eds) (2000) *Cognitive Neuroscience of Emotion*, New York: Oxford University Press.

LeDoux, J.E. (1996) *The Emotional Brain*, New York: Simon and Schuster.

MacLean, P.D. (1990) *The Triune Brain in Evolution*, New York: Plenum.

Meaney, M.J. (2001) 'Maternal care, gene expression, and the transmission of individual differences in stress reactivity across generations', *Annual Review of Neuroscience* 24: 1161–92.

Panksepp, J. (1979) 'A neurochemical theory of autism', *Trends in Neuroscience* 2: 174–7.

——(1981) 'Brain opioids: a neurochemical substrate for narcotic and social dependence', in S. Cooper (ed.) *Progress in Theory in Psychopharmacology*, London: Academic Press.

——(1993) 'Neurochemical control of moods and emotions: amino acids to neuropeptides', in M. Lewis and J. Haviland (eds) *The Handbook of Emotions*, New York: Guilford Press.

——(1998a) *Affective Neuroscience: The Foundations of Human and Animal Emotions*, New York: Oxford University Press.

——(1998b) 'The periconscious substrates of consciousness: affective states and the evolutionary origins of the SELF', *Journal of Consciousness Studies* 5: 566–82.

——(1999) 'Emotions as viewed by psychoanalysis and neuroscience: an exercise in consilience', *Neuropsychoanalysis* 1: 15–38.

——(2001) 'The long-term psychobiological consequences of infant emotions: prescriptions for the 21st century', *Infant Mental Health Journal* 22: 132–73.

——(2005a) 'Affective consciousness: core emotional feelings in animals and humans', *Consciousness and Cognition* 14: 19–69.

——(2005b) 'On the embodied neural nature of core emotional affects', *Journal of Consciousness Studies* 12: 161–87.

Panksepp, J. and Bishop, P. (1981) 'An autoradiographic map of 3H diprenorphine binding in the rat brain: effects of social interaction', *Brain Research Bulletin* 7: 405–10.

Panksepp, J. and Burgdorf, J. (2003) '"Laughing" rats and the evolutionary antecedents of human joy?', *Physiology and Behavior* 79: 533–47.

Panksepp, J. and Harro, J. (2004) 'The future of neuropeptides in biological psychiatry and emotional psychopharmacology: goals and strategies', in J. Panksepp, (ed.) *Textbook of Biological Psychiatry*, Hoboken, NJ: Wiley.

Panksepp, J., Bean, N.J. , Bishop, P., Vilberg, T. and Sahley, T.L. (1980) 'Opioid blockade and social comfort in chicks', *Pharmacology Biochemistry and Behavior* 13: 673–83.

Panksepp, J., Siviy, S. and Normansell, L.A. (1984) 'The psychobiology of play: theoretical and methodological perspectives', *Neuroscience and Biobehavioral Reviews* 8: 465–92.

Panksepp, J., Lensing, P., Leboyer, M. and Bouvard, M. P. (1991) 'Naltrexone and other potential new pharmacological treatments of autism', *Brain Dysfunction* 4: 281–300.

Panksepp, J., Moskal, J., Panksepp, J.B. and Kroes, R.A. (2002) 'Comparative approaches in evolutionary psychology: molecular neuroscience meets the mind', *Neuroendocrinology Letters* 23: 105–15.

Panksepp, J., Burgdorf, J., Turner, C. and Gordon, N. (2003) 'Modeling ADHD-type arousal with unilateral frontal cortex damage in rats and beneficial effects of play therapy', *Brain and Cognition* 52: 97–105.

Petrovic, P., Kalso, E., Petersson, K.M. and Ikngvar, M. (2002) 'Placebo and opioid analgesia: imaging a shared neuronal network', *Science* 295: 1737–40.

Plato (2000) *The Republic*, ed. G.R.F. Ferrari, trans. T. Griffith, Cambridge: Cambridge University Press.

Reddy, V. (2003) 'On being the object of attention, Self-other consciousness', *Trends in Cognitive Sciences* 7: 397–402.

Riva, M.A., Molteni, R., Bedogni, F., Racagni, G. and Fumagalli, F. (2005) 'Emerging role of the FGF system in psychiatric disorders', *Trends in Pharmacological Sciences* 26: 228–31.

Rolls, E.T. (1999) *The Brain and Emotion*, Oxford: Oxford University Press.

Scott, E. and Panksepp, J. (2003) 'Rough and tumble play in human children', *Aggressive Behavior* 29: 539–51.

Siviy, S.M (1998) 'Neurobiological substrates of play behavior: glimpses into the structure and function of mammalian playfulness', in M. Bekoff and J. Byers (eds) *Animal Play: Evolutionary, Comparative and Ecological Perspectives*, Cambridge: Cambridge University Press.

Spinka, M., Newberry, R.C. and Bekoff, M. (2001) 'Mammalian play: can training for the unexpected be fun?', *Quarterly Review of Biology* 76: 141–68.

Spitz, R. (1965) *The First Year of Life: A Psychoanalytic Study of Normal and Deviant Development of Object Relations*, New York: International Universities Press.

Sunderland, M. (2006) *The Science of Parenting*, London: Dorling Kindersley.

Trevarthen, C. (2001) 'Intrinsic motives for companionship in understanding: their origin, development, and significance for infant mental health', *Infant Mental Health Journal* 22: 95–131.

Vanderschuren, L.J.M.J., Niesink, R.J.M. and van Ree, J.M. (1997) 'The neurobiology of social play-behavior in rats', *Neuroscience and Biobehavioral Reviews* 21: 309–26.

Zubieta, J.K., Ketter, T.A., Bueller, J.A., Xu, Y., Kilbourn, M.R., Young, E.A. and Koeppe, R.A. (2003) 'Regulation of human affective responses by anterior cingulate and limbic mu-opioid neurotransmission', *Archives of General Psychiatry* 60: 1145–53.

# 4

# A NEW ERA FOR PSYCHOTHERAPY

Panksepp's affect model in the context of neuroscience and its implications for contemporary psychotherapy practice

*Roz Carroll*

## Introduction

Jaak Panksepp (1998) is one of a handful of key contributors to the emerging field of neuropsychoanalysis and neuropsychology.[1] He stands alongside others such as Antonio Damasio (1994, 1999), Mark Solms (Solms and Kaplan-Solms 2000; Solms and Turnbull 2002), Colwyn Trevarthen (Trevarthen and Aitken 2001) and Allan Schore (1994, 2003a, 2002b, 2003b) who have bridged the worlds of science and psychotherapy in recent years (Carroll 2003). All of these thinkers are involved in overturning the 'perspectives handed down to us from the pre-neuroscientific behaviourist and cognitive eras' (Panksepp, Chapter 2 in this volume, p. 14).

This discussion of Panksepp's chapters for this book aims to set his thinking in the context of other developments in neuroscience, as well as considering its implications for psychotherapy. Neuroscience is useful to psychotherapy where it can confirm, or reframe, or challenge intuitions which have become established clinical theory (Corrigall and Wilkinson 2003; Carroll 2005b). One theme of this chapter is that many different approaches to psychotherapy have been 'on track' one way or another.

Panksepp's work is based on the study of affective states as they emerge from the neurodynamics of brain circuits. These are being mapped with increasing precision through the combination of animal research, molecular biology, evolutionary psychology and experimental and behavioural psychology with humans and animals. In the first of these chapters he makes a case for studying affect in its own right (apart from cognition) and briefly describes seven basic emotional systems which mediate core psycho-behavioural states. He argues: 'At least half of the scientific problem for understanding mental disorders is a clarification of the neural nature of affective processes in the brain' (Panksepp, Chapter 2, p. 16). In Chapter 3 Panksepp illustrates this by commenting on autism and ADHD, with their very different genetic and social-developmental profiles.

The 'emotional operating systems' identified by Panksepp organize complex neurobiological processes for priming communicative and action states and for shaping relational responses. They can be divided into the primordial set, FEAR, RAGE, and SEEKING, which are basic to survival, and the social set, LUST, PANIC, CARE and PLAY, which are characteristic of mammals, and which depend on the creation and maintenance of social bonds for survival. It is this differentiation of basic affect states that opens up the possibility of radically restructuring psychiatric and psychotherapeutic diagnostic categories around new principles.

## Affect, cognition and the body

Historically, from a behaviourist perspective, certain complex behaviours in animals and humans were seen as largely reflexive responses to the environment involving an automated symphony of actions and physiological changes (Hess 1957). Affect was not considered central to the understanding of animals, and it was perceived to be too ephemeral in humans to be studied through brain research which instead focussed on cognition (Panksepp 1998). Panksepp's work is of outstanding importance because of its wide interdisciplinary research base, which enables him to navigate the 'difficult triangulation' of studying 'affective experience, behavioural/body changes, and the operation of neural changes *concurrently*' (1998: 34).

Part of Panksepp's rationale for drawing on animal research is that the core structure of the mammalian brain is very similar across all mammalian species. Although species vary in terms of the strength and fine details of various basic emotions, the main difference in their brains is a great variability in the size and interconnecting complexities of the neocortex. In mammals these underlying structures of behaviour – mating, nurturing, defending territory, etc. – are explicit observable activities within a relatively predictable range. The neural circuits and neurochemistry which underpin and correlate with these fundamental behaviours in mammals are closely paralleled in the neurobiology of the human sub-neocortical limbic regions.[2] Panksepp stresses that the deep organizational structures of affect can be distinguished from higher cortical systems that are essential for most cognitive activities.

The neocortex is a mushrooming structure with rapidly firing neural systems generating vast networks of sensory and semantic associations. Whereas the sub-neocortical limbic regions seem to initiate or 'prime' affects, the cortex enables emotions to be filtered, elaborated and extended in time. Patterns of behaviour which are clear in animals are often obscured and interrupted by the human capacity for self-reflexivity. Many cortico-cognitive activities tend to suppress (or heavily modulate) subcortical emotional processes.

Although everything in Panksepp's argument implies the body, it is worth spelling out more fully how the body fleshes out our multidimensional emotional nature. The robust but slowly firing systems of the sub-neocortical limbic regions are rich in neurochemicals which influence attention, emotions, and motivations, as well as perceptions and memories. Neuro-modulators like hormones and other peptides, produced in endocrine glands and organs of the viscera, generate very specific effects which feed back into the brain. It has been established that many neuro-chemicals found in the brain, such as serotonin, are produced in the gastrointestinal system as well (Gershon 1998). The brain is not the sole executor, but rather part of a complex system of feedback loops (Damasio 1994).

What we experience as affect involves dynamic movement at many levels of the body: cellular processes, blood circulation, muscular contractions, facial expres-sions, changes in electrical conductivity of the skin, and shifts in the peripheral nervous system (Carroll 2005a, 2005b). These changes are perceived and regis-tered through the processes of proprioception (the felt sense of muscular changes and the position and orientation of the body in space), kinesthesis (a subset of proprioception which refers to the perception of the sensation of movement) and interoception (perception of neurochemical and visceral activity in the body). This information from the body is registered in many different parts of the brain. In fact, Douglas Watt has proposed that 'emotion binds together virtually every type of information the brain can encode . . . [it is] part of the glue that holds the whole system together' (1999: 1).

Panksepp argues that, from a practical evolutionary perspective, 'affect has to be grounded in action tendencies' (Chapter 2, p. 18). In other words, affect is accompanied by the impulse to move, express, or act in some way which fulfils the function of the emotional operating system. With the FEAR system, for example, freezing is evoked at low levels of arousal and at higher levels the flight reflex is triggered, demanding that the body run. With the activation of the PANIC system, we are wired to cry and wail. In RAGE, muscles tense especially around the fore-arms and hands, the eyes glare, etc. In terms of psychotherapy, this does not means that clients need to act out those impulses, but that therapist and client must recog-nize the reality of the feeling (Orbach 2005). Otherwise, as Panksepp suggests, we are vulnerable to 'psychosomatic disorders from repressed bodily urges' (Chapter 2, p. 15). Reich (1972) was one of the first to recognize the link between illness and chronic disconnection between body, impulse, and affect, and research into the suppression of specific affects supports this (Traue and Pennebaker 1993).

It is common for people to be unaware of powerful feelings. For some, talking to another opens up the possibility of getting in touch with feelings. However, Panksepp's model sheds some light on why other approaches are valuable too. Body psychotherapy, dance movement therapy, psychodrama, Gestalt psychotherapy, process oriented psychology, arts therapies, all provide therapeutic contexts for the client to find the hidden affective imperative through moving or expressing or tuning in to the body (Carroll 2005a; Totton 2005). Much of the data used by the brain is secondary, deriving from the body, which has sensory nerve endings in every cell (Damasio 1994). Whereas the subcortical areas respond rapidly to (unconscious) perceptions, the cortex, especially the left cortex which is related to language, may be the last part of the brain to know.

## A little help from Jung

The implications of Panksepp's model do not stop with active body-centred modalities. In fact, there are interesting parallels between Panksepp's model of core affects and Jung's ideas about archetypes, instincts and affect. Jung's interest in the self-regulating psyche led him to proposals which can be used to extend and enrich the perspective offered by Panksepp's rigorous theoretical model:

> Though 'instincts' or 'drives' can be formulated in physiological and biological terms, they cannot be pinned down in that way, for they are also psychic entities which manifest themselves in a world of fantasy peculiarly their own. They are not just physiological or consistently biological phenomena, but are at the same time, even in their content, meaningful fantasy structures with a symbolic character. An instinct does not apprehend its object blindly and at random, but brings to it a certain psychic 'viewpoint' or interpretation, for every instinct is linked *a priori* with a corresponding image of the situation.
>
> (Jung 1955: 602)

Jung was influenced by ethology (the study of the evolution of animal behaviour patterns) and anthropology in the relatively early phase of their development as disciplines. These and other sources such as mythology and philosophy inspired his idea of the archetype as a structuring principle (*Collected Works*) (CW8: 748). Jung suggested that 'instincts are typical modes of action' (CW8: 273), while 'archetypes are typical modes of apprehension' (CW8: 280, cited in Haule 2005). He argues that instinct and archetype 'determine one another' (CW8: 271), and he suggests that the archetypal may be experienced as an affective state through an image or a metaphor (CW9: 267).

Jung's theory emphasizes the dynamic creativity of the human mind in which the unconscious is 'the totality of all archetypes' (CW8: 339). Jung's archetypes represent both a collective pattern and a state that can be experienced in a highly personal and individual way. Panksepp insists: 'Certain states of the nervous system may have affectively experienced contents without any objects in the world to which they are *intrinsically* attached' (Chapter 2, p. 20). In other words, we may experience a particular affect before we have ascribed meaning and a set of associations to it. Let me give an example. In *Affective Neuroscience* Panksepp (1998: 230) writes about 'vasopressin, a molecule which is important in the mediation of courtship and territorial marking'; it is associated with aggression and jealousy. It is one element of the chemistry of care, the maternal/paternal instinct. As I was reading about this, I vividly remembered a moment in 1995 when I was eight months pregnant. I was in an Authentic Movement group, moving with my eyes closed, feeling the fullness of my belly, sensitive to the preciousness of the life inside me. I had an image of myself as a brown bear in the wild, standing and alert to my environment. I had a very clear sense that if any creature approached to threaten my baby, I would swipe them with my great heavy paw. At the time I felt a certain awe at the fierce clarity of motive and action embodied in this image, which resonated so powerfully in every cell of my body. I had of course had experiences in my life of feeling protective, possessive, jealous etc., but at this moment, without external stimulus, I was aware of an impulse arising from deep inside. The image was 'the instinct's perceptions of itself' (CW8: 277).

Of course, these heightened moments of connection to instinct become relatively rare after childhood, so huge is the part played by socialization and the effects of language on human beings. Internal bodily information (interoceptive processes) and information from external senses (exteroception) are sent to specific areas of the cortex to be processed, and then this information is forwarded into association cortices where it is reinscripted, leading to increasing abstraction and recategorization. The neuroscientist Llinas ((Llinas and Churchland 1997) compares the processing in association cortices to 'sympathetic chords', internal resonances that are self-activating. These intrinsic continuing processes of the brain often become more prominent than new information, as we increasingly project our expectations on to the world, rather than grasping each new moment afresh (Solms and Turnbull 2002).

Jung's interest in the image as a means of access to the underlying structure of an experience has influenced many forms of psychotherapy. Whether the image is identified by client or therapist, and whether it is perceived through the emergence of a metaphor in a verbal narrative, or felt to be present, or visualized quite distinctly, or made or drawn, it can enrich and deepen the exploration of a process (Samuels 1989). Some images are simply useful for bringing out unconscious thoughts or feelings, while others connect the client to intense feelings. Beverley Zabriskie, in Chapter 14 in this book, gives remarkable examples of how some of her patients' dreams offered comment on physical disease and impending deaths through symbolic images. Images sensed by the therapist may also be important countertransference clues (Carroll 2005a). Susie Orbach in Chapter 5 in this book describes how she felt as though her body was on fire after a session with a client whose brother was burned to death. This account suggests that instincts are not only perceived but also communicated to others via embodied images.

## Libido, the seeking system and psychotic states

While some of Panksepp's emotional operating systems (FEAR, RAGE, LUST) are predictable, others radically reformulate our established categories of affect with surprising implications. The SEEKING system was originally conceived of as a reward system but it has subsequently been found that it is not the possibility of reward per se that reinforces seeking but the pleasure of investigation and pursuit. Its prototype is foraging behaviour, with the search for resources (food, shelter, a mate etc.) initiated through receptor systems that detect bodily imbalances. Its chemistry is characterized by dopamine, a neurotransmitter described as the 'power switch' because it energizes and invigorates the individual in relation to their environment. Cocaine, for example, works by increasing dopamine availability.

In animals, seeking behaviour is quickly spotted: sniffing and persistent forward locomotion are indicators of the SEEKING system in action.

SEEKING behaviour is triggered by need and its activation orients the subject towards any object that might fulfil that need; as Lewin said, 'need organizes the field' (1926: 443). From an evolutionary perspective, it is critical for survival that we experience seeking as affectively positive (as intrinsic desire) and that it is focussed and goal-directed. Hope, excitement, anticipation, determination and curiosity provide the motivation and force to keep going, to move forward, to follow the scent.

The SEEKING system engages the frontal cortex which is involved with 'fore' thought, planning, and expectancy. As with each of these affect systems, SEEKING operates across a spectrum from the immediate and concrete, e.g. looking in the fridge when you are hungry, to more sophisticated needs such as searching for meaning, satisfaction or solace. Panksepp suggests that SEEKING may be 'similar to the psychoanalytic concept of libido' (Chapter 2, p. 25). It interacts with other systems, such as LUST, CARE, PANIC and PLAY, as well as FEAR and RAGE, and especially with memory, to create representations of options based on prior learning. Dopamine release stimulates active associative networks correlating with the drive to formulate meaning and causality. Dysregulation of the SEEKING system leads to an excess of meaning-making with a tendency to 'confirmation bias' (that is, you see what you want or expect to see). Paranoid schizophrenia is characterized by excessive dopamine activity, and anti-psychotic drugs work by reducing dopamine activity at specific receptors (Panksepp 1998: 162). Over-arousal of the seeking system can lead to other kinds of addictive or displacement activities as well (Panksepp 1998: 161).

Psychotherapy depends on the SEEKING system. It holds out the possibility of self-discovery and plays a key role in learning and making connections. For the client in despair of getting any help from psychotherapy, it may be the awakening of curiosity which provides initial and continued motivation for coming. However, although seeking can be used in the service of relationship, it can also be highly self-sufficient and potentially obsessive. Dreaming, investigating, pioneering, hunting, surfing the internet, activities which do not need an*other*, which in fact generate extraordinary amounts of pleasure and satisfaction that can lead away from social contact, are the hallmark of 'seeking'. Ideally psychotherapy is a form of exploration which does not avoid the shadow side of seeking – frustration, disappointment and despair (Carroll 2002). One crucial aspect of this is the attention given to the interplay between what's going on inside the client, and what's going on in the therapeutic relationship, 'the explicit acknowledgement, and exploration, of the realm between, created by, and in some way greater than, both participants' (Hycner and Jacobs 1995: 203).

Seeking is a primordial state common to all animals, including reptiles. Although all the senses may be engaged in searching, in evolution seeking is particularly linked with smell, the only exteroceptive source of information that goes straight into the sub-neocortical limbic region. Even though SEEKING is implicated in many forms of spiritual, intellectual, and creative activities, its roots are in a primitive, pre-relational, self-stimulating instinct. Panksepp states that SEEKING has 'a super-ordinate function, as an essential infrastructure and scaffolding for all of the other basic emotions' (Chapter 3). This may be why the dysregulation of SEEKING (as a result of genetic or environmental factors) is so critical to 'mental' health. From a diagnostic perspective it is of considerable significance that the SEEKING system is the only system where overactivation is firmly linked to psychotic states.

## Panic and play in relation to attachment theory

While SEEKING may be super-ordinate in terms of generating raw energy, it is through bonding and the attachment relationship that the sense of self-in-relationship is developed (Schore 2003a). Panksepp has contributed to the more general field of attachment theory through his very specific focus on PANIC (separation distress), social bonding and PLAY. Panksepp's investigation of the brain chemistries of opioids, oxytocin and prolactin have proved central to the understanding of social bonding, pleasure, and emotional dependence in all creatures. Studying a range of young mammals showed that contact comfort in the form of touch and physical play generated positive feelings mediated by these chemistries (Panksepp 1998). A surge of oxytocin (such as accompanies orgasm and breastfeeding) is correlated with deep feelings of contentment and love. But it still depends on the actual social environment to make it relevant – putting oxytocin directly into rat brains doesn't make them happier unless there are other rats to play with. Panksepp's research suggests that depression, social withdrawal, and panic attacks are 'linked with the activation of the distress response' (1998: 274–5); autism, on the other hand, has been linked with 'interruptions to bonding mediated by opiates which soothe distress' which probably reflects 'some type of dysfunction in normal neural development originating in the second trimester of pregnancy' (Panksepp 1998: 276–7).

Panksepp highlights the importance of vocalisation, both in separation distress (crying and wailing) and in joy (laughter) (Panksepp 1998; Chapters 2 and 3 in this volume). He does not go into the detail of development but looks rather at core affective states, such as the dependence of the very young on the proximity of the attachment figure, and the more exuberant, exploratory physical play which stimulates the growth of the social brain. In Chapter 3 he shows that autism may be a largely genetic disorder, treatable with a combination of drugs and plenty of human warmth and attention (Panksepp, Chapter 3). This expands the perspective on autism originally proposed in psychoanalytic theories (Tustin 1992).[3] On the other hand, he argues that ADHD is basically a 'social-developmental disorder', requiring treatment consisting of 'a regular diet of physical play, each and every day' (Chapter 3, p. 41). This confirms what has been known for many years by those working therapeutically or in a mentoring capacity with children and adolescents (Meade 1992; Biddulph 1997). Or even further back, if we think of Winnie the Pooh taking Tigger to the woods to work off his excessive bounciness (Milne 1926).

Panksepp's theory of emotional operating systems complements the work of neuroscientists and psychotherapists studying the fine-grained transactions of parent–infant attachment. Allan Schore's (2003b) work on the regulatory function of attachment relationships gives us an understanding of how complex neurochemistry with a particular developmental timetable can go seriously awry. He shows how brain organization is affected by the baby's experience of relationship. Schore argues that through repeated intricate and subtle aspects of interaction, or non-interaction, the infant internalizes the mother, and/or the major caregiver(s). The mother's face has particular importance as a 'hidden biological regulator' of the infant (Schore 2003b: 44). Intense face-to-face transactions, traumatic or loving, become imprinted in long-term memory and act throughout the lifetime of the individual as an internal regulating object, whether consciously remembered or not (Beebe and Lachman 2002; Schore 2003b).

Schore's interest is in attunement, the micro-element of behaviour, and the reciprocal influence of mother and infant on each other's nervous system. In particular Schore (1994) focuses on the orbito-frontal cortex, which is the main interface between the sub-neocortical limbic regions and the cortex. Appropriate regulated responses by the mother to her infant's intense affective states help transform the instinctual into the relational. Without some constancy, empathy and mutuality the infant is otherwise left to cope with a string of dissociated states organized around rage, fear, and panic (Schore 2003b). As a result, feelings may become inhibited, prohibited or distorted (De Zulueta 1993).

A secure attachment enables the development of resilience and wellbeing; it has a stabilizing effect on the sense of self. There is increasing evidence that depression as a phenomenon is related to persistent early experiences of feeling rejected or abandoned (Gerhardt 2004). More serious abuse or chronic neglect in infancy and childhood have an even more damaging effect on an individual's capacity to cope, then and later, with their feelings and with the normal stresses of life. This can lead to more severe disorder such as borderline personality disorders and antisocial personality disorder (Schore 2003b).

Attachment theory has proved of enormous value to psychotherapy, where the relationship with the therapist is often the central vehicle for change and growth in the client (Pollard 2005). Engaging with the client in a way which brings feelings explicitly into the therapeutic relationship where they can be felt, responded to and acknowledged is critical to working in depth. In particular, it is understood that small details such as the timing of comments, the words used, the exchange of looks or smiles, have a significant impact on the client's sense of self. This attention to the quality of contact and relating enables affects which may never have been consciously felt or recognized, or which may have been experienced as overwhelming and painful, to be shared and explored in a safer context as Diamond (2005) explains. As clients become attached to their therapists, there is often an increase in both tears and laughter.

## Differentiating fear and panic

The development in the understanding of the FEAR system has been of major significance to the study of anxiety disorders and trauma (Van der Kolk et al. 1996; Levine 1997). It is now recognized that humans have a genetically based fear response which may be triggered automatically by certain stimuli such as dark places or unprotected heights, while other fears are learned through experience (Panksepp, Chapter 2). The characteristic of fear is alarm, a state of strong activation of the sympathetic nervous system manifest as increased heart rate, sweating, and increased muscle tension (Carroll 2000). The FEAR response may be initiated in a startle reflex, which is an especially strong orientation reflex, preparing the body for avoidant action (ducking, diving), freeze and/or flight. The striking appearance of some clients, for example their raised shoulders, severely contracted diaphragm, a frozen posture suggesting up-tightness with readiness for flight, and fright etched into the facial expression, is vivid evidence of chronic fear.

It is now established that there are two circuits for triggering FEAR: the longer, slower one which takes information about stimuli and associates it to a time and place (hippocampus) and also makes it available for conscious reflection (cortex), and the short circuit which sends sensory information directly to the amygdala to makes a rapid assessment. Overactivation of the amygdala, shutting down of important areas for information processing (hippocampus) and verbalizing (Broca's area), and dysregulation of the autonomic nervous system are now recognized as underlying trauma-related conditions such as borderline personality disorder and post traumatic stress disorder (PTSD) (Scaer 2001; Schore 2003b). In Chapter 2 Panksepp emphasizes that an understanding of the FEAR system is more important for understanding the feelings of fear and anxiety than the study of learned inputs to the FEAR system.

Panksepp's model gives a very useful differentiation of FEAR as the response to threat to physical survival, and PANIC as the response to the loss of the attachment object. In panic an object is sought, in fear it is fled from. The fight/flight system is unambivalent: it says 'danger – attack, freeze or get out'. Attachment is often bound up with ambivalence, and the maturation of the relationship requires increasing separation and the development of independent resources. When the attachment object is the source of fear, not a source of comfort, the conflict between PANIC and FEAR interrupts the development of the capacity to regulate feelings (Schore 2003b). One of the mistakes sometimes made by therapists is to encourage and support the emergence of an intense affect which has overwhelmed the client in the past. If the therapeutic relationship is unable to contain what gets stirred up, the experience can be retraumatizing.

Trauma therapy is one of the fastest growing areas of psychotherapy and it has benefited directly from neuroscience's new understanding of fear. In fact, it is becoming a necessary clinical skill to recognize the activation of a trauma response and the potential for dissociation in the client (Rothschild 2000). Many therapies such as Cognitive Behavioural Therapy, Cognitive Analytic Therapy,

Eye Movement Densensitisation Reprocessing, and Somatic Trauma Therapy, have evolved specialist tools for trauma related to life-threatening situations. All employ some degree of structured procedure that requires cognitive elaboration by the client. This can help modify the reflexes of the FEAR and PANIC circuits, and create some integration where fear relates to things and events. Chronic fear and anxiety stemming from insecure or even traumatic attachment are coloured by amygdala reactions, which are hard to reach through cognition. Here, an understanding of and capacity to work with attachment patterns, implicit memory and internal models of self and other which manifest in the transference, is critical (Diamond 2005).

## Navigating the log jams

Panksepp's differentiation of emotional operating systems, with their particular neurochemistries, behaviours, and other bodily and cognitive aspects is of major relevance to psychotherapy. Internalised relationships and conflicting parts of self may be linked to the over- or under-use of particular affects. Affect that can be tolerated and elaborated has the capacity to bring some sense of coherence, of meaningful, feelingful acts and relationships. But what if clients are torn between strongly opposed feelings which threaten to destabilize them? It is often the case that clients bring not simply unresolved or unexpressed or unfelt feelings, but a dense intertwined tangle of feelings, much like the undergrowth in a jungle.

Clients who have endured early abuse or major injustices as adults may suffer from a log jam of affects which may be mutually inhibitory. Often they may be stuck in the conflict between anger and hurt. RAGE involves adrenalin, strong arousal, hardening of muscles, an upward and outward movement, a puffed up chest, narrowing eyes: a fight response. Hurt, on the other hand, belongs to the PANIC system, which relates to attachment and safety. Hurt is the loss of trust in an individual, system, group, even in life itself – what has been relied upon as a secure base has been disrupted. The client needs to grieve to heal this wound, just as the puppy separated from its mother needs to howl with increasing mournfulness. The PANIC system has totally different effects in the body – it engages the opposite side of the autonomic nervous system, which is associated with withdrawal, crying, collapsing or a caving-in of the chest. The need to grieve (to let go, to accept) and the need for protest (to seek redress) can become chronically deadlocked. Shifts into a more detached SEEKING state or repeated activation of the FEAR system may complicate the process further.

When affective states become objects of consciousness, they can bring awareness of environment, relationship and motivation (Perls et al. 1951). When they are unconscious, they maintain a relentless presence in the body. The therapist has to be skilful in recognising and facilitating the elaboration of these basic affects, and understanding their place within the current intersubjective context of the therapy. For this, the sensitivity to the cycles of each system (Aposhyan 2004), to body process, to core images and countertransference responses, is critical (Carroll 2005a).

## The future of psychiatry and psychotherapy

Panksepp's models are derived from accumulating evidence in multiple disciplines, each with their own limitation in frame, scope, and complexity, but he has brought them together through his scientifically informed imagination and capacity for conceptualization. His work stands at the juncture which potentially bridges some of the division between psychological and pharmacological models, as well as challenging the psychiatric classification system based on diagnostic syndromes (*Diagnostic and Statistical Manual of Mental Disorders IV* 1994), as opposed to emotional endophenotypes (characteristics stemming from the interaction of genes and environment).

In practice, psychotherapy and psychiatry do overlap but Panksepp's elucidation of deep organizational principles of human behaviour gives a more coherent model for precise prescriptions as well as human relational interventions. In particular it addresses two interrelated questions which have caused psychotherapy to be such a contentious discipline, namely 'what is primary and what is compensatory or defensive in human behaviour?' and 'how do nature and nurture interact?' The answers to these are not simple but his work has made new inroads into the extremely complex epigenetic developmental landscape. Furthermore, Panksepp's firm emphasis on the significance of affect, especially when combined with research on attachment (Fonagy 2001; Schore 2003a) can counterbalance the arguments of those, such as the UK government adviser Professor Richard Layard, who suggest that National Health Service provision should focus exclusively on therapies which offer cognitive solutions to human distress and difficulty (Layard 2004).

## Notes

1  This chapter reflects on Panksepp's Chapters 2 and 3 in this book.
2  Panksepp argues that the widely used term 'subcortex' is misleading since it implies that the referent is still 'cortex'. He has since globally replaced it with the longer but more correct phrase, 'sub-neocortical limbic regions'; the 'neo' is needed since he has never left *limbic cortex*, which is not neocortex, out of the affective equation.
3  While psychoanalysis recognized from early on that genetic factors played a part in autism, Tustin's work strongly emphasised the child's difficulties in separating from mothers who were 'cold, intellectual and rejecting' (1992: 14). More recently there have been fertile collaborations between neuroscience and psychoanalysis in exploring the aetiology and effects of autism, such as the Symposium on Autism: Neural Basis and Treatment Possibilities (Bock and Goode 2004)

## References

Aposhyan, S. (2004) *Bodymind Psychotherapy: Principles, Techniques and Practical Applications*, New York: Norton.

American Psychiatric Association (APA) (2000) *Diagnostic and Statistical Manual of Mental Disorders*, 4th edn, Washington, DC: APA.

Beebe, B. and Lachman, F. (2002) *Infant Research and Adult Treatment: Co-constructing Interactions*, Hillsdale, NJ: Analytic Press.

Biddulph, S. (1997) *Raising Boys*, Lane Cove, NSW: Finch.

Bock, G. and Goode, G. (2004) *Autism: Neural Basis and Treatment Possibilities*, Novartis Foundation. Online. Available http://www3/interscience.wiley.com (accessed 4 January 2006).

Carroll, R. (2000) *The Autonomic Nervous System: Barometer of Intensity and Internal Conflict*. Online. Available http://www.thinkbody.co.uk (accessed December 2005).

——(2002) 'Intrinsic potentials: panic, seeking and play in psychotherapy', *The Psychotherapist* 19: 41–5.

——(2003) 'On the border between chaos and order: neuroscience and psychotherapy', in J. Corrigall and H. Wilkinson (eds) *Revolutionary Connections: Psychotherapy and Neuroscience*, London: Karnac.

——(2005a) 'Rhythm, re-orientation and reversal: deep re-organisation of the self in psychotherapy', in J. Ryan (ed.) *How Does Psychotherapy Work?* London: Karnac.

——(2005b) 'Neuroscience and the "law of the self": the autonomic nervous system updated, re-mapped and in relationship', in N. Totton (ed.) *New Dimensions in Body Psychotherapy*, Maidenhead: Open University Press.

Corrigall, J. and Wilkinson, H. (eds) (2003) *Revolutionary Connections: Psychotherapy and Neuroscience*, London: Karnac.

Damasio, A. (1994) *Descartes' Error: Emotion, Reason, and the Human Brain*, London: Putnam.

——(1999) *The Feeling of What Happens: Body, Emotion and the Making of Consciousness*, London: Heinemann.

De Zulueta, F. (1993) *From Pain to Violence: The Traumatic Roots of Destructiveness*, London: Whurr.

Diamond, N. (2005) 'When thought is not enough', in J. Ryan (ed.) *How Does Psychotherapy Work?* London: Karnac.

Fonagy, P. (2001) *Attachment Theory and Psychoanalysis*, New York: Other Press.

Gerhardt, S. (2004) *Why Love Matters: How Affection Shapes a Baby's Brain*, Hove: Brunner-Routledge.

Gershon, M.D. (1998) *The Second Brain*, New York: HarperCollins.

Haule, J.R. (2005) *Language: The Biology of an Archetype*. Online. Available http://www.jrhaule.net/evol-atp/02Lang.html (accessed July 2005).

Hess, W.R. (1957) *The Functional Organisation of the Diencephalon*, London and New York: Grune and Stratton.

Hycner, R. and Jacobs, L. (1995) *The Healing Relationship in Gestalt: A Dialogic Self-psychology Approach*, Highland, NY: Gestalt Journal Press.

Jung, C.G. (1953–79) *The Collected Works* (Bollingen Series XX) trans. R.F.C. Hull; H. Read, M. Fordham and G. Adler (eds) Princeton, NJ: Princeton University Press.

——(1937) *Psychological Factors Determining Human Behaviour*, Vol. 8.

——(1947) *On the Nature of the Psyche*, *Collected Works*, Vol. 8.

——(1949) *The Psychology of the Child Archetype*, *Collected Works*, Vol. 9.

——(1955) *Mysterium Coniunctionis*, *Collected Works*, Vol. 14.

Layard, R. (2004) *Mental Health: Britain's Biggest Social Problem*. Online. Available http://www.strategy.gov.uk/downloads/files/mh_layard.pdf (accessed 30 December 2005).

Levine, P. (1997) *Waking the Tiger*, Berkeley, CA: North Atlantic Books.

Lewin, K. (1926) 'Vorsatz, Wille and Bedurfnis (intention, will and need)', *Psychologische Forschung*, 7: 440–7.

Llinas, R. and Churchland, P. (1997) *The Mind–Brain Continuum*, New York: Carfax.

Meade, M. (1992) *Men and the Water of Life*, San Francisco, CA: Harper.

Milne, A.A. (1926) 'In which Tigger is un-bounced', in *Winnie the Pooh: The Complete Collection of Stories and Poems*, reprinted 1995, Godalming: The Book People.

Orbach, S. (2005) 'The psychotherapy relationship', in J. Ryan (ed.) *How Does Psychotherapy Work?* London: Karnac.

Panksepp, J. (1998) *Affective Neuroscience: The Foundations of Human and Animal Emotions*, Oxford: Oxford University Press.

Perls, F., Hefferline, F.R. and Goodman, P. (1951) *Gestalt Therapy: Excitement and Growth in the Human Personality*, New York: Dell.

Pollard, J. (2005) 'The value of attachment theory in understanding how psychotherapy works', in J. Ryan (ed.) *How Does Psychotherapy Work?* London: Karnac.

Reich, W. (1972) *Character Analysis*, reprinted 1990, New York: Farrar, Strauss and Giroux.

Rothschild, B. (2000) *The Body Remembers: The Psychophysiology of Trauma and Trauma Treatment*, London: Norton.

Samuels, A. (1989) *The Plural Psyche*, London: Routledge.

Scaer, R. (2001) *The Body Bears the Burden: Trauma, Dissociation and Disease*, New York: Haworth.

Schore, A.N. (1994) *Affect Regulation and the Origin of the Self*, Hove: Lawrence Erlbaum.

——(2003a) *Affect Regulation and the Repair of the Self*, New York: Norton.

——(2003b) *Affect Dysregulation and Disorders of the Self*, Hove: Lawrence Erlbaum.

Solms, M. and Kaplan-Solms, K. (2000) *Clinical Studies in Neuro Psychoanalysis*, London: Karnac.

Solms, M. and Turnbull, O. (2002) *The Brain and the Inner World: An Introduction to the Neuroscience of Subjective Experience*, New York: Other Books.

Totton, N. (ed.) (2005) *New Dimensions in Body Psychotherapy*, Maidenhead: Open University Press.

Traue, H.C. and Pennebaker, J.W. (eds) (1993) *Emotion, Inhibition and Health*, Toronto: Hogrefe and Huber.

Trevarthen, C. and Aitken, K.J. (2001) 'Infant inter-subjectivity: research, theory and clinical application', *Journal of Child Psychology and Psychiatry* 42 (1): 3–48.

Tustin, F. (1992) *Autistic States in Children*, London: Routledge.

Van der Kolk, B., McFarlane, A. and Weisaeth, P. (eds) (1996) *Traumatic Stress: The Effects of Overwhelming Stress on Mind, Body and Society*, New York: Guilford Press.

Watt, D.F. (1999) *At the Intersection of Emotion and Consciousness: Affective Neuroscience and Extended Reticular Thalamic Activating System (ERTAS) Theories of Consciousness*. Online. Available http://cognet.mit.edu/posters/TUCSON3/Watt.html (accessed 4 January 2006).

——(2003) 'Psychotherapy in an age of neuroscience', in J. Corrigall and H. Wilkinson (eds) *Revolutionary Connections: Psychotherapy and Neuroscience*, London: Karnac.

# CONTEMPORARY APPROACHES TO THE BODY IN PSYCHOTHERAPY

## Two psychotherapists in dialogue

*Susie Orbach and Roz Carroll*

## Introduction

This chapter comes from the dialogue and discussion, chaired by Bernd Eiden, held at the conference 'About a Body'. We, as authors of this chapter, decided to keep our introductory statements and the ensuing discussion as it was on the day, with some minimal changes made for clarity. We have done this to preserve the immediacy of the points we were making as they emerged in the discussions with each other and with members of the audience.

## Roz Carroll

My basic proposal is that the sense of the self is rooted in the body and catalysed by relationships and the environment. Neuroscience confirms two things that have always been basic parameters of body psychotherapy: that the body is essential to the sense of self and that we are social creatures designed to interact with other humans (Damasio 1994; Trevarthen and Aitken 2001).

I am going to map out some of the basics of body psychotherapy which include characteristics which are general to most therapies, and specifics which are more particular to the body psychotherapy field. There are four broad aspects to working with the body, some of which of course apply to therapists in all traditions.

First, basic relatedness, attunement, ordinary empathy, all require responsive-ness to the client's body (Schore 2003a). Second, a more sophisticated elabora-tion of this basic relatedness is the use of self, the use of the therapist's embodied awareness of their own process (sensations, images etc.) which we know of as countertransference. Thirdly, there are interventions designed to highlight the client's awareness of sensory elements, impulses, breathing, feelings and defences. A defence in body psychotherapy terms, for example, would be the muscular ten-sion that holds back, distorts or cuts off a basic impulse or sensation (Reich 1972). And finally, there are the specialized body work skills. These are quite wide-ranging skills including working with knowledge of specific developmental patterns such as reflexes, with body systems (fluid, motor, digestive) and working directly to re-establish healthy functioning of the nervous system. It encompasses the dance movement field, and body psychotherapists working with or without touch (Totton 2003).

Following and facilitating a body process depends on a perceptual capacity in the therapist. The kinds of bodily phenomena to be perceived fall into three broad groups. First are the visually observable signs: colour change, breathing, levels of tension in the client's body, posture, gesture, facial expression and micro movements. Second is the sense of contact quality that we know through a variety of senses. We assess how present the client is: what their eye contact is like, their voice quality. We sense the variations and shifts in mood and attitude. And third the therapist uses their countertransference. This is the therapist's awareness of their own body, of sensations, images, impulses, feelings and fantasies that offer a link to the client's process and the intersubjective field (Orbach 1999; Carroll 2004).

In psychotherapy, the therapist is constantly making decisions about which level to engage with, moving back and forth between levels. All interventions – interpretations, questions, bodywork, attention to breath, sensation, and image – are forms of feedback that can heighten the client's sense of themselves (Carroll 2003). Most people have a preferred sense (vision, hearing, and proprioception) and a preferred mode of access. Some clients are very tuned into dreaming; others like narrative, and have immense curiosity for the detail of the stories of their life. Some clients gain most from exploring contact-specific sensory detail; others, from free association through movement. There are many royal roads to the unconscious. Some clients like to go with the sense that feels more developed – where they have a sense of mastery. Others choose the undeveloped sense. Often clients choose to come to body psychotherapy because they have an underdeveloped sense of their own body (Carroll 2002). By increasing body awareness through the process of therapy, they get more immediate access to unconscious and unprocessed feeling. This links with Jung's idea of inferior and superior functions (Jung 1968).

Strengthening or amplifying one aspect or sense can lead to a greater connection in the whole. As Panksepp argues, 'all levels of information processing in the generation of emotional responses interact with each other' (Panksepp 1998: 33). If there is enough information coming through, you don't need to set up special ways to increase it. Indeed, body-based interventions are often about finding a point of equilibrium or containment – this is especially true of working with clients who dissociate (Rothschild 2000). Many clients have come to body psychotherapy because they want to work with explicit body interventions. This presents its own challenge – the desire for touch, or to move, or to release through catharsis may come loaded with a fear of the inner world and of relating. The client may have an unconscious need to re-enact – or a wish to expel – painful and intolerable feelings and sensations. In this case the therapist may need to support the client in slowing down, focusing on how it is to be with the therapist and noticing what is already happening.

When my new client, Tony, comes in and talks about his family, he appears to be a long way away. 'How are you?' I ask. Referring to his strained forward posture, I ask him if he is uncomfortable. His head moves back to rest on the chair with a sudden movement. He closes his eyes and his hand waves desperately in my direction. Making physical contact with a client is a process I'm confident with, but I don't want to rush in here, because this is very dramatic. I want to address both his anxiety about contact and the urgent communication of his gesture, so I ask him, 'Shall we experiment with the distance between our chairs and see what feels right?' Having found a position that feels right for him, he talks about his feelings of longing, and we explore how much he can manage, and not manage, eye contact.

With any client, there are issues around timing and focus: when to wait, listen, and hold the pieces that a therapist hears, sees, feels and senses or when to draw attention explicitly to contact. By contact I mean the experience of being with another. This may involve physical contact, eye contact, or a sense of connectedness through a shared feeling, or an idea. Body psychotherapy, like other integrative and humanistic therapies, employs a variety of structures to support the client in exploring ways of being. The therapist considers when to suggest or support a structure that brings in the experiential element to develop something embryonic, emerging, stuck or unconscious and when to bring him or herself in directly to heighten or make explicit a dynamic in the relationship.

It is widely recognized now in contemporary psychotherapy that the client needs to experience feelings in the relationship with the therapist. Surviving intensity of feeling, transitions between feelings, and identifying of unfamiliar feelings, are all part of embodied insight (Carroll 2003). Embodied insight includes the survival of intense feelings, becoming aware of transitions between feelings, and the identification of unfamiliar feelings. And so the therapist's work involves moving between supporting the client's self and meeting it (Hycner and Jacobs 1995). Relationship feeds the sense of self, but the elaboration of self also occurs in a self-preoccupied way, as the client takes time to tune into the self. It's a pulsation back and forth.

Some clients have their most powerful therapeutic experiences through exploring in a particular modality, such as working with movement, or touch, or sensing, even though the most valuable thing in the end is the relationship with the therapist. Some clients experience a particularly strong sense of agency or self through moving. Others find a sense of connection and containment through touch – which feels like a vital food for them. Others don't require touch and wouldn't dream of moving spontaneously as a way of processing, but discover aspects of the self through sensing, through tracking the breath in the body and discovering their own innate imagery (Landale 2002). And still others find the greatest satisfaction in words, in recognizing the self through the act of finding the right words, exploring the detail of the story.

When awareness is felt to come from inside the client, it registers as experience. This enhances agency because it creates a sense of ownership. The function of experiential work is not only to express or to gain insight, but also to find out what helps the client self-regulate. Psychotherapy is, among other things, about finding how to help the client get to what they need. What increases anxiety for some lowers it for others. So, for example, with some clients actually asking about a movement they make or the sensation in the body would be a bit counterproductive, because it would feel intrusive or invasive or scary, because they have no sense of their body. So we would have to proceed in other ways, perhaps just by talking more directly, allowing the client to get to know the therapist.

What begins as an experiment in bodily processes within psychotherapy develops into a relational experience of psychotherapy. As the client is talking, they may make spontaneous gestures or movements. The therapist's work would be to bring awareness to these spontaneous movements by drawing attention to them, or perhaps moving with the client, or interacting with them.

> A client who came with a tremendous feeling of shame from being looked at told me about a man who had looked at her in a sexual way. She had felt very humiliated and wanted to disappear. Those were her words. She had a history of being very uncertain about sexual signals and it was something we had been exploring in the therapy. We talked about this for a while but then she moved on to talk about the experience of going to see a Spanish dancer. She became very animated as she spoke. It was a single male dancer surrounded by adoring women. As she was talking about him I noticed that her colour was rising, her face was wreathed in smiles, her eyes were sparkling, and her movements were very animated and alive. So I took the risk of feeding back to her this excitement and wondering with her where she would place her feelings in her body right now on a spectrum of sexual feeling from just pleasure in observing him, or flirtation, or was she turned on? As we were talking about this I noticed that she kept going back into his posture which involved expanding her chest, lifting her head and her chin. She looked as though she was really enjoying this posture, so I encouraged her to go into this movement more, to become him, to see how it felt to be this gorgeous man surrounded by adoring women. This led to her contacting the other side of the polarity of shame: from being exposed, to feeling the part of her that wanted to be surrounded by attention and to feel attractive. It was from the movement pattern rather from any words she used that I went from thinking that she fancied him to thinking that she fancied being him.

Body psychotherapy is associated with the use of touch although some body psychotherapists don't use touch and it is not a given. Using touch within psychotherapy is not an intervention; it is a multiplicity of possibilities, each with a context in a specific therapeutic relationship at a particular moment. Touch can be provoking, intensifying feelings of fear, rage, loss, shame, helplessness, sexual desire etc. Touch can equally have a profoundly containing effect, providing safety and contact, through a connection to the client's own body in the context of a therapeutic relationship (Carroll 2002).

> With Tony, some sessions later, I suggested that he lie down on the mattress and I did hold his hand. With this, waves of feelings came up, as well as an anxious driven need to be doing something therapeutic, like having insightful connections to his childhood. I was more interested in whether he could actually allow the experience of me being there with him.

A small proportion of clients really get a lot from touch. A skin-hunger from early deprivation is key, and working with touch begins to initiate an experience of self. A connection to body is possible because of the combination of touch with attention and the therapist's sensitivity to understanding and working with the defences against touch. The effect of physical contact, together with a sense of being held emotionally, is mutually enhancing and can enable the client to experience support, relaxation, acceptance and self-recognition. And on some occasions I use my body literally to support the client in states of distress, trembling and shaking.

Much of the process of body psychotherapy is about weaving together an experience of the body with an understanding of process and the developing sense of self-in-relationship. Sometimes I will ask certain question that may help to increase the client's own awareness of their body. I might ask them to be aware of their breathing, or guide them with specific questions 'How does your chest feel? Can you feel your feet?' in order to build a sensory picture. I might particularly do this with areas that either look very charged or look quite cut off. Then perhaps I feed back the details that they have given me (using their words, not mine) to heighten their awareness of their body. Then I might ask the client what they see or sense or feel and whether a character or metaphor is evoked from this process.

> One client, Julian, who was addicted to looking at porn sites on the internet, found that when I asked him about his body picture in this way he connected to a sense of his body being inflated. He became aware of a subtle feeling of his body changing size and becoming huge, almost as if he might burst out of his clothes, 'like the Incredible Hulk' he said. From there he could sense for the first time his rage, and remembered himself as a child setting fire to his toys (this case is described in more detail in Carroll 2005a).

Finally I want to comment on countertransference, which is a term I use to mean a sophisticated relational response to the client. The elements of countertransference include the therapist's perception of sensation, images, fantasies within herself, as well as catching unusual details or incongruence in the client's behaviour. When we feel any of these, I believe we are responding with an extreme sensitivity to relational cues. For the therapist, these responses often exist on the border between compulsion and improvisation, receptivity and activity. So, when I am observing my countertransference responses, I ask myself: 'What role does this client want me to play?' I need to consider whether what is being evoked in me is a therapeutic response, a relational response, or an impulse that is drawing us both into a re-enactment (see Michael Soth, Chapter 8 in this volume).

## Response from Susie Orbach

The starting point for my interest in the body as a psychoanalyst is Roz's remark: 'There are patients who don't have a sense of their body'. I am really interested, intrigued and perplexed by people who I see in therapy whose transformations with their body are so profound that it is almost as though they don't have a body. In very complex ways, with enormous creativity, they engage with their bodies many times a day to create something that for them doesn't exist and is not right.

For me, the body is constructed. What do I mean by this? I don't assume the body as simply existing by virtue of its being a physical entity. Nor do I see the body as an elephant – a place of remembrance or as a site of a deeper truth. I think that is a way that many people conceptualize or express an interest in the body. I am interested in the question of how we get a body. I am interested in the developmental history of the body and the ways in which it is amenable to distress and what it tells us, this amenability to distress, about the history of that body.

The origins of psychoanalysis were about the interplay between the body and the mind and particularly the attempts to understand bodily symptoms that had no organic basis. The tic, the paralysed arm, the person who spoke in a different language than their own on an involuntary basis, the swelling of a belly that looked like pregnancy, such symptoms were what Freud and Breuer termed hysteria and were what they studied.

Since the mid 1950s within psychoanalysis there has been a mentalist turn, so that the body is now seen as a dustbin for that which the mind cannot cope with. So it's a dumping ground and it's a bit player with the mind having the central activity. I've been rather disturbed by this tendency, which is also present, I believe, in many of the body therapies, even though the therapist is working directly on or with the body. I find the formulation that the body is the dump for the mind very unsatisfactory. I think there are interesting questions to be asked about how and why we, and the people who seek our help, are able, so exquisitely, to override what seems to be the materiality of the body. This is why Roz's work interests me, and Panksepp's (1998) work and Damasio's (1994) work. Their work is implicitly developmental and constructivist. They don't present the body as the truth or a royal route to unconscious processes, which is the unintended message of both contemporary psychoanalysis and many body therapies.

If I can encapsulate my position very quickly, I would say that the body is not so much the truth but it's a relational outcome of the intersubjective field of the carer and the baby just as much as the mind is. Winnicott frequently tells us that 'there is no such thing as the baby. Whenever you see a baby you see a mother and baby pair' (Winnicott 1971). I would like to extend this idea to say there is no such thing as a body. Whenever you see a body, you see a body that has been internalized in the context of a relationship with another body.

The body is an outcome of an intersubjective field and relationship. All the cultural, class, religious forces: everything about the body is an outcome of relationship. If you are raised to speak French, you are raised in the French language, the motion of your mouth, the way you hold your head, gesticulate, the shape of your maximilian facial muscles, everything about the way in which your body is structured is a cultural relational event. Many of us who have seen people in our practices who have what we might call different self-states or dissociated states of mind, may explicitly incorporate different body-states within that. Valerie Sinason (2002) captured this on film very beautifully with some people with multiple self-states and showed us the differing body relations that accompany these different states of mind.

To underscore my position, when we look at a body we are looking at the history of that body and the history of the difficulties in that body to body relationship. When an individual comes to therapy there is the creation of a therapy relationship, and if the individual has a disturbed or distressed or unhappy or shaky body, this may well have an impact on the therapist's own body, if the therapist listens. Most of you in the room seem to be body therapists, so you know this very well indeed. In my bit of the field, they don't know this well at all. In fact some of my colleagues are so disturbed at the idea of the body being in the room, that they sit behind their patients. So for me, particularly when working with people who come in with active body distress, I anticipate a pretty interesting journey for my own physical corporeal experience, what Roz has called and I would call the countertransference or my subjective bodily experiences. I've had all sorts of completely unexpected bodily feelings in the therapy room and it is those feelings that stimulated my thinking.

In trying to understand these body countertransferences I've found it useful to see if they can help us engage with:

- the physical distress of the individual we are working with, the difficulties they experience at the corporeal material level
- the instability of their body subjectivity
- what they might have missed developmentally and still are searching for at a physical material level
- how we might understand the constant fretting or involvement with the body, let's say as in anorexia or in eczema, where somebody has to pay a certain kind of physical attention to her or himself constantly.

To take up the fourth point, most psychoanalysts and a lot of body therapists would think or say 'You're picking at the body because you are weeping'. I'm interested in why the body is weeping. I am quite interested in disrupting, for the moment, the question of why the soul or heart is weeping and looking at what it is about the body that needs to announce itself as a weeper or, with an anorectic, asking what are those rituals doing in relation to the basic instability about the body. I do not think we can help the individual sufficiently if we do not address the body distress as a distress about the body directly.

That is one level of question. Simultaneously, I am curious about what my body may have to offer to the bodies of my patients. How does my body enter the inter-subjective field between us? How does it affect the other body in the room? In what ways can my body be of value to my patient? How can they use it as a site of provision, as a site of identification, as a site of stability or as a site of projection?

I'd like to give a couple of interesting body countertransference responses, one from my practice currently and one from a very long time ago. In the last year I left a session and went to write up my notes, it's something I do, it's my way of trying to understand or free-associate or contain and also hold something, and as I was typing my notes up for this particular session, I felt that my body was on fire. I was really out of my skin, it was so unusual a feeling, and I felt I was burning. I am not histrionic in relation to the body – a headache is about as bad as it gets with me and that is a very occasional occurrence. This burning sensation was terribly upsetting and it took a while to calm down. Fortunately I didn't have a session immediately following. In the next session with this particular patient, she proceeded to tell me a story of her brother falling from a shelf above a stove and burning to death when he was an infant. She wasn't alive at the time. The tragic event is part of her family history. Consciously she wasn't much touched by it in her growing up. You can well understand the terrible reticence and anguish of her parents whose child died in this ghastly way.

To me, this burning sensation was a really interesting transfer of information. We are very accustomed to that kind of funny smell or pain that we get working with people who have experienced explicit abuse, which we do not understand, and we wait for what it is. But this was really inexplicable in the first instance (Orbach 2006).

The other dramatic instance of body countertransference is about my experience of working with a woman who was extremely troubled. She had colitis as an adult. As a baby she used to sick up her feed. This had not been received very well and by the age of 6 she developed a full-blown symptom of involuntary vomiting when she was upset. The treatment for this in the 1950s was behavioural management. She was made to reimbibe her vomit. This turned her into a bed-wetter. One could say she was terribly creative in terms of letting everybody know that her body wasn't OK, except nobody was listening (Orbach 1995).

In this therapy the interesting countertransference that I think is worth trying to discuss, is that I suddenly felt like I was a purring pussycat. I just had this abso-lutely, wonderfully embracing, enveloping internal feeling of the most wonderful contentment; an adult purr, not a real pussycat purr, I just don't have a word that's

associated with humans for purring, and it struck me that this woman had an exquisite capacity to create in the therapeutic field and in the therapist, a body that she
could make use of in the room, from which she could start to deconstruct her very
pained, and what I would call rather false, body identification (Orbach 1995). To
begin to deconstruct this body she needed to be safe in the knowledge that there
was a body for her in the room that was rooted and OK.

What this kind of countertransference does in terms of the process of therapy
is to allow the hated body defence structure to be dissolved, to be looked at, so
that the person temporarily becomes a person without a body, which is what they
experience themselves as being. We then face that bodylessness that Roz is talking
about in the process of being able to find a way to develop a body that is actually
robust, vulnerable and can feel anguish, can hurt, can cry, can have joy. We are
used to doing that and providing for that with the psyche. That is what we all do.
We assume that people use our psyches to deconstruct their psychic difficulties,
their defence structures and to be psyche-less if you like or terribly empty and
lonely and distressed in the short term. Then through identification they find a way
forward to develop a more authentic self. And that is what I think I've been trying
to do with the body.

## Dialogue

ROZ: I think there is quite a lot that we agree on, even though how we actually work
with clients might look very different. There is a strong area of agreement
between us, particularly about the importance of relationship and the early
environment in developing a sense of the body. There is one thing I would
like to qualify though about your emphasis. You actually said, 'Everything
about the body is an outcome of relationship'. I agree with you that there's
something, (and neuroscience is really showing this very clearly now) about
the quality of early environment, the caretaking, the mother's responsiveness
to her baby, that has a very significant effect on the body (Gerhardt 2004).
It affects the stabilization of the autonomic nervous system and the capacity of the person to self-regulate. Self-regulation depends on many variables,
and includes being able to translate body sensation into awareness of affect
(Schore 2003a). I believe that the self-regulation of the body translates into
something like the experience of having a body.

When you talk about instability, it is a breakdown and there are various ways
in which our self-regulation can break down. The thing I want to qualify about
Susie's statement is the 'everything'. The role of the mother, the father and
siblings is fundamental, as is the cultural environment. These help or hinder
the establishment of regulatory processes and identifications. As you say 'the
child picks up the mannerisms, the modes of their culture'. But there are other
components to getting a body than human relationships. These include the
way the baby spends hours rolling on the floor, crawling, putting objects in
its mouth. This is part of an innate curiosity (Panksepp's SEEKING system)

that stimulates us to go out and explore territory, to smell the earth, to feel the sun on our bodies. These are very crucial components to getting a body as well (Hartley 1994; Frank 2001). I think we would both agree that there is a necessary basic level of safety that an infant has to have before they can make use of the sensory environment. But nevertheless I don't want us totally to exclude factors beyond the human relational context. This is why I think the experiential element of psychotherapy can be very important, because it takes somebody back to the act of discovery which is part of how we get a sense of our body.

SUSIE: It is really interesting because Jaak Panksepp characterized psychoanalysts as going backwards, and I see myself as working with bodies in the present, so it's really interesting that your description stems from a deficit in self-regulation; someone getting a sense of something that they didn't have and thus having a notion of something that then can break down. To return to the question of how we get a body, if you are a wild child, whether it is in India or whether you are raised with the wolves, you do not have many aspects that are associated with being human. You mimic everything to do with the situation in which you develop. So we know that wild children do not have sexual feelings, they don't have language; they don't necessarily walk on two feet.

ROZ: But those are very extreme.

SUSIE: They are, but I think that is what we have to look at. They give us clues to our own experience.

ROZ: No, we don't disagree on that.

SUSIE: I want to pick you up on this idea of a breakdown, as though there was integrity and then a breakdown. You see, for me, my thinking about the body – and I don't know if this is useful or not to you – is that because of the kind of difficulties that mothers, particularly today, experience, many of them are unstable in their bodies, and this is partly because of the cultural forces that are operating on them. For example if you are a woman who believes she has somehow to look like she never had a baby four weeks after she has had a baby, and if she is freaked out about her own eating and she doesn't know how to feed her baby or herself, she is going to create a baby that has a disturbed relationship to its body and its appetites. I tend to think of the body as developing with a set of defences. Winnicott would say, you've got a false self and then there is a true self underneath. This to me is a kind of nonsense formulation much as I love Winnicott, because what can be so true, and yet can be hidden forever. But if we reformulate that and we call the false self an adapted self and the true self an undeveloped self, then I think we have something to use which we can apply to the body, which I think allows us to . . .

ROZ: Yes. I want to relate this to neuroscience and contemporary body psychotherapy. When I use the word 'breakdown', I don't mean there was one point when something occurred and something was broken down. Organisms have basic self-regulating capacities: homeostasis which keeps the body going, and means that it spontaneously seeks out that which it needs. Sadly it can be the human environment itself (but not only the human environment) that actually damages these basic intrinsic capacities. And part of the difficulty . . .

SUSIE: What if we said that the human environment 'shapes' these basic intrinsic capacities, because then I think we might agree. You say 'damage' as though there is an ideal body out there; I would say 'shapes'; shapes the neural pathways, shapes the . . .

ROZ: I am using 'damage' more in the way that you were, in referring to those wild children. That is, in the sense where children experience very severe early trauma, something in their development, in the structuralization of the autonomic nervous system, in the basic functioning of the body systems, has broken down (Schore 2003b). Then there is a constant attempt, which is what you are describing in your clients, to re-establish the functioning of those systems. But that needs support in various ways. I wanted to come back to your point about Winnicott, because I think what he intuitively put his finger on was what he called mental activity for its own sake. I think that a state of being overdriven or hyper-aroused (for example, in a strong state of anxiety) creates this sort of false mental function where the cognitive thinking about what one ought to be and how one ought to adapt to the environment overrides the deeper and more spontaneous processes (Winnicott 1958). And so in body psychotherapy what we are interested in is how to reconnect the client to spontaneous processes of self-regulation.

SUSIE: Let me push this one bit further and then maybe we should talk about body countertransference. I think what's important about what Winnicott says is something different. He says in the absence of the baby's gesture being received, the mother substitutes her own gesture. When the baby then acknowledges the mother's gesture and substitutes it for its own, that becomes the way in which their relationship operates. He then goes on to say that the baby actually exists on the basis of a set of impingements, because it has this mother's gesture, which is not a meeting gesture but an imposition gesture. What the individual then requires as they develop, is a set of impingements all the time that create a sense in them that they exist because they survive those impingements. It's not the impingements that let them exist, but it's the crisis around them. One could apply that formulation to most of the somatic symptoms that we see. Or to people who have to pass every exam, or climb every mountain. They need a crisis, a challenge, because in mastering that crisis they are able to feel they exist. I think this is another piece of the body story which is quite interesting. I'd love to learn from the body therapists, more about the physical feel of that kind of impingement and false gesture.

ROZ: To answer one of the points that you've made about this idea that some body psychotherapists think there is 'truth' in the body, I think we need to put in some historical perspective. Body psychotherapy has undergone enormous change and development in the last ten or twenty years and has incorporated much of the relational sophistication from object relations (Totton 1998; Soth 2003; Asheri 2004). I am very glad that my colleague Michael Soth will present exactly this battle between the client's idea, not necessarily formulated, of what they think they need to do, how they are objectifying their own body in attempt to get to a certain kind of state, versus the therapist's sense of what is needed to support the client. I gave the example of holding the client's hand where he wanted this because he was in quite an overdriven state. He wanted to do what he thought therapy required of him. But his idea of therapy was coloured by the way his mother related to him – he had internalized her. What I wanted to explore, not as an agenda, but as a process of exploration was: how can you have the experience of being here with me and me holding your hand? How can you actually allow that experience to occur within you?

SUSIE: I think that doesn't account for the titles of the books that I just looked at outside.

ROZ: What were the titles?

SUSIE: 'The body remembers', 'Your body speaks its mind' and a workshop title 'Do bodies tell the truth?' I mean that's kind of what I'm talking about and what I think is my challenge to you. You have multiple challenges to me – this is my challenge to you.

I also want to address the contemporary understanding of countertransference, which as you said is about the internalization of relationship or about the relational field. It's not, as we used to think about it, this simple diagnostic tool, which is 'if I'm feeling this, it's either a version of what you are feeling or it's what you need'. This is the level of the pathology, and I think we no longer think about countertransference only in those terms, and we no longer think it's my craziness versus your craziness. We don't even *think* of it in those terms any more. In the relational psychoanalysis field we have done a lot of work on the co-construction of affects but we haven't looked at the co-construction of bodily feelings because most people don't tend to talk sufficiently about the body in psychoanalysis.

ROZ: And yet I think the countertransference is always a body phenomenon.

SUSIE: A physical . . .

ROZ: No, not a physical – a bodily phenomenon.

SUSIE: But what do you mean by that, because so is speech production?

ROZ: Yes, what I mean by that, well this is not really my thinking; it is Alan Schore's. I want to acknowledge that his proposal is that countertransference occurs within the body of the therapist. The right cortex is the part of the brain that is devoted to novel thinking, creativity (synthesizing large amounts of information), and very speedy perception of bodily emotional information about the objects in the environment. The right cortex also processes bodily emotional information of the perceiver (the therapist), who is resonating with the client (Schore 2003c). This is a very fast-acting, unconscious, highly developed human skill. Countertransference occurs as a result of relationship, although obviously there are responses like that that exist outside therapy. It is fundamentally a powerful perception of the other that then is elaborated and developed. I think there is a lot that we can explore about countertransference and you are right that we have a lot of questions to ask. I think it is a very broad phenomenon, but it's a creative phenomenon and therefore something that is worth pursuing.

SUSIE: I suppose that one of the difficulties that has happened recently is that while we have jettisoned dreams as the royal road to unconscious processes, we could now see the countertransference in that way. I think that would be an unfortunate tendency, because there is so much else going on in therapy. There is also the person's narrative and their physical presentation and all sorts of things. I am an absolute fan of the countertransference, and I have written a book about countertransference and the experience of therapy from the analyst/therapist perspective (Orbach 1999) but just as we need to look at the body in order to get it somehow reintegrated, so we need our present views of countertransference in order to reinvigorate our other systems.

ROZ: Absolutely! I do see it as a fine-tuning mechanism, but not the whole therapy.

## Questions from the audience

QUESTIONER 1: My question is addressed to both of you. I'm intrigued by talking about bodies in this way. My thing really is that if the body doesn't exist as a separate entity, then also you could say that the mind doesn't exist as a separate entity. And my feeling is that it is almost impossible not to talk about them separately because language drives us all the time. I feel the enduring myth of our time is that the mind and the body are separate entities and that we are constructed as people through society and through language and through all our interactions, but the body and the mind are sort of different aspects of the same thing. Susie's example of her body feeling on fire, with that girl whose brother had burnt in the fire, shows the sort of resonance between people. You've picked it up from your patient, who's picked it up from her family or whatever. It's just passed through in a sort of unconscious way, if you like.

SUSIE: If we take something like anorexia, we can understand it psychologically through internal object relational means. We can see it as, in part, the creation of an admirable self out of a self who feels awful. We can see that the only meaningful thing to be is somebody who overrides appetite and desire; who is need free and acceptable and this has been self created. If you look at this simply at the cerebral level, it wouldn't solve the anorexia because the individual is left bodiless. There are a lot of fancy interpretations and most psychoanalytically or psychodynamically oriented therapists are in the translation business partly because they cannot bear the pain of what happens when the body comes into therapy. Who wants to listen to the fact that your patient's just sliced through her breast? I don't just mean a little nick, but a serious 'rush-through-triage ahead-of-everybody-else' slice. Who wants to hear that? It's too painful. So we are in the translation business and I suppose from my side I don't want to translate, I want to know what the hell that means at the body level that somebody can be doing that. What is it they need to be feeling and enunciating at a physical level? I don't know whether that's a response.

ROZ: I could respond as well, but my answer is much more boring and dry: just about all the body/brain, and the social environment, how they all fit together. The short answer is that body and mind are not separate, but there are feedback loops, at different levels (from the cellular to the social) which are experienced as mind or body. Feedback loops enable and trigger spontaneous adjustment to and interaction with objects and the environment. These are all interconnecting systems but we have different ways of describing them (Carroll 2003).

QUESTIONER 2: I wanted to address a question to Susie. I was very struck by the throwaway remark that a lot of body therapists dismiss the body or see the body as a dumping ground. I started as a psychodynamic psychotherapist and I am now training in body psychotherapy and one thing I've been very struck by in the training, in which we work on ourselves a lot, is that we actually very much see the body as a resource and that has been very important for me personally but also seems enormously important in the whole way of body work. So, I suppose I wanted to know from you why you dismiss the body therapists in that way.

SUSIE: Well, I don't mean to dismiss, and I'm sorry if I have as I feel I have a great deal to learn from all of you. But when I've gone and talked to body therapists or have done workshops, body therapists seemed to me to say the same sort of thing as the things that my colleagues say that drive me nuts, like 'The real truth is here', 'The trauma is held here'. This is why I said I thought there was a sense of the body as a place of remembering and of truth and that's the piece I have difficulty with.

QUESTIONER 2: I suppose it does hold the traumas, but it can also provide the resources and the way to move forward in my experience.

SUSIE: Well, I think I tried to illustrate it by saying in the countertransference what kind of resources I felt those two people had brought via their bodies right into the room at a completely unknown level, call it unconscious or call it whatever. But for me to feel like a purring pussycat or to feel on fire is to have profound experiences, one of provision and one of communication, that are exquisitely creative. So they are using their bodies as a dynamic resource, absolutely, I agree with you.

QUESTIONER 3: First of all, I am really appreciative of listening to the dialogue, because five years ago or ten years ago we wouldn't have had this dialogue, and so I'm grateful to each of you for coming forward to do this. I would like to come back to the title, though, of the conference and it's 'the embodied mind' and I'd like to suggest that we are working as we all do within our own conditions here. The Western psyche has always had trouble with the body, the mind and the spirit as separate. I'd like to suggest we widen the field to our colleague in neuroscience, Francisco Varela (Varela et al. 1991). He did not locate the mind in the brain; he located the mind in the body and the heart of course. In Buddhism there is one word for body/mind, which is 'namarupa'; they are not separate and it includes the spirit. And I think that we are looking developmentally for understanding, but if we were to broaden the inquiry and I think Susie you've been talking about this. You've not been using the words, you've been talking about field and there's been so much work done in fluidic consciousness with people like Dr Emotu in the work on fields of consciousness of light. Now these are scientists that don't usually get represented and I'd just like to say that the mind perhaps is a mind of field as opposed to location on a personal level. We are located within a mind as opposed to we are the mind. And if we take on board, and I think this is really for Susie, the possibility that there are people who explain why we have this burning experience, understanding the past, present and future within an embodied relationship, the future is here as well as the past. Not just in the memory of the client, but a much vaster mind and I'm not just using mind as memory, consciousness, beyond the individual. And I'd like to take that on board since we don't get into these cause and effect scenarios, because I think it limits what each of you are bringing into the room.

SUSIE: I think the answer is 'fair enough'.

QUESTIONER 4: My question is addressed particularly to Roz, but first of all I would like to say how appreciative I am of what you both were saying and I saw you both reflecting on your practice of psychotherapy. But my question is this. I would you like to ask you, Roz, why do you look to neuroscience for confirmation of your experience? Now, it seems to me that psychotherapy is a reflection upon experience and the neuroscientists would have nothing to work on if we didn't bring them the experience that we've got. And neuroscience certainly can elucidate our experience to some extent, but it is like 'Do I need to know a lot about physiology in order to ride a bicycle?'

ROZ: Well, I look to neuroscience for dialogue, not confirmation. It is about difference. Because I think if you hang out with people who think the same as you, you only develop your thinking in that part. If you go and meet people who have a totally different way of looking at the world, sometimes you feel like banging your head on the table and running away, other times you hear something really striking, you think 'Gosh, that's interesting. I wonder how that relates to what I do, what I think'. That's why I am interested in neuroscience (Carroll 2005b).

QUESTIONER 5: I think the dialogue got a bit aborted there, about the truth of the body. I think the first thing for body psychotherapists to say is that your challenge I think is absolutely valid. Most of my training, most of the traditional body psychotherapy as far as I can see, has treated the body as you describe it, and I think that is absolutely a blind alley, so I think in terms of a dialogue that's one thing to say. But then the next question that I'm busy with, you clearly talked about the impositional gesture, which the child or the baby takes in. So the implication of that is that somehow through that imposition the child loses that sense of – in Winnicott's phrase – 'the psyche indwelling in the soma', because it takes on somebody else's gesture. So then I am wondering, how are we thinking about the process by which that can transform into an experience where the person later then does experience their psyche as indwelling in the soma? How do we think about that process and what are the resources in that? I think this is mainly a question of understanding in the way like you are saying, is it a mental listing of 'Oh, yes, I understand that process that happened there, I understand the dynamic by which I took that in' – is it that kind of process or is there a possibility, is there a kind of wisdom in the body coming through the body, not that is pure or not constructed, but is there some process or spontaneity that is the psyche indwelling in the soma? Do you see what I mean?

SUSIE:  I absolutely see what you mean, and I think what I was trying to say is that the person who has to run up and down stairs and cut themselves compulsively every half an hour is trying to enunciate a body that is still making a demand to be taken seriously, to be indwelling. I thought you were going to go in a different direction, which is how we understand the impositional gesture which gets internalized and one is revolted by at a physical level and therefore has to incorporate the wrongness of it, versus how we understand internalizing the appropriate gesture, the gesture that allows for that yummy feeling. But you weren't going there. So now let me go back to what it is you were saying. Can you reformulate your question or your challenge to me?

QUESTIONER 5:  That wasn't a challenge. Body psychotherapy has quite a sophisticated theory about the internalization of the external relationship, what you just described that is the introjection and internalization of a relationship which is not yummy. What do you do with that person that is running up and down the stairs? And what is happening with their body in the room?

SUSIE:  Actually most people don't move around in my room. I try to create a kind of physical space that isn't about running around.

QUESTIONER 5:  Why?

SUSIE:  Why? That's what I'm comfortable with. I have to work within the constraints of what I am able to do. I might get a version of the buzzing – and I might or might not talk to them about that buzz. I might talk about my body, or my body might be symptomatic if you want to think of it in those terms, and it's not that I wouldn't have an acute sense with somebody about the interpersonal body field if I could talk about it that way. Will I go and do this? I don't know how to do that.

QUESTIONER 5:  What do you mean 'Do this'?

SUSIE:  I know how to soothe, or I know how to . . . therapy is always an adventure. One sometimes knows what might be soothing and one sometimes knows what might produce the kind of emotional space to go more deeply into the distress in a safe way. So I can do that. One might do it by moving the body, but I do it with words. I might do it by moving forward or back. I'm quite a physical person, I am not one who sits absolutely still – but I don't have the body therapy skills you possess. And I've talked to body therapists and asked 'What is it that I need to do for the person who's running up and down the stairs every half an hour?' They can't just give me a piece, because you have a whole field of experience, you can't abstract it and when it does get abstracted it sounds ludicrous to me, because it sounds like, 'well, you touch somebody in order to push some emotion', which to me is so crude and horrible that it's offensive.

QUESTIONER 5: I agree.

SUSIE: It's like me using a word like 'anguish' if I wanted to – I don't know – whatever it would be. So I don't know what it is I need to put in more.

QUESTIONER 5: No, I wasn't actually asking what you need to put in more, I'm asking, I was more concerned, what is happening to the client's body like we know that some of the time she is running up and down the stairs clearly in pain and distress and what happens with . . .

SUSIE: Hopefully in the fifty minutes she gets to have an experience which takes the frantic away, as well as communicating it to me. It's like Roz's initial statement 'There's attunement, developed self regulation, and so on'. These states happen, get verbalized and they also get felt between the two of us in therapy. There would be some hope of a body-to-body communication. I do an awful lot of one-off consultations and I say this, not to say 'Gosh, you're so skilled', but because if you do a lot of one-off consultations you get a lot of similar sort of phrases and what I often hear is somebody looking out of the window saying 'This is such a calm room'. Well, it isn't particularly calm, because there is activity outside on the pavement and I'm sure that we all get that, but it's interesting that one can get that on an assessment, because obviously one is providing a little space for some kind of soothing attachment into which the horror can be allowed.

QUESTIONER 6: This is more to Susie, but I would also be intrigued by Roz's take on it. Wittgenstein said that the best picture of the human soul 'Seele' (the word Freud would have used) is the human body and I've been racking my brain as somebody who's crossed the floor from the psychoanalytic section to humanistic and integrative section, but still has very deep roots in psychoanalysis, what it is Susie that makes you still a psychoanalyst in everything you are saying and this is a rather sloganeering formulation but nevertheless . . .

SUSIE: You're inviting me over?

QUESTIONER 6: No, no, no, I actually came to a conclusion which I would actually be interested in your response to and as I say it is a bit stereotyped and over simple, but it struck me much of what you were saying is very similar to what someone like Groddeck would say in terms of the id being manifest simultaneously . . .

SUSIE: The 'what' being manifest?

QUESTIONER 6: The id – das Es – you know Freud wrote a book 'Das Es und . . .'

SUSIE: Yeah . . .

QUESTIONER 6: Groddeck was the originator of that notion and he had a holistic notion of the id as a totality encompassing all rather than a segment that was walled off by repression, which was Freud's notion. And what came to me was in a sense you were speaking of something like the id as it manifests through the body in its meaning and therefore, again this is sloganeering, what struck me is that you are becoming a body-psychoanalyst.

SUSIE: Well, thank you very much. The only problem with that is that I don't go for the formulation of the id. I mean contemporary psychoanalysis, at least the school that I belong to, doesn't use those categories at all. Incidentally, I should just say I did come from humanistic psychology.

ROZ: I just wanted to say, I think psychoanalysis is at a turning point and the relational psychoanalytical field marks a new way (Mitchell and Aron 1999). We don't know where that new way will go, but I want to bring in what Nick Totton (1998) has said and others have said this too, that Freud was attempting a body psychotherapy and he got stuck and the tradition carried on with Reich (1972) and Perls et al. (1951). Perhaps in this new integration with this new dialogue between you and me and others, there will be another form of body psychotherapy.

SUSIE: The two most important questions in our field relate to the body. One is about how we get a body, that's my question, and the other is what is sex and the erotic? I think they are terribly interesting questions and we need serious study groups to try and understand those. I'm very happy to be called a body psychoanalyst.

QUESTIONER 7: I wanted to come from the opposite direction and address Roz. In a way it's the other side of the coin from the discussion we've been having. I'm sure you simplified it for effect, but when the guy comes into the room and expects to talk about his distress and you say, 'Lie down on the floor and hold my hand', it made me wonder what's your thinking about this and partly reflects where I am coming from. I can understand more clearly Susie's aims – but I wasn't sure. Can you just say a little bit in a sense about your use of body work and that particular technique perhaps? What are you aiming for?

ROZ: The first aim in that instance was to make contact with the client and create a set-up where he might begin to feel safe to connect with his feelings. And yes, you are right, it is a very simple example and I chose it to spell out some basic things and to take in some of the rawest stuff that the body psychotherapists work with and it's very preliminary. In terms of what I am aiming for, it is just to begin to make contact with another human being. What evolves through the years, down the years, is any kind of complex rich journey that a client goes through.

SUSIE: And I think I may know the difference right there. Let me see if I could articulate this, and I'm sure there is a version in body therapy. Perhaps my version of making that contact is to acknowledge the discomfort. A crucial piece of how I would make that contact is to find words to talk about the dilemma.

# References

Asheri, S. (2004) 'Desire in the therapy room', *Association of Chiron Psychotherapists Newsletter*, 26 (spring): 32.

Carroll, R. (2002) 'Biodynamic massage in psychotherapy: re-integrating, re-owning and re-associating through the body', in T. Staunton (ed.) *Body Psychotherapy*, London: Brunner-Routledge.

——(2003) 'On the border between chaos and order: neuroscience and psychotherapy', in J. Corrigall and H. Wilkinson (eds) *Revolutionary Connections: Psychotherapy and Neuroscience*, London: Karnac.

——(2004) 'Emotion and embodiment: a new relationship between neuroscience and psychotherapy', unpublished training manual, www.thinkbody.co.uk.

——(2005a) 'Rhythm, re-orientation and reversal: deep re-organization of the self in psychotherapy', in J. Ryan (ed.) *How Does Psychotherapy Work?* London: Karnac.

——(2005b) 'Neuroscience and the "law of the self": the autonomic nervous system updated, re-mapped and in relationship', in N. Totton (ed.) *New Dimensions in Body Psychotherapy*, Maidenhead: Open University Press.

Corrigall, J. and Wilkinson, H. (eds) (2003) *Revolutionary Connections: Psychotherapy and Neuroscience*, London: Karnac.

Damasio, A. (1994) *Descartes' Error: Emotion, Reason, and the Human Brain*, London: Putnam.

Frank, R. (2001) *Body of Awareness: A Somatic and Developmental Approach to Psychotherapy*, Cambridge, MA: Gestalt Press.

Gerhardt, S. (2004) *Why Love Matters: How Affection Shapes a Baby's Brain*, Hove: Brunner-Routledge.

Hartley, L. (1994) *The Wisdom of the Body Moving*, Berkeley, CA: North Atlantic Books.

Hycner, R. and Jacobs, L. (1995) *The Healing Relationship in Gestalt Therapy: A Dialogic Self-psychology Approach*, Highland, NY: Gestalt Journal Press.

Jung, C.J. (1968) *Analytical Psychology: Its Theory and Practice*, New York: Vintage.

Landale, M. (2002) 'The use of imagery in body-oriented psychotherapy', in T. Staunton (ed.) *Body Psychotherapy*, London: Brunner-Routledge.

Mitchell, S. and Aron, L. (1999) *Relational Psychoanalysis: The Emergence of a Tradition*, Hillsdale, NJ: Analytic Press.

Orbach, S. (1995) 'Counter transference and the false body', *Winnicott Studies* No. 10, London: Karnac.

——(1999) *The Impossibility of Sex*, Harmondsworth: Penguin.

——(2003) 'There is no such thing as a body', *British Journal of Psychotherapy* 20 (1): 3–33.

——(2006) 'How can we have a body? Desires and corporeality', *Studies in Gender and Sexuality* 7 (1): 89–111.

Panksepp, J. (1998) *Affective Neuroscience: The Foundations of Human and Animal Emotions*, Oxford: Oxford University Press.

Perls, F., Hefferline, F.R. and Goodman, P. (1951) *Gestalt Therapy: Excitement and Growth in the Human Personality*, New York: Dell.

Reich, W. (1972) *Character Analysis*, reprinted 1990, New York: Farrar, Strauss and Giroux.

Rothschild, B. (2000) *The Body Remembers: The Psychophysiology of Trauma and Trauma Treatment*, London: Norton.

Schore, A.N. (2003a) *Affect Regulation and the Repair of the Self*, New York: Norton.

——(2003b) *Affect Dysregulation and Disorders of the Self*, Hove: Lawrence Erlbaum.

——(2003c) The seventh annual John Bowlby Memorial lecture: 'Minds in the making: attachment, the self-organising brain and developmentally-oriented psychoanalytic psychotherapy', in J. Corrigall and H. Wilkinson (eds) *Revolutionary Connections: Psychotherapy and Neuroscience*, London: Karnac.

Sinason, V. (2002) John Bowlby Memorial Conference presentation, London, 2002.

Soth, M. (2003) 'What is working with the body?' A response to Maggie Turp's paper from a body psychotherapy perspective, *European Journal for Counselling, Psychotherapy and Health* 5(2): 121–33.

Totton, N. (1998) *The Water in the Glass: Body and Mind in Psychoanalysis*, London: Rebus Press.

——(2003) *Body Psychotherapy: An Introduction*, Maidenhead: Open University Press.

Trevarthen, C. and Aitken, K.J. (2001) 'Infant inter-subjectivity: research, theory and clinical application', *Journal of Child Psychology and Psychiatry* 42, (1): 3–48.

Varela, F., Thompson, E. and Rosch, E. (1991) *The Embodied Mind: Cognitive Science and Human Experience*, Cambridge, MA: MIT Press.

Winnicott, D.W. (1958) 'Mind and its relation to the psyche-soma', in *Through Paediatrics to Psychoanalysis*, London: Hogarth Press; reprinted 1992, London: Karnac.

——(1971) *Playing and Reality*, London: Tavistock.

# 6

# ONE HUNDRED AND FIFTY YEARS ON

## The history, significance and scope of body psychotherapy today

*Courtenay Young*

### Historical overview

Freud founded psychoanalysis over one hundred years ago in 1892. However, it has been largely forgotten that the work of Dr Pierre Janet (1889) preceded him by at least three years, and Janet (also influenced by Charcot) can also be considered as the first proper body psychotherapist. David Boadella (1997) wrote elegantly about Janet's early work and makes a clear connection between body psychotherapy and the work of Janet going back to at least 1885.

> William James, writing in 1894, in a review of Janet's work commented that two Viennese physicians, Josef Breuer and Sigmund Freud, were in the process of confirming many of Janet's findings.
>
> (Boadella 1997: 47)

Freud's psychoanalysis grew out of this basically body-oriented work, but it ended up as a limited verbal specialization, a 'talking cure' that tended to ignore Janet's

> integrative approach which gave equal value to the body, into an approach tending to neglect the body and the importance of non-verbal communications as studied by Janet, and to concentrate on primarily verbal communication.
>
> (Boadella 1997: 47–8)

Janet reported on his own theory of hysteria in 1907 at a conference in Amsterdam and Jung reported at the same conference that 'the theoretical presuppositions for the thinking work of the Freudian investigation reside, above all, in the findings of Janet's experiments' (Boadella 1997: 47, quoting De Bussy 1908). However Freud, in a letter at the end of his life, denied ever having met Janet or having been influenced by him.

Boadella (1997) describes how Janet's work included significant findings about:

- the diaphragmatic block
- the connection between emotional tensions and constrictions in the flow of fluids in the body

- massage work
- the formative process of the embryological stages of development
- visceral consciousness
- channels of contact
- the kinaesthetic sense
- movement and intentionality
- the importance of working with the body with traumatized patients
- the significance of a change in (or lack of change in) the patient's own body image.

So the idea that is increasingly put forward nowadays, that there are new forms of psychotherapy that include the body, is something of an incorrect anachronism. The body *was* at the centre of psychotherapy when it first started, and then Freud and his followers left the body out of psychotherapy. The body has been subsequently ignored for a considerable period of time, but is recently coming into prominence again. It is some of the forces behind this movement that I wish to explore.

Janet's concept of rapport was possibly the foundation of Freud's concept of transference, though it has much more of an empathic and body-oriented sense. Janet is also believed to have influenced Jung and there is some evidence that Jung went to study with him in 1902 in Paris, though this is not mentioned in his auto-biography. Jung's concept of psychological complexes is certainly derived from Janet, as is his concept of the introverted and extroverted personality types, an adaptation of Janet's concepts of 'hypotonia' (sense of cohesion) and 'asthenia' (lack of psychological force). Adler also acknowledges that his inferiority complex constituted a development of Janet's observations on 'le sentiment d'incompletitude' and he linked this to organ inferiority and organ neuroses in a similar way to Janet's work in somatic psychology.

Piaget, another student of Janet's, was influenced by his concept of integration and synthesis especially in the development of cognitive functions out of sensory, motoric and emotional experiences. Despite Freud having originally described the ego as 'first and foremost a body ego' (Freud 1923: 364), the emerging practice of psychoanalysis chose to remain within the confines of how the psyche can affect the body, and not the reverse, essentially by just pursuing the 'talking cure'. This trend began to ignore the body and psychoanalysts also began to seat themselves in such a manner that there was no proper view of the client's body, which also effectively removed the possibility of most non-verbal communication.

However, body psychotherapy did receive some benefit from psychoanalysis and eventually developed a significant level of integration of the concept of the therapeutic relationship within body-oriented approaches. Reich's own approach to the therapeutic relationship was quite confrontational and this was carried further by some of the later neo-Reichian developments, so the proper use of transference and countertransference within body psychotherapy is a significantly later and welcome development. Nowadays the concept of somatic resonance, essential for many body psychotherapists, is becoming increasingly popular in many fields of psychotherapy as an important aspect of the therapeutic relationship: a form of somatic transference. The therapist's body is, at least, being recognized as relevant as well (Shaw 2003).

Elsewhere in the history of body psychotherapy, another significant figure, also long forgotten is Albert Abrams, based in San Francisco between 1891 and 1910, who produced an impressive volume of works (Abrams 1910). While these were actually published slightly later than Janet's first works, they still predate much of Freud's work. Abrams was coming from a very different stream, basing some of his theories on the work of Franz Anton Mesmer (1779) who had preceded him by 130 years or so, and these earlier works form some of the research and theoretical bases for another, somewhat disowned branch of psychotherapy, that of hypno-psychotherapy.

The influence of Mesmer led to significant work by Armand-Marie-Jacques de Chastenet and Marquis de Puységur, who published 'Mémoires pour servir a l'histoire et a l'établissement du magnétisme animal' in 1784. These ideas about defined links between the mind and body eventually spread to the United States and influenced William James (James 1890) and the New Thought movement, as well as Abrams and others. In Europe, there was a steady and continual development of these concepts, despite considerable medical criticism and disownment, through-out the eighteenth century and well into the nineteenth, with the work of Noizet, Cuvillers and Bertrand. These theories, based more on classical mechanics, set the young science of psychology on its mentalist and separatist path. However, being basically reductionist, psychoanalysis and early psychotherapy faced similar criti-cisms to the Helmholtz school; that of being too mechanistic, too materialist; and too facile. Janet's ideas, with their more organic basis, were anything but this.

Therefore there was, at the end of the nineteenth and the start of the twentieth centuries, several other philosophical, natural medical and cultural perspectives that conflicted with the narrow deterministic path that the emerging discipline of psychology seemed to be being directed down. The counterculture that existed at that same time emphasized free sexuality, vegetarianism, non-religious spiritual-ity, the body, and basic feminist principles. It was perhaps most widely expressed in the Wandervögel, a movement that then was the equivalent of the later Hippie trends in the 1960s and 1970s. A strong health movement existed, interested in natural healing, and artists and writers like Herman Hesse and D.H. Lawrence, as well as dancers like Rudolph Laban, all expressed a widely embracing philosophy with a strong bodily connection. Additionally there was a strong, and surprisingly influential, spiritual movement that resulted in the school of Theosophy, founded by Madame Blavatsky in 1875 and later popularized by Annie Besant and others, which gained wide approval. These were all very body-oriented with Theosophy advocating that the path to wisdom (self-knowledge) was best conducted through the practice of Yoga.

My main contention is that body psychotherapy can be dated back at least 120 years, through the legacy of Pierre Janet, and that other influences go back considerably further. So my claiming 'One hundred and fifty years of body psychotherapy' is slightly presumptuous but I feel that I am not very far out.

In this history we can see two main opposing factors: a growing trend of disownment of the body, paralleling the growth of understanding about the mind. It is almost as if one is necessary for the other to exist and develop. The inclusion of bodily reality is thus not a new phenomenon within psychotherapy, but rather a disavowed aspect of it. What I want to suggest is that psychotherapy, without reference to the body, is a somewhat lesser study, a specialization that (perhaps) misses out on something quite fundamental to human existence, a jigsaw with several quite significant sections missing.

Around 1929–30, and for a variety of complex reasons, possibly connected with Freud's then current fascination with 'thanatos', and possibly as a reaction to Reich's interest in Marxism, socio-political theory and sexuality, the body in psychotherapy became formally disowned. With Reich's expulsion from the International Society, it became definitively split-off from psychoanalysis and the main trend of developing psychodynamic psychotherapies.

Psychoanalysis shifted exclusively from the more instinctual, organic, and drive-based models of understanding to a more object-relational understanding, with a focus on transference and countertransference and psychodynamic history without any reference to or appreciation of the body. This, I claim, limited psychoanalysis.

It took seventy years (1934–2004) before mainstream psychotherapy began to reclaim its body at the UK Council for Psychotherapy conference in 2004 entitled 'About a Body: Working with the Embodied Mind in Psychotherapy'. So the mind–body split epitomized by Descartes' 'I think, therefore I am' is only now just beginning to heal. Within psychology, neuroscience is helping to re-establish something of a more unified field approach to the human and his/her body and recent discoveries in psycho-neuro-immunology further assist this trend.

## Disownment of the body

When we disavow something, we are acknowledging the significance of the 'other' in a negative form, and perhaps also our own inability to deal with that negative aspect at that time. The 'disavowed' is not something insignificant that we overlook, forget, or misplace. It is an active process of enforced separation and we will inevitably eventually pay a price for that denial. We often react 'despite' or 'against' the denied part of our self. Laing writes:

> THE UNEMBODIED SELF: In this position the individual experiences his self as being more or less divorced or detached from his body. The body is felt more as one object among other objects in the world than as the core of the individual's own being. Instead of being the core of his true self, the body is felt as the core of a false self, which a detached, disembodied, 'inner', 'true' self looks on at with tenderness, amusement, or hatred as the case may be.
>
> (Laing 1969: 69)

The body has been significantly disavowed in many different aspects of society, aside from psychotherapy. There are many reasons for this denial, and it is by no means a new phenomenon: it might even extend back to the growth of patriarchy 6000 years ago. Reich wrote about some of these aspects in *Character Analysis* (Reich 1945, 1972) and later, very graphically illustrated, in *Listen, Little Man!* (Reich 1948, 1972) He felt that the basic rejection made was through a quintessential fear of libidinous free movement.

The rigidities of the body that Reich spoke about, often experienced as a social norm for so many years, have caused a basic denial of and a phenomenological resistance to the open acceptance of the body in society. This open acceptance can feel natural and wonderful: however, instead of these feelings permeating through all aspects of society, there have grown various distortions in people's relationship to their bodies.

Over recent years the body has been seen as:

- a repository of sin by various religious groups
- a disgusting sexual object by the Victorians
- holding baser impulses to be sublimated by Freudian analysis
- a disposable asset to the military, especially in the First World War
- something to be medicated or fixed by the medical profession
- a dysfunctional object incapable of bearing a child unassisted
- something to be perfected and controlled through diet and exercise
- something exploited by multinationals selling medicines, alcohol and cigarettes
- something to be transcended by belief, prayer, drugs, free love or meditation
- an object of scientific research by biology and neuroscience
- something to be used politically by suicide bombers (more recently).

These are all phenomena of the separation of mind and body. But how can this possibly happen? The mind–body separation is intensely painful and so thus we must have anaesthetized ourselves over generations to our lack of aliveness. Laing (1976) writes:

> When I look at my body from the outside, it is still there, but it may have disappeared years ago as a real alive experience from within. As we become numb, we are numbed to our own numbness. The less we care, the less we care about caring less. We stiffen, harden, shrivel, become bent, but can't bend, twist, run, hop, dance and sing, walk, sleep, even. We lapse painlessly into the complacent ease of bodily vacuity. We may have to think about it before we realize how unfamiliar this most intimate of all our feelings may be.
>
> (Laing 1976; 7)

This separation between mind and body is slowly being overcome and the body is gradually beginning to come back into the whole psychological picture. Damasio writes:

> (1) The human brain and the rest of the body constitute an indissociable organism, integrated by means of mutually interactive biochemical and neural regulatory circuits (including endocrine, immune, and autonomic neural components); (2) The organism interacts with the environment as an ensemble: the interaction is neither of the body alone nor of the brain alone; (3) The physiological operations that we call mind are derived from the structural and functional ensemble rather than from the brain alone: mental phenomena can be fully understood airily in the context of an organism's interacting in an environment.
>
> (Damasio 1994: xvi–xvii)

Various branches of psychotherapy are now including aspects of the body in their theory and practice. Cognitive Behavioural Psychotherapy now accepts Eye Movement Desensitization and Reprocessing (EMDR) and includes Buddhist mindfulness practice (for example, Segal et al. 2002). Clinical psychology also accepts a bio-psychosocial model and psychoanalysis accepts somatic counter-transference as a legitimate therapeutic technique. However, these disciplines may accept something fundamental to body psychotherapy: the mind–body unity.

Body psychotherapy nowadays still tries to attain Janet's, Reich's and even Freud's original goal of a true understanding of the whole person, believing that this is possible only if the person's capacity for full intellectual freedom, emotional expression, free movement, and social connection is regained. Reich (1945, 1972) held that this was synonymous with, and dependent on, the release of the chronic bodily tensions that make up and maintain the person's essential defences, their character armour. This neurotic holding pattern is what we all long to transcend, from an innate desire for freedom, and, at the same time, we also desperately hold on to these restrictions out of a sense of fear or a need for safety. The way in which we survived emotionally has become the basic pattern for our lives, and this can, not only affect our whole lives, but also our physiological shape. Stanley Keleman (1986) illustrates this very well in his book, *Emotional Anatomy*.

There is a Japanese saying: 'A true man thinks with his belly'. And the Chinese discipline of Tai Chi considers the belly as the 'Dan'tien', the centre of the body, the source of all action. Boadella (1987) writes of three main centres of the body – the Head, the Heart, and the Hara – and the dynamic morphology of the body, and relates these to the three main embryological layers: ecto-, meso- and endoderm. Much has been written about the 'armouring' of the ectoderm (which includes the skin and the brain) and its examination of distortions in our patterns of thinking in the cognitive psychotherapies: much has also been written, by Reich (1945, 1972), Lowen (1958) and others, about muscular armouring (in the mesoderm). Less has been written about the armouring of the endoderm.

Keleman (1986) studies people's morphology, calling these various shapes or distortions 'insults to form' and examines the various main types very graphically, looking at the internal forces which constrict and warp the complex tubes and spaces of soft tissue. This is not armour in the sense of the muscular tensions that Reich worked with; however it is a set of tensions that are softer, deeper and more difficult to work with. Reich (1945, 1972) claimed that 'character armour' was fuelled by our emotions, and these later realizations about visceral armouring or shaping are similar. Gerda and Mona-Lisa Boyesen's (1980) work on psycho-peristalsis is also very relevant here.

I therefore maintain that our bodies carry the scars of our historical traumas, not only physically, but also in behavioural holding patterns, in deep muscle structures, in visceral tensions, in our shape and morphology, in patterns of psychodynamic transference, and in distortions of our perceptions. Our bodies have become, in effect, our psychic dustbins, and we need to find ways of working with all of these aspects constructively. We cannot ignore the body in psychotherapy.

## Body psychotherapy today

Some of the changes in body psychotherapy have come from the influences of Humanistic Psychology, developed in the 1960s and 1970s particularly from the work of Maslow (1968). This incorporates a hierarchy of human needs as well as an acknowledgement of the body, the mind and the human spirit.

Goodrich-Dunn and Greene (2002: 77) make the point that body psychotherapy is 'unusual in that it embraces 2 of the 3 core ideas in psychology – perception, motivation and learning – while most other areas encompass just one'. They feel that academically oriented learning theory

> was primarily associated . . . with behaviourism and experimental psychology . . . and more recently with cognitive theory, [and] histori-cally has not had as much affinity for Body Psychotherapy.
>
> (Goodrich-Dunn and Greene 2002: 78)

Whereas

> Perception, which is linked to Body Psychotherapy via humanistic psychology, which in turn is linked to phenomenological and existen-tial psychology, and the Gestalt philosophers and psychologists, is one. Motivation, which is linked to body psychotherapy via psychoanalytic psychology, is the other.
>
> (Goodrich-Dunn and Greene 2002: 110)

In body psychotherapy there are specific views of the body which are carried by most forms of body psychotherapy, although there are distinct differences in emphasis between the different schools. In clinical work, body psychotherapists tend to work with all of these aspects. The client's body is seen as

- a source of information about the client's state of being – both in visible body language, and in creating an emotional atmosphere
- the repository of emotions and memories: there is a significant body of research to indicate that memories are also 'held' in the body, i.e. somatically
- an entry point for change, bypassing potential intellectual resistance to change, avoiding transferential projections, and softening the character armour
- a vehicle for psychological intervention, whereby attention paid to body awareness can benefit the client considerably
- significant as the mind and no different from it
- a source of somatic countertransference.

(Steckler 2004)

From clinical experience, body psychotherapists often know what someone is feeling when they are speaking with their body language. Body positions affect us through what are being called mirror neurones that cause us to try to 'mimic' another person's positions or movement, especially if we are familiar with that movement. It is also been established that a significant part (estimated at over 65 per cent) of all human communication is non-verbal (Knapp 1978: 30).

Society appears to be slowly demanding a more inclusive and holistic approach. There is a long history of considering the implications of the body–mind connection in the field of psychosomatics. However, this discipline still maintained an essential mind–body dualism until sometime in the late 1970s.

Nowadays it is much more acceptable to say that psyche and soma are aspects of a unitary process and that mind and body refer to frameworks that we impose on that process.

(Holman 1979: 1)

Janet and Reich, and body psychotherapists such as Keleman, Boyesen, and Boadella – and more recently van der Kolk (1994), and Rothschild (2000) – all affirm that we cannot do effective work in psychotherapy, especially with people with trauma, without significantly using body psychotherapy awareness. Mainstream psychotherapy is now addressing the issue of the body in psychotherapy, almost as if it is something new.

Along with seeing ourselves not only as a functioning body–mind unity, perhaps it is now time to begin to see this body–mind unity as an entity that is also continually interacting with its environment. What is happening to create this new climate where the body is being seen as central in psychotherapy again? I believe that what is changing is a realization being found simultaneously in science, philosophy, metaphysics, biology, ecology, and also now in psychotherapy, that there is no subject or object; observer and observed; that dualism is a false perspective. Various respected scientists, such as Bohm (2002), are putting forward theories that the whole universe is essentially 'holographic' and that elements of all the distant galaxies can even be found in every microscopic particle. There is no separation; no duality.

Neuroscience is finding that emotions exist, not in the forefront of our mind where we might happen to register them, but in the somewhat more primitive mind that is intimately connected with all the other systems of our bodies, where we really feel these emotions; and also in the subconscious neural systems, in the neurotransmitters, and even in the peptides (the molecules of emotion) that circulate throughout our body. Pert's (1999) research on neuro-peptides indicates that there may be a complete chemical basis for emotion with perhaps even one peptide relating to each emotion. This would mean that emotions are literally flowing through the whole of our body, with chemical receptors for these scattered throughout all parts of the body. If this is so, it would revolutionize thinking on emotions. This theory posits that there is evidence that the limbic system contains forty times more receptors than other parts of brain and that similar receptors are found in blood, bones muscles, immune system and richly in the cells of the digestive tract. This could explain the common experience of touch eliciting an affective response and could also indicate how emotion influences even the immune system. Perhaps the peptide receptors in the digestive tract could give us another form of physiological basis for Gerda Boyesen's theory of emotional digestion via psycho-persistalsis (Boyesen and Boyesen 1980).

A quick trawl through the variety of research on the neurobiology of trauma indicates many connections with the body and physiology (Rothschild 2003). Some of these are:

- Autonomic nervous system (ANS) shock is shown by fight/flight or freeze.
- Freezing (or inability to act) leads to greater incidence of post traumatic stress disorder.
- Experience is dissociative in nature.
- There is a need to regain internal self-regulation lost through ANS hyperarousal.
- Porges' (2001) ventral vagal nerve theory postulates that there is an aspect of the parasympathetic nervous system that connects viscera to face via the brain stem.
- In Möberg's (2003) 'Oxytocin theory', oxytocin seems to be an antagonist of adrenaline.
- 'Effective work' means the prevention of retaumatization through the client staying 'present' in any somatic experience.
- Implicit versus explicit memory: as stress hormones suppress activity in the hippocampus, this leads to the theory that 'body memory' is being stored in the 'body map' of the hippocampus.
- Levine's (1997) work on movement interruption and completion are important aspects in trauma work.
- Bodynamic running: imaginal movement stimulates the same nerve pathways as actual movement.
- Beneficial touch therapies indicated through research by Tiffany Field (2003), Eva Reich (e.g. Kogan 1980), and others working (particularly) with detraumatizing newborn infants.

Additionally, in body psychotherapy, we find that there are many subtle ways of working with patients or clients, either in pain, in trauma or just in distress. These techniques really have to be learned experientially, and include:

- Body awareness as: an access to emotional states, gestures, facial expressions, posture, attention to subtle changes in clients' respiration, eye contact, dampness, colouring, energy level, etc.
- Movement techniques: micro-movements, re-imaging movement for trauma, developmental movement patterns, Authentic Movement.
- Methods of touch as: boundary creation, facilitating energy flow, remover of armouring, facilitating relaxation, facilitating awareness and sense of self, balancer of ANS, antidote to dissociation.
- Mindfulness: (all kinds) physical and dietary health, anti-stress techniques, body–mass ratios, relaxation techniques, environmental factors, etc.
- Body as metaphor: many emotional words relate to 'the body' – heart-felt, belly laugh, handy, armful, stiff-necked, etc.
- Looking after our own bodies for wellbeing.

(adapted from Steckler 2004)

When the dualistic approach is dropped, as being increasingly insignificant, and a much more inclusive approach is adopted, we discover a very different 'bigger picture' which includes all these subtle intricate forces being revealed. Does this tell us anything about the role of the body in psychotherapy? Lowen in his autobiography writes:

> In therapy, I do not favor verbal analysis now; I favor working energy. To do good therapy, you must understand human nature. Human nature is a combination of an individual's intricate aspects – ego, sexuality, understanding of his life and how nature is expressed in an individual. However, the body itself is the most important aspect. . . . Going deep into the [body's] energy concept is working energy, not exercising. Doing good therapy is understanding that human nature is the body itself. Reich said that no one cheats nature, and I believe this fully. Because we are part of nature, if we cheat on nature, we are only cheating ourselves. The danger in the modern world is the megalomania that tells us we can do whatever we dream. This ungrounded statement verges on self. That self for me is the bodily self, the only self we will ever know. Trust it, love it and be true to yourself.

(Lowen 2004: 243)

## Conclusion

Our bodies, in themselves, don't provide many of the answers. Neither do our minds, by themselves. Separated, they are considerably less than one half of that which makes us human. Only when the circuit is fully complete, can we begin to find some really significant answers. Only when we fully include the mind *and* the body as an interfunctioning whole, as a unity, do we begin to get a sense of something much larger than ourselves: then we get a sense of the 'circle' in which we sit; or the environment in which we operate: the multidimensional hologram or the 'field' of our existence.

What body psychotherapists carry collectively is something fundamental. Body psychotherapists are aware that the body is mostly a physical manifestation of something much larger, and less definable – a multilayered collection of different systems and energetic exchanges. These are all interconnected in ways that we cannot even name, let alone describe. The synthesis of these connections is also much greater than the sum, and carries many mysteries: the greater 'something' that even allows us to carry a human potential: a spirit or soul. And there is still another layer: the greater 'field' in which all of these systems operate.

So, if something of this perspective can be used as a method to expand psychology and psychotherapy towards being more meaningful and exciting professions, then it may be possible to help people with what concerns them, and in ways that really address these concerns. Maybe it can also really help to change the world a bit as well.

I hope that my exploration of the history and the main dynamics within body psychotherapy have helped outline some of the connections and possibilities that exist with psychology and other psychotherapies, and set the scene for further explorations and developments with the body.

## References

Abrams, A. (1910) *Spondylotherapy; Physiotherapy and Pharmaco-therapy, and Diagnostic Methods based on a study of Clinical Psychology*, San Francisco, CA: Philopolis Press.

Boadella, D. (1987) *Lifestreams*, London: Routledge.

——(1997). 'Awakening sensibility, recovering motility: psycho-physical synthesis at the foundations of body-psychotherapy: the 100-year legacy of Pierre Janet (1859–1947)', *International Journal of Psychotherapy* 2 (1): 45–57.

Bohm, D. (2002) *Wholeness and the Implicate Order*, London: Routledge.

Boyesen, G. and Boyesen, M-L. (1980) *The Collected Papers of Biodynamic Psychology, Vols 1 and 2*, London: Biodynamic Psychology Publications.

Damasio, A. (1994) *Descartes' Error: Emotion, Reason and the Human Brain*, New York: Avon.

De Bussy, J.H. (1908) Discussion at the *Premier Congrès Internationale de Psychiatre*, Amsterdam.

Field, T. (2003) *Touch*, Cambridge, MA: MIT Press.

Freud, S. (1923) *The Ego and the Id, Vol. 11*, Penguin Freud Library, Harmondsworth: Penguin.

Goodrich-Dunn, B. and Greene, E. (2002) 'Voices, a history of body-psychotherapy', *USA Journal of Body Psychotherapy* 1 (1): 53–117.

Holman, P. (1979) *Introduction to Psychosomatics*, London: Biodynamic Psychology Publications.

James, W. (1890) *Principles of Psychology*, New York: Henry Holt.

Janet, P.M.F (1889) *L'Automatisme psychologique: essai de psychologie expérimentale sur les formes inférieures de l'activité humaine*, Paris: Ancienne Librairie Germer Baillière et Cie.

Keleman, S. (1986) *Emotional Anatomy*, Berkeley, CA: Center Press.

Knapp, M.L. (1978) *Nonverbal Communication in Human Interaction*, 2nd edition, New York: Holt, Rinehart and Winston.

Kogan, G. (ed.) (1980) *Your Body Works: A Guide to Health Energy and Balance*, Berkeley, CA: And/Or Press and Transformations Press.

Laing, R.D. (1969) *The Divided Self*, Harmondsworth: Penguin.

——(1976) *The Facts of Life*, New York: Pantheon.

Levine, P. (1997) *Waking the Tiger*, Berkeley, CA: North Atlantic Books.

Lowen, A. (1958) *The Language of the Body*, New York: Collier.

——(2004) *Honoring the Body: One's Home is One's Body*, Alachua, FL: Bioenergetics Press.

Maslow, A.H. (1968) *Toward a Psychology of Being*, New York: Van Nostrand.

Mesmer, A. (1779) *Mémoire sur la Découverte du Magnétisme Animal*, P.F. Geneva: Didot le Jeune.

Möberg, K.U. (2003) *The Oxytocin Factor, Tapping the Hormone of Calm, Love and Healing*, Cambridge, MA: Da Capo Press.

Pert, C. (1999) *Molecules of Emotion*, New York: Pocket Books, Simon and Schuster.

Porges, S.W. (2001) 'The Polyvagal Theory: phylogenetic substrates of a social nervous system', *International Journal of Psychophysiology* 42: 123–46.

Reich, E. (1980) 'Prevention of neurosis: Self-regulation from birth on', *Journal Biodynamic Psychology* 1: 18–50.

Reich, W. (1945, 1972) *Character Analysis*, New York: Touchstone.

——(1948, 1972) *Listen, Little Man!* London: Souvenir Press.

Rothschild, B. (2000) *The Body Remembers: The Psychophysiology of Trauma and Trauma Treatment*, New York: Norton.

Segal, Z.V., Williams, J., Mark, G. and Teasdale, J.D. (2002) *Mindfulness-Based Cognitive Therapy for Depression: A New Approach to Preventing Relapse*, New York: Guilford Press.

Shaw, R. (2003) *The Embodied Psychotherapist: The Therapist's Body Story*, Hove: Brunner-Routledge.

Steckler, L. (2004) PowerPoint presentation: EABP Conference, Marathon, Greece.

Van der Kolk, B.A. (1994) 'The body keeps the score', *Harvard Review of Psychiatry* 1: 253–65.

# 7

# IMPLICATIONS OF EMDR AND ENERGY THERAPIES

## The limits of talking therapy

*Phil Mollon*


### Introduction

Psychoanalysis and other talking therapies can be helpful – in acquiring insight, self-knowledge, a greater capacity to think, and in exploring new emotional possibilities or ways of being with self and other. However, many would agree that the results of talking therapy, of whatever variety, are often less than one might have hoped – and that fundamental patterns of feeling and attitude do not always change. Moreover, even such results as are achieved tend to come only through years of work. It cannot be said that our conventional methods of talking therapy are particularly effective or efficient. We tend to assume that this reflects the inherent difficulty of bringing about deep psychological change. The question I would like to raise is 'Might we be using the wrong methods?'

New and highly effective methods of therapy, which, although using words, are not essentially reliant upon words for the curative effect, present challenges to many prevalent assumptions about the psychosomatic system and its disturbances (Mollon 2005). Basically, I will argue that we can achieve very little in psychological therapy if we ignore the body, the brain, and the energy system.

In 1995, a group of clinicians and researchers in the United States, dismayed by the lack of effective therapies for trauma, established the 'Active Ingredients Project' (Figley and Carbonell 1995) in an endeavour to stimulate research on better and faster treatments for PTSD. They contacted thousands of clinicians worldwide, asking for submissions of potentially effective new treatments. Two of these were Eye Movement and Desensitization Reprocessing (EMDR) and a method within the new genre of Energy Psychology, called Thought Field Therapy. Both were found to be greatly more effective and faster than traditional talking therapies – and both make use of eye movements.

## Eye Movement Desensitization and Reprocessing

EMDR has been around since about 1990 and is now a well-established therapeutic modality (Shapiro 2001, 2002). It is the most highly researched treatment
for PTSD and has many other applications. We can use it with confidence as a
highly 'evidence-based' method. It must be used with caution, only by clinicians
trained by the EMDR Institute and its affiliated organizations (such as EMDR
UK and Ireland). This method employs bilateral stimulation – such as side-to-side
eye movements, or alternating sounds in either ear, or tactile stimulation of either
side of the body, perhaps using vibrating buttons held in each hand. While there
are various theories about how and why this works, a common proposition is that
the bilateral stimulation of each cerebral hemisphere facilitates inter-hemispheric
communication and the associative processes of the mind and brain. I would see
this as facilitating free-association – and for me EMDR is profoundly psychoanalytic in its action. Indeed I often use it very much as a tool to enhance free-
association, leading to useful material of emotion and fantasy. Such use is not the
method outlined by Francine Shapiro (2001), the founder of the method, but it is
one that I find very helpful.

When using EMDR, we ask the client to focus on the troubling experience,
while making the eye movements (or other bilateral stimulation), and we ask
them to 'just notice' what they experience – including what is experienced in the
body. The therapist is usually not particularly active, although highly attentive.
Interpretive comments may occasionally be included (Shapiro calls them 'cognitive interweaves') – but mostly the client does the work of processing without
interference from the therapist. Emotional reactions to the troubling event subside
(are desensitized), cognitions (about the event and about the self) spontaneously
change. When given the facilitation of bilateral stimulation, the mind – indeed
the whole psychosomatic system – moves towards health, optimism and joy. This
can be quite awesome to witness. A psychoanalytic process of change occurs, but
without active introduction of content by the therapist. It does not depend on clever
interpretations, and does not rely upon working in the transference.

I believe contemporary psychoanalysis has become somewhat less effective
than it could be – ironically through the very development that many would regard
as an improvement on Freud's original position. Freud developed the technique
of free-association – the patient was encouraged to say whatever came to mind,
regardless of how relevant or polite it might be, and the resistances to the free-
associative flow were seen as representing the defensive dynamic forces within the
mind that were giving rise to the troubling symptoms. Freud noted that often these
resistances would centre around some thought or feeling in relation to the doctor
– and that this disturbing constellation of cognition and emotion would derive
from childhood experiences and conflicts, a phenomenon he called transference.
The analyst would be listening to the free-associative mind and its complexes.
However, what has happened increasingly in more recent years is that the analyst
is listening to an object-relating infant. Instead of listening to the free-associations,
as revealing of intrapsychic conflict, the analyst is looking for the disturbances in

the patient's relationship with the analyst – and the therapeutic process is seen as one of struggling to help the patient achieve a better way of relating to the analyst (see Mollon 2005: 71–95). Moreover, all the patient's communications tend to be seen as unconsciously referring to the so-called transference relationship. This, to my perception, is not a particularly helpful way of proceeding. The traumas and intrapsychic conflicts are not processed – and in a very odd and ironic way the work becomes a kind of interpersonal psychotherapy rather than psychoanalysis based on processing the intrapsychic. At the same time, the therapist is imprisoned within a role restricted to that of interpreting the transference – almost to the extent that any conversational activity other than this is seen as a breach of appropriate boundaries. Within such a framework, it is not easy for the psychoanalytic therapist to introduce the patient to EMDR!

It is enormously refreshing to be able, through the medium of EMDR, to return to the intrapsychic, and to be released from the tyranny of excessive preoccupation with the transference. This does not mean that I use EMDR in the same way that a cognitive behavioural therapist might – I think we all find our own ways of engaging with EMDR. For me the most important feature of EMDR is the way that it powerfully facilitates the free-associative process. This is often quite startling when a client is otherwise unable to produce relevant material. For example, a woman reported that she had been feeling somewhat low that day – but she had no idea why. I asked her to make some eye movements and to ask herself what might be troubling her. After just a few eye movements, she said that what occurred to her was that she had had an alarming dream about her mother. Her associations to the dream rapidly led to her awareness of feelings of anger and conflict in relation to her mother – and thus her mood of depression then began to make sense. Without the EMDR we might have waited a long time for this material to emerge.

With another patient, recently, I selected from her discourse a theme of feeling rejected and asked her to hold this in mind while making eye movements. She remarked that it was like watching a film of her life – she saw a pageant of scenes of rejection beginning with her mother's complaints that she was like her father and her father's complaints that she was like her mother, through to circumstances in her current life at the age of 40 – all within a minute or two of eye movements.

Psychoanalysis is, at least in my view of it, fundamentally to do with free-association – indeed it is to do with freedom – freedom of feeling and freedom of thought (Bollas 2002). Neurosis, to use an old-fashioned term, is a result of curtailment of inner freedom, for reasons of defence against anxiety – anxiety about unacceptable or frightening feelings, perceptions and impulses. The neurotic anxiety brings about a narrowing of consciousness and a restriction of the flow of the energies of thought and feeling – resulting in unfree-association and a diversion of the flow into symptom formation. Therefore the therapeutic activity is one of kick-starting the free-associative process and liberating the flow. EMDR does this very nicely – stimulating the conversation between the emotion-processing right hemisphere and the linguistic left hemisphere. It is precisely this conversation that is inhibited in traumatized states of mind – and also in states of repression of warded off feelings. In a state of repression, a person may vaguely remember an event but not have access to the associated feelings and the emotional significance of the experience. If the brain were an electrical circuit – which, of course, in one sense it is – EMDR seems either to increase the voltage or lower the resistance of the circuitry so that more parts are lit up and functioning. Pursuing the analogy, in states of trauma, or states of repression, it is as if areas of the circuitry are shut down or insulated from the rest.

Dreams tend to reveal a lowering of the resistance of the circuitry – and Freud (1900) argued that dreams are the 'royal road' to the unconscious. Indeed, in dreams, the main pathways of motor discharge are blocked (the person is asleep) and the less direct neuronal paths are facilitated. This shift to less direct paths of association – this reversal of the facilitation of direct associative paths charac-teristic of waking consciousness – gives dreams their peculiar quality of seem-ing utterly at odds with waking perceptions of reality. Dreaming may be a crucial component of the 'digestion' of mental experience, enabling it to be absorbed into the wider neuronal ocean (to use another metaphor) and used as a basis for 'learn-ing from experience', which Bion (1962) saw as the fundamental nutrients for the growth of the mind. Here of course we have the oft-cited point of contact between the eye movements of EMDR and the REM movements of dreaming. Although there are other forms of bilateral stimulation, such as auditory and tactile, this does not invalidate the comparison since all of these may reflect the facilitation of indirect association.

We might also consider repetitive cognitions addressed by cognitive therapists – the automatic thoughts and the deep self-related beliefs and self-images – as another form of insulated association. These beliefs and habits of thought are rela-tively immune to modification by evidence. Thus they show the same constric-tion of associative dispersal and creative recombination as is found in traumatic associative paths. Again, it is necessary to free up the associative flow, to bring the patterns of thought and feeling into dynamic interaction with the environment and the ongoing stream of experience. And again, EMDR does this nicely.

Of course the down-side of free-association is that it can flow endlessly away from the areas of pain, trauma, and anxiety. This is most apparent in manic states of mind – where the patient's accelerating spiral of thoughts flies centrifugally away from areas of most crucial distress. It is also commonly observed in the process of EMDR – we might begin with a target experience or emotion, but the patient's associations move rapidly away from it. In psychoanalytic work (at least as Freud conceived it) this is a normal expected feature – the patient's free-associative dis-course expresses a conflict between the forces of emotional expression and the forces of repression. The analyst has to try to discern the leakage of the repressed, disguised within the manifest – and then must interpret this to the patient, assum-ing that the patient has not reached the repressed first. This is quite a difficult task, requiring much skill and knowledge of the forms of expression of the unconscious mind. However, things are a bit simpler with EMDR. We can simply keep taking the patient back to the target problem. Moreover, if we discern that the patient is associating, not towards crucial areas of mental pain, but away from these, we can gently bring his or her attention back into a more fruitful direction. If necessary we can insert a cognitive interweave – or we might simply ask 'Do you think you might be trying to keep away from something that would be disturbing to you?' – or 'When have you felt like this before?'

Freud's psychoanalysis began with the body. He worked with patients whose bodies had, in some instances, been violated. He worked with patients whose bodies had ceased to function normally even though there was no anatomical damage. He developed a theory of sexuality – the libido – based on the infantile investment of pleasure in different bodily zones. He remarked that 'the ego is first and foremost a bodily ego' (Freud 1960: 20). Similarly EMDR is a body-oriented therapy. We ask the patient 'Where do you feel it in your body?' – and at the end of processing we may check whether this is complete by asking him or her to scan the body for experiences of discomfort. Indeed, EMDR involves bodily activity and bodily, sensory, stimulation. We are not surprised when PET scans reveal changes in brain function, in neurobiology, after EMDR treatment (van der Kolk 2002). It is very obvious to us, from the dramatic changes observed and experienced, that EMDR brings about alterations at a neurobiological level.

In explaining free-association to his patients, Freud (1913) used the analogy of watching scenes pass by from the window of a train. Francine Shapiro used the same analogy in explaining to patients how they should observe and report their thoughts, images and memories during EMDR (Shapiro 2001). Both Freud and Shapiro were thereby facilitating a stance of 'mindfulness' in their patients – and this is something that has also been encouraged by some cognitive therapists recently.

## How do I use EMDR?

Although I sometimes use EMDR according to the standard protocol for trauma, often I employ it much more flexibly as a means of facilitating emotional exploration. Of course in the very process of exploring, the mental constellations (of affect, cognition, image and fantasy) are being processed and digested. This was a feature of psychoanalysis too – a method of enquiry into the mind that was at the same time therapeutic. Sets of eye movements may be interspersed with long periods of more ordinary free-associative talk. On other occasions I may offer the patient the possibility of wearing headphones providing continuous bilateral stimulation while we undertake an otherwise ordinary psychoanalytic therapeutic conversation.

Sometimes a patient may report events, from childhood, for example, and EMDR will then rapidly take them into the emotions associated with those memories.

## *Marlene*

Marlene, a rather sensitive and spiritually oriented woman in her thirties, sought help for feelings of depression and insecurity after reading about EMDR. One issue that emerged was her feelings of resentment and anxiety in relation to her husband's daughter from his previous marriage. She told me, in the first session, of growing up in a rather disturbed family that had suffered the trauma of her mother's death when she was age 2; she had no conscious memory of her mother. After half an hour of this discourse I invited her to make some eye movements and to think of what she had been speaking of. She then described a vivid feeling of being an observer within this troubled family, feeling that she did not belong – and yet feeling very aware that she must construct some kind of social identity for herself in order to function in the world. Moreover she spoke of a childhood feeling that she had lived before – recalling remarking to her grandmother, when she was aged 4, 'It was different when I was here before'. She felt she could recall her birth – and floated back to what she perceived as a scene of her dying in a previous life. I did not express a view on the historical validity of her past life memory. It did seem to express her sense of being a kind of visitor to her family, not feeling that she really belonged there – and perhaps also alluded to the radical rupture of continuity brought about by her mother's death in Marlene's second year of life. Over the course of three sessions, interspersed with much EMDR, we were able to understand very clearly how Marlene experienced her husband's daughter as triggering childhood feelings of oppression by her sister – and how this evoked her internal child feelings of being very lonely and unprotected. These emotional recollections, and the association between the sister of childhood and the stepdaughter of the present, emerged with a vividness and rapidity that I am sure would not have been possible using a merely conversational method. Marlene accomplished what she felt she needed to do in therapy in three sessions.

## Energy methods: Emotional Freedom Techniques

In recent years, a family of therapeutic methods have developed, based on releasing blockages or patterns of dysfunctional information that are stuck in the energy system of the body – a kind of psychological application of acupressure. Generically these are known as 'Energy Psychology' (www.energypsych.org) – and one of the most popular methods is called Emotional Freedom Techniques (EFT), and was developed by Gary Craig.

The origin of these lay in innovations in the 1960s and 1970s by a chiropractor, George Goodheart, who developed a means of interrogating the body using muscle testing, and also began to link his work with principles of acupuncture – developing a field called Applied Kinesiology (see, for example, Krebs 1998; Frost 2002). One of Goodheart's students was a psychoanalytically oriented psychiatrist, John

Diamond (an Australian member of the British Royal College of Psychiatrists, now residing and working in New York). He began in the 1970s to apply Goodheart's principles to emotional and psychiatric problems, discovering deep patterns of association between different emotional states and the acupuncture meridian system, as well as using sophisticated muscle testing to enquire of the body's deep attitudes and reactions – one of his most famous books being *Your Body Doesn't Lie* (Diamond 1979). He used a combination of verbal affirmations and tapping on meridian points to cure psychiatric conditions. Diamond, who was born in 1934, still continues to develop his work and to write and has produced a vast compendium of astonishing knowledge, linking energy principles with psychoanalysis (and a great deal else as well), that goes far beyond that of any other practitioner (although unfortunately not all of it is readily accessible).

One of Diamond's colleagues was a clinical psychologist, Roger Callahan, who discovered that phobias, anxiety states and other emotional distress, could often be eliminated rapidly when the person thought of the problem and tapped on a sequence of acupressure points. Different tapping sequences were required for different problems. Drawing on principles of Applied Kinesiology, Callahan developed a method of diagnosing the required sequences, using muscle testing. Commonly recurring sequences for particular emotional problems were termed 'algorithms' and these would often be successful without the use of muscle testing. Callahan's method – which he called Thought Field Therapy – has evolved since 1980 into a therapeutic approach which can claim a very high success rate, vastly superior to that of conventional verbal methods (Callahan and Callahan 2000; Callahan 2001).

A crucial feature of Callahan's innovative framework is the notion of 'psychological reversal' (similar to some of Diamond's ideas), whereby a person's conscious desires to recover, or to be successful, are sabotaged at a deep level. The energy flow is literally reversed, along with what Diamond (1988) called a 'reversal of the body's morality', such that in some cases good may register as bad and bad may register as good. Obviously we can link this with psychoanalytic ideas about death instinct, resistance, perversion, negative therapeutic reaction, and so on. Callahan developed simple corrections for this kind of reversal, based on tapping particular points while making a statement of acceptance of self and of the problem. As Callahan developed and refined his method, the results were more consistently good, as well as rapid. He also incorporated various eye movements and other 'brain balancing' procedures – all of which were guided by muscle testing.

Callahan's student, Gary Craig, simplified the tapping sequence, eliminating the role of muscle testing, diagnosis, and the need for detailed knowledge of the meridian system, and placed more emphasis upon the importance of rapport with the client and the crucial role of seeking the correct issues and aspects on which to focus the statements and phrases used during the tapping sequences. While making use of the meridian energy system, Craig does so in a manner that is more psychotherapeutic, drawing upon empathy, mirroring and attunement to the client's energy system. He also teaches ways in which the therapist can use his or her own bodily responses as feedback regarding the client's energy body. It is Craig's method that is called the Emotional Freedom Techniques. One of the important differences between Craig's EFT and Callahan's TFT is that Craig argues that sequencing of tapping is unimportant, whereas within TFT it is regarded as crucial. While the TFT practitioner will target a precise and often relatively short sequence of acupoints, Craig advocates tapping on all the main meridians (although he often uses a short form). This seemingly fundamental cleavage of perspective becomes potentially bridgeable when it is realized that many common TFT algorithms will be covered within the basic EFT tapping sequence, and certainly if there is repeated tapping round and round the sequence.

There are now many methods within the field of energy psychology (see www.energypsych.org) most of which, but not all, are derived from, or influenced by, Thought Field Therapy (Lammers and Kircher 2002; Diepold et al. 2004; Feinstein 2004; Hartung 2005). The research evidence so far suggests that these methods are very effective indeed (see summary in Mollon 2005). Energy medicine in general is highly congruent with emerging paradigms (Oschman 2000).

One crucial implication of these methods and their effectiveness may be that if emotional information (based on traumatic experience, for example) is patterned into the energy system – or if the energy system is a controlling interface between the 'thought field' and the body – then methods that work purely with conscious and unconscious thoughts, and with experienced emotions, may be limited in what they can achieve, because the energy pattern constrains the person within the same old reactions. By contrast, energy methods may be accessing the highest point of organization of the psychosomatic system, so that work at this level releases the constraining cognitive-emotional information rapidly and without the client having to re-experience the trauma.

The one drawback of energy methods is that they can be confusing for the client – the brain cannot make sense of the change because it cannot track the process in terms of experienced thoughts and emotions. This will sometimes lead the client to confabulate an explanation of the change – perhaps arguing that he or she is merely distracted from the problem, or sometimes concluding that there never really was a problem in the first place. Callahan referred to this well-known phenomenon as the 'apex problem' (Callahan 2001). It can often be remedied by simple explanation by the therapist.

EFT is procedurally somewhat similar to EMDR – except that a sequence of acupoint tapping substitutes for the eye movements, and, unlike with EMDR, the client experiences the emotions only minimally (see Hartung and Galvin 2003). Each round of EFT tapping begins with a statement of acceptance designed to counter 'psychological reversal'- and follows the formula 'Even though I have this problem [stating whatever it is], I accept myself'. This is followed by a statement of a brief reminder phrase at each tapping point 'This problem [stating the problem] . . . ' Once the basic process of EFT is grasped, it becomes possible to use it very intuitively and free-associatively (see Hartmann 2002, 2003a).

Usually, in clinical practice, the client taps his or her own body.

102

## Mrs D – compulsive hair pulling

Mrs D is a 35-year-old woman who had suffered from compulsive pulling of her eyelashes for twenty years. This was a significant problem for her, involving mutilation of her appearance. It was treated in one session of energy psychology. A further and more general problem emerged following this, which was then successfully resolved in the second session.

Mrs D did not know why she compulsively pulled her eyelashes. However, she was able to tell me that the problem began when she was age 15. At the time, her grandmother, who was dying of ovarian cancer, was living with the family – and Mrs D was given many of the tasks of looking after her. She had resented this.

She mentioned that her father travelled a lot and they were not close. At age 10 she had discovered his collection of pornography, which had greatly disturbed her.

Mrs D told me that she often experienced very angry dreams about her mother. In these dreams she would be screaming at her mother for putting her down. Sometimes she would hit her mother. We clarified that she was angry with her mother for (a) putting her down continually, (b) for letting the grandmother live with them for so long, and (c) for letting her father have pornography in the house.

Mrs D also mentioned that she did not have a satisfactory sexual relationship with her husband, whom she described as 'very patient'.

After a brief explanation, Mrs D readily agreed to using energy methods. It seemed reasonable to target her feelings of rage at her mother, since these obviously troubled her and one hypothesis was that her hair pulling symptom was an expression of this rage – especially since it had developed during a period of intense anger towards her mother.

Intuitively I felt we could make use of a method I use sometimes, whereby an agreed code word is used to refer to certain emotional experiences. The advantage is that (a) the person does not then need to think of the disturbing events directly, and (b) several situations can be loaded into the code word at once.

Thus we chose the word 'red' as a code word – and I told her that we would represent the following feelings with the word 'red': (1) rage at her mother for putting her down, (b) rage at her mother for letting the grandmother stay with them for so long, (c) rage at her mother for letting her father have pornography in the house. We did a few rounds of EFT tapping on the word 'red' – beginning with the standard opening phrase 'Even though I have these red feelings, I completely accept myself'. Then I asked her to shift to the statement 'Even though I channelled my red feelings into pulling my eyelashes, I completely accept myself.' All this took about five minutes.

We then tested the result by having her think about her mother and the various situations that had previously made her angry – specifically asking her to note whether she experienced any tension in her body. She reported greatly reduced emotion, but a slight feeling in her stomach, that she described as being like 'scribbling on paper'. We then used EmoTrance to release this. EmoTrance (Hartmann 2003b, 2004) is another energy method that basically involves placing attention on the bodily experience of emotion and using intention to soften this 'trapped energy' and allow it to flow. Mrs D reported a rapid experience of this tension dissolving away.

I then asked her to notice whether she experienced any impulse to pull her eyelashes. She reported a slight inclination to 'fiddle' (as opposed to 'pull'). We then did a further round of EFT tapping, starting with the phrase 'Even though I want to fiddle with my eyelashes, I completely accept myself.' She reported a complete cessation of any desire to fiddle.

Mrs D returned for a follow-up the next week. She was smiling broadly and her opening remark was: 'I have to say I am absolutely astonished: since seeing you last week I have not picked at my eyelashes once.' She followed this by saying that she had had another dream in which her mother was making demeaning comments, but this time Mrs D was just laughing it off. She said she felt generally lighter in her step – and, moreover, she and her husband had had sex for the first time in a year.

This seemed a good result – and indeed the kind of thing we have come to expect quite often with EFT. I was assuming that we could stop at that point, and explaining to her that she could now use EFT to address any distressing emotion in the future, when she then remarked that the problem was that she tends not to be aware of her emotions. So we did a round of EFT tapping, using the phrase 'Even though I am not in touch with my emotions, I completely accept myself . . . '. I then asked her to tell me whether she experienced any tension in her body and, if so, to describe it. She reported a sensation like a metal door between her head and her body. We then used a muscle test to ask her body whether it was safe for her to be in touch with her emotions. This indicated a clear 'no'. So I asked her what she thought might be the reason for it not being safe to be in touch with her emotions. She said it might open a 'can of worms'. We then used EFT tapping and EmoTrance for her fear of a can of worms. Muscle testing revealed a lessened sense of danger, but still some. I asked her whether she thought the can of worms was still there. She replied that perhaps there was still 'a worm'.

So I asked her what the worm might be. In response she remembered a dream from a few days previously. The dream was that her father was looking at her lasciviously. I asked her what she felt about her father when she thought of him at that moment. She reported feelings of disgust – in relation to his pornography – and a feeling of not being protected. She also mentioned that at age 10, after discovering his pornography, she had feared he would rape her – i.e. that he would do to her what she had seen in the pictures. She recalled being very frightened in her bedroom, worried that he would come in and assault her. However, she was quite clear that he had not actually assaulted her.

We used the code word method again – using the word 'black' for all her disturbing feelings about her father. After a few rounds of EFT tapping on 'black feelings', we checked with a muscle test again. This indicated that it was now safe to be in touch with her feelings. At this point we ended the work.

A telephone follow-up at two months indicated there had been no return of the hair pulling symptom and that she was no longer troubled by rage at her mother. She did return later for further work on other issues. The methods of energy psychology are extremely effective, but since psychological problems can be structured in complex and multi-layered networks, the resolution of one issue may then reveal another – and so on.

## Jane – inhibition of painting

Quite often I have clients coming to me who have previously undergone years of conventional psychoanalytic therapy and wish to experience one of the new therapies, such as EMDR or energy methods. One such client was a psychotherapist whom I shall call Jane. Since she lived in Scotland, she arranged to see me for just a few sessions of energy work, travelling down to the London area once a month.

Jane had had several years of psychoanalytic therapy during her training. She had found this helpful in certain ways, but felt some issues were left unresolved and unchanged. One theme was that her real passion is for painting and sculpture, but she felt somehow frustrated and inhibited in her endeavours. In our initial discussions, I explained to Jane that my experience with energy work had led me to the conclusion that there are limits to what can be achieved in talking therapies alone. She was somewhat startled to hear a psychotherapist stating this, but she also reported great relief – a sense of recognising truth in what I said.

### Shame and rage

We agreed to proceed with EFT. Using my free-associative style of EFT, we focused first on an experience of panic that she had felt on her analyst's couch. Tapping on this issue gave rise to thoughts and feelings of great rage. Further tapping then took us to feelings of shame – and, in particular, to thoughts of shame about sex. The following experiences came to mind, associated with shame, all of which were tapped on: her mother's anxious and disapproving messages about sex; an old feeling that one should not have sex on a Sunday afternoon, but only at night; at age 18 having sex with a waiter on holiday, followed by guilt and shame and praying in church; age 7 sitting astride a pointed roof and experiencing sexual pleasure; age 20 various exciting sexual encounters while working in London, these being followed by deep shame; age 21 a sense of lost innocence, and crying, after watching a film of innocent love – her mother saying, 'I know why you are crying'; teenage experience of penetrative sex with boyfriend, after which he ended the relationship, leaving her very upset and full of shame; the anxious and shameful experience of her wedding night when she and her husband were so tense; falling in love with other men and feeling shame about this. She then shifted to speaking of her passion for painting – and her feeling that she has tended to try so hard with the technicalities of painting that she stifles her creativity and spontaneity. A theme emerged of how she tries to do everything properly rather than spontaneously – this being driven by shame. We continued tapping on these issues. At the end of the session, Jane reported feeling relieved.

### What would my mother say?

At our next meeting, Jane reported that following this session she had woken in the night in a state of great panic – with thoughts that she was being drawn into something weird (that is, this strange therapy that I had introduced her to). She also said she had felt even more frustrated with her painting and had got into a rage with it. She thought she also had felt rage with me for leading her astray and for giving her instructions. She spoke of a pattern in which she would go along with other people, not asserting herself, and then be furious with herself, and feel foolish. Her further associations were as follows: feeling humiliated by her mother; her mother laughing at her because she was upset by a pretend spider, feelings of being 'taken in' by someone; worries that she would look stupid; worries that her husband would think this therapy was stupid; fears of her mother's scorn if she knew about this therapy; her mother's snobbery; how her mother's attitudes and behaviours would make feel enraged. She agreed with my comment that the thoughts underlying her panic on waking in the night were 'What would my mother say?' and 'What would my analyst say?'. She went on to associate to the way that her mother would tell her how to do everything – 'Mother knows best'.

We commenced further EFT tapping on these themes. She then associated to feeling that her psychotherapist had been scornful of aspects of her work. She spoke of her psychoanalytic therapy as having been a nightmare – painful and addictive. She recalled how her psychotherapist would tell her she was destructive – and how this would make her enraged. As she continued the tapping she spoke of her rage that she would just 'lie there and take it': 'Why didn't I get up and walk out and say "fuck you?"' She then spoke of fears of others finding out how badly her psychotherapy had ended.

There were various other events and experiences, with similar themes, that emerged during this series of tapping. She spoke of real-izing that she had been in a rage for most of her life – and how she would be in a rage when sitting with her patients. The final fundamental issue that emerged, which was articulated most succinctly, was 'I want to be me – but that risks my mother's scorn'.

At the end of this session, Jane commented: 'It's been a revelation – of how angry I am – how angry I feel when I am with clients – and how central is my fear of my mother's scorn.'

Subsequently, Jane reported feeling greatly liberated by this ses-sion – saying she felt as if something toxic had been released from her system.

### Protective enclosure

In a third session, Jane wished to focus on her inhibitions and frustra-tions in her painting and sculpture. As she began tapping on this, she associated to how her father would batter her with criticisms – and how she felt something of this had been re-enacted in her analysis. She also associated to a recent experience in which she felt a colleague had battered her during a peer supervision. Further childhood humiliations emerged – with criticisms and scorn from both parents. She referred to worries about what colleagues would think if they knew what she was like, and if they knew the kind of therapy she was engaged in. She spoke of pubertal embarrassment about her developing breasts. A general and pervasive childhood sense of being angry was apparent – which she linked to feeling constrained and frightened. Then she began to speak of a childhood state of creating a protective enclosure around herself – she had developed this in response to the sense of having no privacy from the intrusions of her mother.

One of the features of more advanced and intuitive forms of EFT is that it is possible to reframe the client's problems, highlighting the posi-tive intention behind a symptom or inhibition. These emerge intuitively rather than through advance planning. I suggested to Jane that she begin a tapping sequence with the statement 'I was creative in establishing a protective enclosure around myself – which kept the creative core of me safe – and I choose now to release this creativity'. She clearly found this statement very congruent and ran with it. At the end she seemed deeply moved and awed by the process. I received a message subse-quently saying that her inhibitions in painting and sculpture appeared to have gone.

## Summary and comments regarding the work with Jane

The basic, or core, conflictual theme (Luborsky and Crits-Christoph 1998) that emerged in these three sessions with Jane was that she had felt dominated, emotionally violated, and shamed by both her parents – had developed a protective covering, a false self of compliance, behind which lay great rage and shame. She had wanted to express herself authentically and creatively, but this fundamental desire had come up against her fear of criticism and shame – and so she continually monitored the environment for dangers of shaming disapproval from others. As we moved into this area with the energy tapping work, she encountered the shaming internal figures – of her mother and her analyst. Continued tapping through these themes released her rage – allowing her authentic and creative self to emerge.

No doubt many of these same areas had been explored in the conventional psychoanalytic work. It required the additional brief work with the energy body to release the constraining structures that had hitherto prevented fundamental change.

Jane had found her psychoanalytic therapy difficult. My impression is that a reliance on talking, and working in the transference, while illuminating and helpful in certain ways, can be disheartening and frustrating for the client – because the patterns of conflict become known but do not change. The addition of an energy component seems to release the constraining information, patterned in the energy system, allowing a rapid move into more positive states of mind.

The tapping seems to allow a rapid journey through thematically linked psychodynamic material – as emotions are located but not plunged into. There is a sense of continued movement – as opposed to the stuck states that may often characterize conventional verbal psychotherapy.

One interesting point that Jane put to me was that she would leave the sessions of energy work feeling better – whereas she would often leave her psychoanalytic therapy feeling worse. A particularly stark and poignant comment was as follows: 'After finishing my analysis, it led me to feel I couldn't bear to think about myself because any thought led to some idea of terrible motivation.' It does seem that often psychoanalysis does focus more on negative and destructive emotions and motivations than upon positive intentions. By contrast energy work (and also EMDR) seem naturally to lead the person into more positive states of mind – the implication being that positive states are natural, if the energy blockages are cleared.

## The contribution of the therapist in EFT

What is the contribution of the therapist? Gary Craig, who originated EFT, has often emphasized that the work is able to reach its higher levels depending on the extent to which the therapist can get him/herself out of the way – allowing the process to flow intuitively and creatively. The therapist's intuition can be manifest in terms of the words used in each tapping sequence and in the choice of tapping points. Implicit interpretations can be embedded in the opening words of each sequence, informed by the spontaneous words that occur to the therapist at each moment. Often these might be a means whereby the therapist gives voice to the client's unconscious – which happens most easily and naturally when the therapist surrenders to the process of resonance, mirroring, or other forms of rapport with the client (just as Freud described how the analyst's unconscious becomes attuned to that of the patient). For example, in one of his teaching videos (*Steps towards the Ultimate Therapist*), Gary Craig works with a man who is unable to urinate in a public lavatory – a not uncommon inhibition, sometimes called 'bashful bladder'. He explores childhood experiences of humiliation by a group of older adolescents, continually tapping on various aspects of these, using different opening statements to address different nuances of experience, thought, desire and fear – and, at a relatively late stage in the session, includes the opening statement 'Even though I want to piss all over them . . . '. The client laughed – and was subsequently able to pee freely. As Freud indicated in his study of jokes, there is relief in the sudden permissive expression of repressed unconscious wishes – and there is indeed often much humour and experience of relief in EFT work.

I think of my own way of working with Emotional Freedom Techniques as 'psychoanalytic energy psychotherapy'; it uses free-association, it addresses psychodynamic conflicts, and it takes the emotional charge out of traumatic memories. Transference may emerge, but this does not become the vehicle of the healing – rather, it is just another issue to be tapped through. Similarly, words are used – but the words alone are not the vehicle. It is the use of words to speak deeply into the client's energy system, accessed through tapping the body, that allows the changes to take place rapidly. Obviously, the work is not psychoanalysis – but I doubt that I could do it if I were not a psychoanalyst.

## References

Bion, W.R. (1962) *Learning from Experience*, London: Heinemann; reprinted in Bion, W.R. (1977) *Seven Servants*, New York: Aronson.

Bollas, C. (2002) *Free Association*, Cambridge: Icon.

Callahan, R.J. (2001) *Tapping the Healer Within*, New York: Contemporary Books.

Callahan, R.J. and Callahan, J. (2000) *Stop the Nightmares of Trauma. Thought Field Therapy: The Power Therapy for the 21st Century*, Chapel Hill, NC: Professional Press.

Craig, G. (2000–) Articles available online from garycraig@emofree.com (accessed 31 December 2005).

Diamond, J. (1979) *Your Body Doesn't Lie: An Introduction to Behavioural Kinesiology*, reprinted 1997, Enfield, UK: Eden Grove.

—— (1985) *Life Energy: Using the Meridians to Unlock the Hidden Power of your Emotions*, St Paul, MN: Paragon House.

—— (1988) *Life Energy Analysis: A Way to Cantillation*, New York: Archaeus.

Diepold, J.H., Britt, V., and Bender, S.S. (2004) *Evolving Thought Field Therapy. The Clinician's Handbook of Diagnosis, Treatment, and Theory*, New York: Norton.

Feinstein, D. (2004) *Energy Psychology Interactive: Rapid Interventions for Lasting Change*, Ashland, OR: Innersource.

Figley, C.R. and Carbonell, J.L. (1995) Active ingredients project: the systematic clinical demonstration of the most efficient treatments of PTSD, Florida State University Psychosocial Research Program, reported in F.P. Gallo (ed.) *Energy Psychology*, New York: CRC Press.

Freud, S. (1900) *The Interpretation of Dreams*, Standard Edition, ed. J. Strachey, Vol. 5, London: Hogarth Press.

—— (1913) *On Beginning the Treatment*, Standard Edition, ed. J. Strachey, Vol. 12, London: Hogarth Press.

—— (1960) *The Ego and the Id*, ed. J. Strachey, trans. J. Riviere, New York: Norton.

Frost, R. (2002) *Applied Kinesiology: A Training Manual and Reference Book of Basic Principles and Practices*, Berkeley, CA: North Atlantic Books.

Hartmann, S. (2002) *The Advanced Patterns of EFT*, Eastbourne: DragonRising.

—— (2003a) *Adventures in EFT*, 6th edition., Eastbourne: DragonRising.

—— (2003b) *Oceans of Energy: The Patterns and Techniques of EmoTrance, Volume 1*, Eastbourne: DragonRising.

—— (2004) *Living Energy: The Patterns and Techniques of EmoTrance, Volume 2*, Eastbourne: DragonRising.

Hartung, J.G. (2005) *Reaching Further: How to Remove Obstacles to Personal Excellence*, Colorado Springs, CO: Colorado School of Professional Psychology.

Hartung, J.G. and Galvin, M.D. (2003) *Energy Psychology and EMDR: Combining Forces to Optimize Treatment*, New York: Norton.

Krebs, C. (1998) *A Revolutionary Way of Thinking*, Melbourne: Hill of Content.

Lammers, W. and Kircher, B. (2002) *The Energy Odyssey: New Directions in Energy Psychology*, Eastbourne: DragonRising.

Luborsky, L. and Crits-Christoph, P. (1990) *Understanding Transference: The Core Conflictual Relationship Theme Method*, New York: Basic Books; 2nd edition, 1998, Washington, DC: APA Books.

Mollon, P. (2005) *EMDR and the Energy Therapies: Psychoanalytic Perspectives*, London: Karnac.

Oschman, J. (2000) *Energy Medicine: The Scientific Basis*, New York: Churchill Livingstone.

Shapiro, F. (2001) *Eye Movement Desensitization and Reprocessing*, 2nd edition, New York: Guilford Press.

—— (ed.) (2002) *EMDR as an Integrative Psychotherapy: Experts of Diverse Orientations Explore the Paradigm Prism*, Washington, DC: American Psychological Press.

Van der Kolk, B. (2002) 'Beyond the talking cure: somatic experience and subcortical imprints in the treatment of trauma', in F. Shapiro (ed.) *EMDR as an Integrative Psychotherapy: Experts of Diverse Orientations Explore the Paradigm Prism*, Washington, DC: American Psychological Press.

# 8

# WHAT THERAPEUTIC HOPE FOR A SUBJECTIVE MIND IN AN OBJECTIFIED BODY?

*Michael Soth*

## Modern psychotherapy as an ambivalent response to the 'disembodied mind'

UKCP would not have organized a conference subtitled 'Working with the Embodied Mind', unless as psychotherapists we all shared an implicit recognition of the 'disembodied mind'. All psychotherapy, whatever the specific approach, is involved with, and affected by, the blessings, the contortions, the vicissitudes of the 'disembodied mind'. Although it has developed special expertise in working with the body since the 1930s, and although it claims to champion the body, traditional body psychotherapy has also subscribed to and exacerbated the culturally prevalent objectification of the body. In this chapter I am attempting to work through some of the shadow aspects of the body psychotherapy tradition. It then becomes possible, I believe, for body psychotherapy to make its own unique and precious contribution towards the development of a twenty-first-century relational psychotherapy, which does (re-)include the body.

### *Max: a case illustration*

Following Freud's idea that extreme cases reveal the dynamics of 'normality', in contemplating how to reinclude the body in psychotherapy, we might want to think of people who are extremely disembodied. Years ago, when I first started out as a psychotherapist, I worked with a client, let's call him Max, who knew he hated his body.[1] He hated his appearance: he thought he looked too thin and weedy. His grandfather had coped with being an immigrant by becoming a boxer, and had taught his son accordingly. My client grew up with the constant certainty of his father's and grandfather's contempt for him. He was not the same kind of man as they, and they were the only kind of men he knew. When he

111

came to see me years later, in his mid thirties, he was habituated to living with that contempt and self-hatred as a constant companion. By that time he had been through quite a therapeutic journey already. He had spent his twenties in a fairly isolated state, without a social life, working long hours in administration. This helped him forget his body and ensured a social status that would protect him from the powerlessness and uncertainty which his father's family had suffered from.

## Objectification of the body

During this pre-therapy period of his life Max illustrates an attitude towards his body which we recognize as fairly common in our culture: the body as an ignored and exploited slave. This is what I would call 'negative objectification'. Ken Wilber puts it neatly:

> I beat it or praise it, I feed it and clean and nurse it when necessary. I urge it on without consulting it and hold it back against its will. When my body-horse is well-behaved I generally ignore it, but when it gets unruly – which is all too often – I pull out the whip to beat it back into reasonable submission.

> (Wilber 1979: 106)

The implicit objectification of the body may remain invisible to its 'owner' as long as the body can be ignored, but it does become apparent when the body gets 'unruly'. When 'normal' disembodiment breaks down, the common reaction is to run to the doctor, some helping professional or other quasi-medical expert, who is obliged to provide the illusion that *somebody* is in control of it all. The doctor gets paid to 'fix the engine', ideally in a scientifically validated fashion, so the patient can go back to 'using' the body in the 'normal' way they are accustomed to. In other words: ignore it and use it as long as it is working, fix it and get it to perform when it's faulty.

Max's body finally did become 'unruly': he developed colitis and started seeing complementary practitioners. They told him his lifestyle was damaging and that he should take care of his body. That is not easy for a person who is consumed with self-loathing, including contempt for his body. No longer allowed to ignore his body altogether, he was confronted again with the underlying hatred; it was staring him in the face. Having always hated the look of his nose, Max reappeared after one summer break, with a new, improved nose, thanks to cosmetic surgery. This is an illustration of the degree of delusion that is possible in the 'disembodied mind' – he thought he was 'taking care', whereas all I could see was a self-mutilating enactment of his hatred for himself and his body. Max being a thorough and conscientious person, he 'took

112

care' of his body in the only way he knew: quite brutally, and in terms of external appearance only. His looks became terribly important to him, especially his physical appearance. He did not go as far as joining a boxing club, but he did make it to the gym. Without improving his physique, he was convinced that his chances of attracting a relationship were non-existent. In fact, he became a regular gym addict. So even when he was tired after a long day's work and resented it, he had to go because otherwise, as he called it, 'the rot would set in'.

The whole thing was, of course, completely irrational because what the world had always seen from the outside was a good-looking attractive man. Now Max started taking his cue from Hollywood celebrities and became obsessed with his fitness, his health and his diet. He went to massage regularly. He showed all the outward behaviour of someone who takes care of his body, long before magazines like *Men's Health* spread the message. During this period of his life he illustrates an increasingly widespread attitude towards his body, modelled by global fashion icons all over the media, an attitude which we might call 'positive objectification'.

The body is fast becoming a postmodern fashion accessory, treated like a car as a substitute for self, an advertisement for self. Maybe with the advances of cosmetic surgery we will all at some point be able to download the perfect designer body off the internet, but that attitude of shaping and training the body to fit our chosen image of it only brings home the full extent to which we use the body. We think we can do to it anything we like, we use it to approximate our ideal image of the body rather than identify with the one we already *are*.

I am obviously not at all criticizing the many wonderful holistic and complementary therapies we have available these days (I myself do Tai Chi, have massage, go to osteopaths, homeopaths and acupuncturists etc.). All of these are helpful and precious practices. But from a psychotherapeutic perspective there is more at stake than turning an exploitative relationship to the body into an apparently caring, positive one. Positive objectification through an attentive attitude designed to perfect and parade the body is still objectification; and does not do any more justice to the spontaneous life of the body than neglectful, callous objectification of the body.

## Disembodiment

The culturally constructed image of the body mirrors our sensation of it. The way we relate to the body reflects our experience of the body. Both kinds of objectification, negative and positive, are the 'far end', both collectively and individually, easily visible manifestations of the extent to which our culture suffers from an underlying pervasive disembodiment, a 'dissociation of mind and body which is a peculiar lesion in the modern and post-modern consciousness' (Wilber 2000: 174).

I can only manipulate my body with that objectifying degree of arbitrary nonchalance, if I am no longer connected or identified with it at all, and, if it is indeed an 'it', which 'I' drag with me through life as an appendage underneath my neck. I can only abuse and exploit the body in such objectifying fashion, if I am already habitually disembodied, if my spontaneous, given, first-hand experience is that 'I' am not in 'it', let alone that 'I' am 'it'.

After a few hundred years of Cartesian duality, enlightenment, positivistic reductionist materialism, we have ended up thinking disembodiment is the human condition. Our culture has lost every sense of identification with the body, to the point that when body psychotherapy elder Stanley Keleman rediscovers it, it sounds like a revelation:

> You are your energy. Your body is your energy. . . . The unfolding of your biological process is you . . . as body. Your body is an energetic process, going by your name. It delights me to say that I am my body. It gives me identity with my aliveness, without any need to split myself, body and mind. I see all my process – thinking, feeling, acting, imaging – as part of my biological reality, rooted in the universe.
>
> (Keleman 1975: 24)

Max never experienced anything like this. That kind of statement was inconceivable to him. Most of his life Max could not actually feel his body, let alone derive an identity from it. He, his identity, his subjectivity (if it was anywhere) was, without a doubt on his part, located in his mind, his principles, his alert and acute mental and cognitive consciousness. His body was an 'it' which he was responsible for, but a hated, disturbing, troublesome 'it' which 'he' was identified against and struggled against. That was a never-ending battle.

He spontaneously experienced his body as an 'it', disembodiment was a given, a fact of existence, an experience which he found himself thrown into'. And through being trapped in his father's hatred of it, which he experienced as self-hatred, he was also internally perpetuating the objectification. This internal relationship between 'his identity in his mind' and his hated body guaranteed his continuing self-objectification. Therapy can easily perpetuate this dynamic and become a vehicle of it: as long as I am using the body in an objectifying fashion (under whatever therapeutic guise), I am not identifying with it, thus perpetuating disembodiment.

These are the two facets of the quintessential objectified body I refer to in the title of my chapter: objectification is both a spontaneous subjective experience which we are landed with (a background bodymind state of disembodiment), and it is an internal, ongoing process (the bodymind relationship is a continuously repeated object relation). His father's relationship to Max was paralleled by (or mapped onto) the relationship between Max's mind and his body, structured into an incessant conflict between his habitual mental state and his spontaneous bodymind processes. He was caught in a constant internal repetitive enactment, which he could not help but act out externally, in his life and in therapy. His unconscious construction of therapy and me as his therapist always already contained these two conflicted poles and the dynamic between them, long before I had even entered the room.

## Using the body: the body as object rather than subject

This was Max's individual version of what is a collective condition: our culture is pervaded by an underlying stance which treats the body as an object rather than a subject. The objectification of the body is rampant in our clients and in the field of counselling and psychotherapy. Generally speaking, the way psychotherapists relate to the body is not free from the disembodied and objectifying tendencies in the culture.

But as long as we are caught in such an objectifying stance *against* the body, we cannot possibly appreciate the potential for spontaneous, autonomous subjectivity emerging *through* the body. We cannot talk about how to 'use' the body in psycho- therapy without some recognition of the 'use', mis-use and ab-use of the body under 'normal' circumstances. We cannot hope to work with the body unless we share an understanding of how much we are always already caught in a culturally constructed stance of working against the body.

We cannot expect profound therapeutic transformation if psychotherapy operates within the limitations implicit in this stance: as long as we take for granted and accept as a given of the human condition the underlying conflicted state of the bodymind and the experience of disembodiment, described as 'character armour' by Reich (1983), the roots of human suffering will continue to elude us. We can- not hope for an experience of spontaneous subjectivity through the mind as long as client and therapist are perpetuating a disembodied, self-objectifying system. We cannot fully address the pain and problems manifesting in the body without addressing the problems inherent in our dualistic conception of the bodymind relationship.

## Overview: two ways of (re-)including the body in psychotherapy

This chapter is based on the belief that the return of the neglected, dissociated and repressed body can inform and transform counselling and psychotherapy as we know it today. If our discipline is to move into the twenty-first century, it is essen- tial that we learn to attend to the therapeutic relationship as a bodymind dynamic. In the attempt to re-include the body, we can draw on the tradition of body psycho- therapy, but not without addressing some of the shadow aspects of that tradition first. Body psychotherapy has important concepts and tools to offer to the rest of the field; without these it will, for example, be hard to apply the precious insights of modern neuroscience to our practice. But first we need to learn from the failures and fallacies of body psychotherapy. There are many, partly justified, prejudices against body psychotherapy, and many misconceptions about it. Inevitably, in championing the body, body psychotherapy has attracted to itself the cultural ambivalence about the body. Surrounded by fears and fantasies, idealization and contempt, exciting and frustrating, libidinal and anti-libidinal objects, the actual body and the actual theory and practice of body psychotherapy can remain elusive and misunderstood.

The challenge to body psychotherapy has been that we idealize the body, and that we tend to short-circuit the depth of pain by providing either directive and invasive or gratifying and soothing interventions. As I will try to show in terms of the development of my own practice, that is an entirely valid and correct challenge: the techniques of the body psychotherapy tradition (including body awareness, touch and bodywork) *can* and *have been* used to 'make better', to evacuate, discharge and sidestep the depth of the pain, and to minimize, counteract and circumvent the heat of the transference. I have used them like that. In trying to counteract the bodymind split and the pervasive objectification of the body, body psychotherapists have 'used' the body to overcome resistances, undercut the ego and the mind, make catharsis and embodiment happen, in pursuit of their own purposes and in a fairly objectifying way. For all its humanistic values and its emphasis on embodied presence and interpersonal contact, body psychotherapy was largely based on an implicit medical model stance which tried to reverse the dominance of the mind over the body. It has access to a differentiated holistic appreciation of transference, but has not taken on board the insights of the 'countertransference revolution' (Samuels 1993).

In the rest of this chapter I propose that there is a way in which the spontaneity of the body, both the client's and the therapist's, can become one avenue, one of the royal roads, into the depths of psyche, into the traumatic depths of disembodiment, into subjective and intersubjective depth and into spontaneous transformation.

This will involve the deconstruction of what I now consider traditional body psychotherapy and the incorporation of a more relational perspective. But I do not think of this simply as a development from an old, invalid way of working to a newer and better one, merely replacing one theory with another one. What I will be proposing is that my original way of working on the one hand, and a more relational perspective on the other, constitute two poles of an underlying paradox inherent in *all* psychotherapy. These two poles disclose two ways of (re-)including the body in psychotherapy which are both helpful and necessary and ultimately complementary. But inasmuch as they correspond to the two sides of the underlying paradox, they are also antagonistic, as they imply radically different therapeutic stances and meta-psychologies (affecting, in turn, therapeutic aims, theories, techniques and potential results, as well as the requirements of the therapist). In order to present these two ways of including the body in psychotherapy, I want first to share with you some details of my own journey from an exclusive reliance on the traditional way to an appreciation of their necessarily conflicted coexistence in the paradoxical core of the therapeutic position.

116

## The diagnosis of disembodiment

When I worked with Max in the late 1980s, my beliefs about the embodied mind were straightforward. I assumed that the 'disembodied mind' is the root of all neurosis, and embodiment is the solution. I thought I had cracked the code, and I was on a mission. At that time, I only knew about the first way of using the body, and my whole therapeutic style, thinking, theory, and meta-psychology was immersed in an idealization of the body and embodiment. That was the time when a friend of mine wrote a book *How to Feel Reborn* (Albery 1985), and I knew what he was talking about, I had been there. We had breathed together, gone through the heaven and hell of regression and catharsis, and we had felt a wondrous sense of aliveness better than anything we had hoped for. If we, and everybody else, could feel like that all the time, there would be no need for war and oppression and addiction and unhappiness. All it apparently needed was surrendering to the body, the feelings and the breath, and everything else would sort itself out.

Consequently, as a therapist, I saw myself as an expert on embodiment, a body magician, whose task it was to make people return to their birthright: a blissful existence in their true home, their physical, sexual, animal being. Wilhelm Reich (1983) said that there was a pure, good, loving core which we could get back to, and I was dedicated to this retro-romantic fantasy (as postmodernists like to call it these days). Expression, catharsis, feeling our feelings, was the key to health, happiness and embodiment. As a therapist I thought I should and could make that embodiment happen.

Whatever our therapeutic approach, sooner or later there will be a client who traps us in our most cherished assumptions about therapy. Max was such a client for me. Being a well-educated, politically aware intelligent man, he had over the years tried to make sense of his condition. By the time he came to me, he had a clear analysis and self-diagnosis of his own numbness, the denial of his feelings and his disembodiment. Through co-counselling (Jackins 1982), he had arrived at a perspective similar to my Reichian one. In fact, that was one of the main reasons he sought me out. You may know that co-counselling is a mutual form of self-help therapy, where client and counsellor swap roles. A key principle is for the counsellor to detect and contradict the client's negative patterns in order to elicit 'discharge' of feeling. Max was so good at it as a counsellor that he even became a teacher of co-counselling. I should have listened up when he said the only problem was that he was very bad as a client. Apparently, he was so good at avoiding and anticipating the counsellor's manoeuvres that nobody could get through to him and his feelings. Coming to see me was a fairly explicit attempt to bring bigger guns onto the battlefield!

## Basic assumptions of traditional body psychotherapy

So we shared a lot of assumptions, Max and I, and in my infinite naivety at the time I assumed that would make the work easier. There is no space here to spell out the theoretical framework of traditional body psychotherapy I was relying on at the

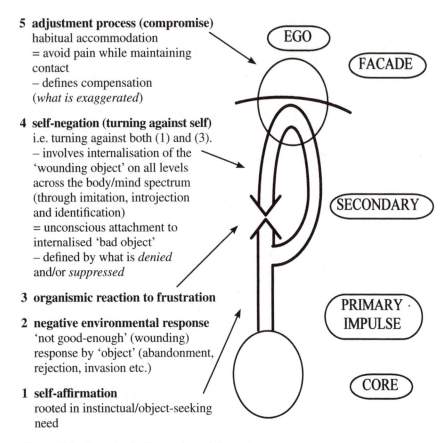

**5 adjustment process (compromise)**
habitual accommodation
= avoid pain while maintaining
contact
– defines compensation
(*what is exaggerated*)

**4 self-negation (turning against self)**
i.e. turning against both (1) and (3).
– involves internalisation of the
'wounding object' on all levels
across the body/mind spectrum
(through imitation, introjection
and identification)
= unconscious attachment to
internalised 'bad object'
– defined by what is *denied*
and/or *suppressed*

**3 organismic reaction to frustration**

**2 negative environmental response**
'not good-enough' (wounding)
response by 'object' (abandonment,
rejection, invasion etc.)

**1 self-affirmation**
rooted in instinctual/object-seeking
need

*Figure 8.1* Steps in the formation of character
*Source:* based on Johnson 1994; Reich 1972

time, but accessible introductions to the subject are available (Rosenberg 1985; Staunton 2002; Totton 2003), especially through Johnson's summary of his life's work (Johnson 1994), integrating Reichian character structures with the developmental theories of ego-psychology, self-psychology and object relations.

According to Johnson's (1994) psychodynamic account, whatever the child's age, developmental stage and corresponding existential need or issue, developmental injury occurs and is internalized in the following sequence of interactions and experiences: the child's spontaneous expressions are met with a negative or 'not-good-enough' parental response which initially generates an organismic, impulsive reaction in the child. When this reaction also meets with a consistent and systematic failure by the caregiver to respond adequately, eventually the child, in a bio-psychological gesture of turning-against-the-self, internalizes the negative environmental response. As this intensely conflicted state is not sustainable, a variety of superficial adjustment mechanisms are necessary which both repress the wound and present a compensating facade to the world (see Figure 8.1).

In line with these theories, both Max and I assumed that his disembodiment was the result of early trauma that had been frozen into his bodymind as character armour. We shared the assumption that behind his mask were buried intense feelings and an aliveness which he was systematically denying and avoiding; by accessing and expressing those feelings, he would return to healthy, alive functioning. But accessing those feelings required a circumvention of Max's defences which, according to his own reports, were rather effective and pervasive. Most therapeutic approaches have their own language for describing the double-edged nature of defences: they are simultaneously protective and self-sabotaging. The Jungian analyst Kalsched (1996), for example, has described the 'self-care system' which traumatized people develop, a defensive-protective mechanism which provides some kind of safety, but at the expense of contact with self and others and to the detriment of spontaneous aliveness. Kalsched describes how the 'self-care system' is intent on defeating the therapist and the therapeutic process, putting me in mind, also, of an early statement by Wilhelm Reich: 'Every patient is deeply sceptical about the treatment. Each merely conceals it differently' (Reich 1983: 120).

If it is clear that it takes severe, systematic trauma to shock somebody out of their body for good, into habitual disembodiment, what actually constitutes trauma is more relative and debatable. In a culture where only what can be seen and measured is real, only extreme, violent, visibly brutal trauma is noticed. This post-hoc adult version was the only form of trauma Max could understand and conceive of. He could not allow himself sufficiently any imagining of his experience as a child, let alone his infantile emotional reality, to appreciate the kind of psychological trauma which attachment theory shows us at the root of developmental damage. Apart from this little difference, we agreed on the hypothesis of early trauma and the project of uncovering it. I completely agreed with his self-diagnosis. I completely agreed with his proposed solution. If we have diagnosed the problem as disembodiment, then the solution must be the opposite, embodiment.

## The project of embodiment

There are two ways in which the body can be used in therapy to counteract the client's disembodiment, contradict the client's life-denying patterns and undercut the client's defences and resistance. We can categorize the interventions of traditional body psychotherapy into two main manoeuvres:

- *The hard, masculine way: crack and break through the 'character armour'.* This has the aim of provoking catharsis at a primal level by challenging the superficial mask-like adaptations of the false self, and accessing both primary and secondary feelings in their raw form.
- *The soft, mothering way: melt the armour.* This has the aim of undercutting the pseudo-autonomy of the social façade by nurturing the pre-verbal self, and reconnecting with the buried and denied primal feelings and needs.

Armed with my idealistic notions, these two main manoeuvres, and the whole toolbox of active interventions (biodynamic, bioenergetic, breathwork, Gestalt) at my disposal, I went to work. Considering Max's explicit demand for (and apparently willing cooperation in) the attack on his armour, it was not that difficult occasionally to break through his resistance, to make him feel feelings, to force cracks in his defences, to touch his longing. These breakthroughs did provide him with glimpses of a different sense of being and of a more alive universe. They were precious experiences. But I only understood later that because they arose in the context of a retraumatizing re-enactment which we were both oblivious of, they could never be fully integrated. In disappointing contrast to what I thought the textbooks said, these peak experiences, therefore, never led to sustained change or improvement.

On the contrary, apart from occasional glimpses which seemed to confirm the validity of our project, the only other result of these breakthroughs was that it was getting more and more difficult to produce them. With every breakthrough he learnt more about the cracks and weak spots in his armour and became more adept at anticipating further breaches. My client's self-care system used every successful embodiment breakthrough to prevent the next one more comprehensively. His self-care system was learning fast, and I was running out of tricks.

## Learning from the failure of the embodiment project

That was a shocking awakening to me. Even when clients say they want their body back after having repressed, excluded and abused it for years, and I offer it back to them on a plate, they do not exactly embrace it with open arms: they resist, they struggle, they deny, they reject me, they leave! There I am, full of good intentions and out of the goodness of my heart trying to lead them back into the pleasures of embodied, grounded, passionate existence, and they throw it back in my face – how terribly unfair! Though it took me a while to learn from this shock, with hindsight now it seems very straightforward and obvious.

Letting go into the body, the first thing we encounter in clients is not a 'noble savage', blissfully self-regulating. The first thing we are liable to meet is the objectified body, the body as 'it', already cleaved away from any sense of self, already excluded, disavowed, the body as carrier of the shadow. It took me a while to translate my failure with Max into a general principle. At first I thought it was just my incompetence, or worse: personal inadequacy. I thought this debacle was some anomaly in an otherwise perfectly valid therapeutic framework. But Max helped me recognize that the same dynamics occurred with other clients, only in more subtle ways.

The problem was not with my perception of the client's conflicted bodymind reality, but with the conclusions I drew from that perception and my therapeutic responses to it. My diagnosis was correct: Max *was* trapped in a habitual conflict, between his spontaneous, organismic reality and his cognitive, reflective identity and self-image. But typically my responses to his habitual trappedness were coming from an equally trapped and habitual place within me: based on my idealizing fantasy of the body, I was constantly taking a one-sided, biased and fixed position. I was siding with what I perceived as his potentially alive body against what I perceived as his habitually defensive mind. This bias was tantamount to an ideology for me, and I was blind to its effects.

As any marital therapist knows, a conflict in a couple cannot be contained if the therapist habitually sides with one party against the other. Taking sides like that does not facilitate the spontaneous reorganization of the conflict into transformation; it actually keeps it going. It was only through Max being such an expert at avoiding embodiment that this began to dawn on me. I realized that the more I pursue embodiment and the more I take the side of the client's body against the client's mind, the more we end up acting out between us the client's war between body and mind. I then 'become' their body, and the client retreats into their already restricted identity with their disembodied mind. The more I champion, out of my own ideological investment, the client's body over and against their mind, the more the client and I perpetuate the bodymind split relationally. Far from helping to heal that split, which was the avowed intention, this was undoubtedly exacerbating it. In the apparent pursuit of embodiment, catharsis and aliveness, I was taking a fixed, habitual position in which I was being relationally oblivious. I was proactively manoeuvring myself into a position in which I was participating in a re-enactment of the client's internal bodymind split between the two of us.

I was forced to conclude that the more I insist on embodiment, the more I end up getting in the way of it. To simply try to make embodiment happen, is not just counterproductive, it is impossible. Regardless of its theoretical validity, apparent 'truth' and 'accuracy', my whole mind-set, fuelled by an idealization of the body and traditional body psychotherapy, was acquiring a profoundly counter-therapeutic function in relation to Max.

Based on a simplistic description of the conflict between the client's body and the client's ego, I had sided with the body against the ego (if I may be allowed to use this multifaceted notion for now without precisely defining it). By equating the body with the uncorrupted core, along the lines of 'the body never lies', I had taken it upon myself to see my task as siding with the body against the restrictive ego (which at the time I saw naively as equivalent with the disembodied mind) and thus to liberate the client from their life-denying inhibitions and repressions. In simple terms I was constructing myself as an enemy of the client's ego, not just with Max, but with all my clients. Because this construction operated within me irrespective of the particular client, I came to consider it as an instance of – what I like to call – 'habitual countertransference'.

I now am grateful to Max and the process with him for helping me deconstruct this limiting mind-set, which I was hiding behind as my therapeutic identity. But at the time, I had severe difficulties with finding myself deconstructed. Then, I did not have the conceptual tools and was in no way prepared for the processes by which the client's unconscious constructs the therapist as an object; let alone could I conceive of the possibility that the ensuing *de*-construction of the therapist might be a therapeutically useful and necessary process.

I was so invested in my therapeutic identity, that I was still miles away from actually surrendering relationally to the transference-countertransference entanglement I was lost in. Max would often comment on his numbness. Typically (and not incorrectly) I would take that as a criticism of my apparent impotence and inability to break through his self-protective, defensive mechanisms. Not being able to bear my sense of failure, I would redouble my efforts to make him feel. But, of course, I could not afford to become too determined and insistent, let alone outright aggressive, lest I start resembling his intimidating father. That was anathema to me. If I understood that his father's brutality had shocked him into disembodiment in the first place, then therapy had to be the opposite, didn't it? What would be the point if therapy was more of the same?

One simple way of thinking about this would be in terms of two levels of working alliance. Based on our shared theoretical assumptions, Max and I had an apparently good working alliance on a verbal level, most of the time. But on the level of spontaneous, non-verbal interaction, which as neuroscience tells us accounts for 93 per cent of communication, we hardly had any. To all intents and purposes, in his sessions with me, a large part of Max's bodymind was in a bio-psychological energetic state where he might just as well have been in the same room with his father: his body was furtive, alert, anxious. Judging by his spontaneous experience he was in an emergency situation, expecting attack.

I was so entranced by our shared pursuit of the holy grail of Max's embodiment, the last thing I was going to notice was that, in the perception and experience of his non-verbal self, I was turning into the very father whom consciously I was obviously trying to help him recover from. My interventions, my assumptions, my whole therapeutic stance in relation to him, was a re-enactment of the father who was unhappy with him and his body as it was. Like his father, I was behaving in an attacking and contemptuous manner towards his current way of being. Everything about me was corroborating the assumption that there was something wrong with him, that he needed to change and be different, and especially have a different body.

I now recognize that unconsciously, and on a non-verbal and pre-verbal level, therapy for Max had always been constructed as a repetition of his relationship with his father, even before he came to see me. But, from the beginning, I had unconsciously fallen into this dynamic and, under the guise of my best therapeutic intentions, proactively acted into it. Our relationship, therefore, descended into a vortex where it was becoming little more than both an internal and external re-enactment of the father.

## Re-enactment

These recognitions are not news for practitioners in the analytic tradition, but in the field of body psychotherapy at that time we were just beginning to discover the extent and pervasiveness of projective identification. It took many years to understand the processes of transference and countertransference in bodymind terms and integrate this understanding with established body psychotherapy principles and techniques. The sustained attempt to do justice to the bodymind complexity of re-enactment later developed into the more comprehensive map of 'the five parallel relationships' (Soth 2005: 44).

The crucial lesson I formulated for myself out of the shreds of my deconstructed therapeutic position, is one which I found to be applicable and useful in all my relationships with clients, and in supervision. I offer you two versions, one formulated in the language of my own approach of body psychotherapy, and one in terms which can be adapted to any psychotherapeutic orientation.

*It is impossible to pursue a therapeutic agenda of breaking through the armour or undercutting the ego's resistance without enacting in the transference the person against whom the armour/resistance was first developed.*

The more we attend to the client's whole bodymind in the here-and-now of the therapeutic relationship, including how the original trauma has become frozen as a particular bodymind structure, the more it becomes obvious that the wound is always already there in the room, and it is always already there in relation to the therapist. I do not think it would have been possible for me to recognize the full extent and pervasiveness of re-enactment as a bodymind process unless I had been trained to attend to the body and its energetic state, in constant, minute detail. But while I stumbled into it through following the body into the depth of the bodymind split and disembodiment, re-enactment is of central significance in all psychotherapy. So here is what I consider the crucial lesson, formulated in terms applicable to any therapeutic approach: *it is impossible for a therapist to follow a strategy of overcoming or changing a dysfunctional pattern, without enacting in the transference the person in relation to whom that pattern originated.*

Regardless of the particular techniques or theories we are using, when we address and focus on any dysfunctional pattern, its relational origin/context is increasingly likely to come into the room and determine the client's perception and experience of both of therapy and therapist in the here-and-now of the therapeutic relationship. Whatever traumatic memory is buried within a dysfunctional pattern, sooner or later it will enter the room as a spontaneous, non-verbal process, and therapist and therapy will be perceived and experienced through it.

In my view, re-enactment happens, anyway, in all therapy and nobody can do anything about it. There is no way out of re-enactment, there is only a way in. Every attempt to minimize or counteract it, actually exacerbates it. There are many ways to deny it, or gloss over it or dress it up (e.g., as the client's resistance, or insufficiencies in the therapist's approach or style). As I have described in terms of my experience with Max, it is perfectly possible for a therapist to be so invested in their own particular therapeutic identity that they would not want to notice the ever-present pervasive dynamic of re-enactment right under their nose.

From within my original framework, therapy was meant to be healing, reparative, good – re-enactment did not appear on my map, therefore it did not have any reality. When it then did become a reality for me, I could not get my head around the paradox that the goals of therapy and the experience of re-enactment are irreconcilably opposed. How can any good come out of the fact that the very wounds for which the client is seeking therapy, consciously or unconsciously, are bound to be re-experienced and re-enacted between client and therapist?

Reflecting my own emotional response at the time, my first attempt to come to terms with this was to distinguish between therapeutic stances which inherently deny the relational dimension – and therefore re-enactment – altogether, and those which allow for it or acknowledge that it occurs.

## 'Third-person medical model' versus 'first-and-second-person intersubjective-relational' stance

In coming up against the limitations of treating the patient and his already objectified body in an objectifying way, I recognized that this had been my default position: as a therapist I can take a 'third-person perspective' and relate to the client as a case, an 'it', objectively, scientifically. This stance perceives and diagnoses the patient's pathology, applies a theoretical framework regarding the aetiology, dynamics and structure of that pathology, and on that basis prescribes and administers a treatment plan. As this is what patients typically expect from a doctor, we may for simplicity's sake call it the medical model.

A first-and-second-person perspective on the other hand recognizes the presence of another subject, another 'I', whom in essence I cannot possibly meet as long as I take an exclusively objectifying attitude. This stance, rooted for example in hermeneutics and Buber's (1923) 'I–Thou', is well established in relational psychoanalysis and in the dialogical principle of Gestalt therapy.

It is only when the medical model stance breaks down, or we deliberately refrain from it, that we notice the persistence with which the client transfers the familiar dynamics of their inner world into the therapeutic space. Through being active all the time in making change happen, an exclusively objectifying quasi-medical stance interferes with an important principle: it interferes with allowing myself to be constructed as an object by the client's unconscious. If I want to allow space for that process, I need to enter the relational experience of that construction while letting it be. Without this, I do not touch the spontaneous origins at the root of the client's being-in-the-world. On its own, the medical model stance is incomplete and counter-therapeutic. It is only through taking what we might call an intersubjective-relational stance that we experience the full extent to which re-enactment presents a problem and a paradox to the therapist.

The tension between these two modes has been with us since Freud and is, in my opinion, one of the most unintegrated issues in psychotherapy. Therapists tend to identify with one or the other polarity in a rather absolute fashion. Some therapists see their practice firmly within the scientific paradigm and construct their therapeutic position as indistinguishable from a medical expert, and denounce everything else as unprofessional. Some therapists vociferously maintain that any medical model attitude on the part of the practitioner is fundamentally inimical to the therapeutic process, as it will abort the authentic meeting, which they see as the core of the therapeutic encounter. Most therapists, as did Freud himself, oscillate uncomfortably between the two polarities, often switching between them in response to transferential pressures.

Re-enactment must obviously appear as irrelevant to therapists who subscribe to an exclusively objectifying medical model stance. I would maintain that it occurs, anyway, but it becomes significant as a transformative possibility only in forms of psychotherapy which put the therapeutic relationship into the centre of therapy, that is in those approaches which include the relational dimension and the transference / countertransference process. As the relational perspective is gathering momentum across the various approaches, re-enactment is going to become an increasingly central concept in psychotherapy.

The distinction between the medical model and the intersubjective-relational model helped me divide the therapeutic field between those who deny or remain unaware of re-enactment and those who at least acknowledge its existence. As exclusive and habitual positions, either stance can clearly be detrimental to the therapeutic process, as each tends to engender particular therapeutic dangers. If the medical model can get lost in the dualism, non-mutuality and the power-over dynamic inherent in the objectifying doctor, the relational model taken to the extreme presents an equivalent danger of the therapist degenerating into a collusive friend. While I could see the respective dangers of each stance, I still saw them as mutually exclusive and was caught in a dualistic either-or conception. Concomitantly, re-enactment, although now recognized, remained a dangerous phenomenon for me, liable to scupper therapy and therefore to be avoided and guarded against.

One of Freud's greatest insights was to reframe transference from his initial conception as an obstruction to therapy to his later view of transference as the royal road into the unconscious. Building on the insights of the 'countertransference revolution' since the 1950s, we may now take a similar turn with regard to countertransference, by reframing re-enactment: to the medical model therapist, re-enactment constitutes the opposite of therapy and therefore presents an unmanageable paradox. However, from within the paradox, the therapist's experience of feeling torn between objectifying and relational impulses becomes another route into the unconscious.

## The paradox at the heart of the therapeutic position

When we stop taking sides between the medical model and the intersubjective-relational perspective, consider them both as valid in spite of their antagonism, and recognize the contradiction between them as necessarily inherent in the endeavour of therapy, we embrace the underlying essential paradox, which – in my view – all therapeutic activity is subject to. I see all therapy as caught between (a) allowing and entering the inevitable repetition of the wound in the here and now of the therapeutic relationship (i.e. the re-enactment of the wound in and through the therapy) and (b) responding to the wound by counteracting it, relieving, soothing, modulating it – the far end of which is a reparative 'making it better'.

If the therapist can bear and hold that tension, and can be in it and both act and relate from within it (that is, fluidly engage from both sides of that tension), then spontaneous transformation of the wound can occur. In order to access the relational information inherent in the therapist's conflict, it is important to grasp the two perspectives as two poles of an underlying paradox. It then becomes possible to link our countertransferential conflict between these two stances to dynamics in the client's inner world. My recognition of re-enactment not only as an inescapable, but also as a necessary and profoundly productive feature of psychotherapy, represented a turning point in my development as a therapist.

Large chunks of what I am proposing are old hat to modern psychoanalysis and may sound as though I am reinventing the wheel. But it seems to me that neither traditional body psychotherapy nor psychoanalysis quite grasp the nettle of the bodymind totality of re-enactment which pervades both the client's and the therapist's bodymind process. The countertransference revolution and the shift towards relational perspectives in psychoanalysis have helped us appreciate the existence and significance of re-enactment. The tradition of body psychotherapy can provide a profound holistic phenomenology of re-enactment across all the levels of the bodymind in both client and therapist. In that sense I absolutely concede that I am not inventing a new wheel. Rather, I am proposing that we take two already invented wheels and get on our bikes and ride them.

## Two ways of re-including the body in psychotherapy

Corresponding to the two sides of the underlying polarities inherent in the therapeutic position, and the paradoxical tension between them, we can now formulate two ways of (re)-including the body: I can use the body to try and contradict the wound, or I can attend to the body as an inescapable dynamic feature in the re-enactment of the wound. I will propose that we need both, and, more importantly, that we need to develop the capacity to work with the tension between the two.

One way of reincluding the body is through working from a third-person, monological perspective. It is, therefore, operating from within the same objectifying paradigm implicit in the client's existing dualistic bodymind relationship, but doing so in order to make embodiment happen. It is about taking a quasi-medical therapeutic position, in order to reverse the client's disembodiment and to counteract the body's exclusion. In this way of using the body, I bring my knowledge, authority and expertise to bear in order to affect change (change through what I call translation and contradiction). Here, I am aware that the client suffers their individual version of the culturally constructed supremacy of the mind over the body. I recognize that where it hurts, they are helplessly trapped in it. Everything they do with their mind, every strategy they use, just makes things worse. So quite naturally, if I love and care, I have an impulse to ease their pain, so this first way is mainly about symptom-reduction. In attachment language it is about modulating and soothing the client's uncontained pain.

In any case, if I want to meet clients where they are, I need to collude with each client's self-objectification, which is inevitably reflected in their expectation for

me to take a medical model third-person stance. This way of using the body therapeutically is, therefore, treating the body as an 'it', which is how the client experiences and treats it, anyhow. It is the logical opposite to overly rational, mentalist
approaches, but it is, in terms of its implicit relational stance, using the dualistic
paradigm even as it is contradicting it.

From a first-and-second-person perspective, I relate to the client's and my own
body intersubjectively, whatever state that body is in (that is, even when we are
both disembodied or trapped in self-objectification). Rather than taking a position
which tries to change the habitual patterns, conflicts and dissociations we find
ourselves in from the outside, I am surrendering to relating from within them. It
is about consciously entering the same experience which the first stance tries to
change (and therefore treats from a third-person perspective), but it is about entering it as a dialogical, relational dynamic. By entering, I do not imply any activity
other than allowing myself to be constructed and being aware of the relational
bodymind reality we find ourselves thrown into. It does, however, require more
than withdrawing into a passive, reflective, or purely interpretive position.

In this stance I do not just act on any of the objectifying therapeutic impulses
which inevitably arise. Instead I reflect on them as possible re-enactments, because
I am holding out for the possibility of spontaneous transformation (rather than
deliberate, strategic change through translation and contradiction). I do not entirely
refrain from such impulses as a policy, but I try to hold the tension between embodiment and disembodiment, spontaneity and reflection, subjectivity and continuing
objectification, enactment and transformation. This way of attending to the client's
body and my own body, therefore, is all about resting in conflict and paradox, as
necessary ingredients in the therapeutic position.

We need this second way of including the body for developing an holistic phenomenology of relationship, and for making sure psychotherapy keeps doing justice to two of its core values: subjectivity and intersubjectivity. In other words it
involves bringing the therapist's full and spontaneous bodymind reality into the
consideration of the countertransference. This is where a bodymind perspective
transcends the reflective-interpretive bias of traditional psychoanalysis.

The first stance is a precious, although in itself limited reversal of disembodiment and the existing power dynamic of mind over body. As history teaches us, the
error and the hubris of too many revolutions is to stop short at such a plain reversal
of the power dynamic. Whereas the first stance is necessary for counteracting and
counterbalancing disembodiment and the still dominant nineteenth-century bodymind paradigm, the second stance is required for actually allowing deconstruction
and transformation of that paradigm.

## Surrendering to re-enactment as a here-and-now bodymind process

From a relational perspective, one of the key issues defining the transformational
capacity of the therapeutic space is the range and depth of human suffering, and the
extremes of pain and joy, which the therapist can bear to feel, to engage with, to be

drawn into. I think the limits of what we can bear as therapists can be extended by theoretically understanding the inevitability and necessity of re-enactment. But a lived understanding of how, paradoxically, profound spontaneous transformation occurs in the pit of re-enactment, can arise only by us surrendering to it, what I call 'entering' it (Soth 2005: 49).

Here we come up against the limitations of psychotherapy's inherited dualistic paradigm, both in terms of our habitual construction of the therapeutic position, and of our theories. An internalized object, as described by modern object relations, is not mainly or only a mental representation, it is a bodymind process (that is, it is not a static object and it is not only in the mind). Its main manifestation is not mainly in the content of our thoughts and fantasies (whether conscious or unconscious), but more importantly, it is structured into the process of our thinking, into our way of thinking. But not just our thinking: it is equally structured into the processes of sensing, feeling, perceiving, imagining, remembering, both in their psychological and their biological (physiological-anatomical) aspects.

On a physical level, more specifically, we could say that every internal object is anchored in particular sensations, particular tensions and mannerisms, particular parts of the body. Moreover, to take it beyond the idea of a singular internal object into an understanding of the relational unit in which each object is constituted, in the sense that 'there is no such thing as a baby' (Winnicott 1987: 88), then both poles of an internalized relationship are actually embodied on a somatic level in the relationship between parts of the body.

> Max's internalized father was, for example, particularly anchored in his eyes. Max had no felt sense of his eyes or the way he was looking. The frightened child anticipating attack lived on, for example, in his chest: the child's whole bio-neuropsychological state was accessible through the sensations in his chest. In his chest, the past was constantly present as if the father's attack was happening now. The relationship between the eyes and the chest whenever he looked at himself in the mirror, encapsulated the whole re-enactment. This was the strongest, but by no means only manifestation of similar parallels throughout his body-mind system.

This is the extent to which patterns of emotional relating (and wounding) actually get embodied, not only in the brain, but throughout primary, immediate body/mind experience. Modern neuroscience, by transcending established bodymind dualisms confirms what body psychotherapy has taken for granted since the 1930s: the attachment relationship affects physiological and anatomical development. We are now capable of tracking the biochemical and neurological processes in detail, but the principle was implied in character structure theory all along, that is that emotional interpersonal processes become internalized and embodied as body/mind processes: see Table 8.1.

*Table 8.1*: Internalization and embodiment of interpersonal dynamic as bodymind process

---

- the attachment relationship affects physiological and anatomical development
- emotional interpersonal processes become internalised and embodied as bodymind processes
- the way the infant is held and related to becomes the way the person's mind is capable of holding and relating to their feelings
- which is reflected in the way the brain relates to body physiology (e.g. endocrine and immune systems: see Pert 1997)
- which is reflected in the way different subsystems of the brain relate to each other (e.g. the cortex to the limbic system)

---

But the recognition of the full spectrum of parallel relational processes across biological, emotional and mental levels still eludes even the most advanced neuroscience. It is, for example, in my opinion a brilliant and helpful insight to have established the existence of seven distinct emotional brain systems (see Panksepp, Chapter 2 in this volume), significantly expanding the information age metaphor of the brain as a computing and thinking machine. But the important point is not only that these functional systems, stretching across anatomical, physiological, neurological and psychological domains, exist. For psychotherapy it is more important how they *relate to each other*. My hunch is that the fragmentation of the body/mind is reflected in a fragmentation of the brain, that body and brain reflect each other mutually, reciprocally, holographically, via parallel process. What gets mapped in the brain (and in memory) is not only content, but also process, relationship.

We will never get at this by chasing after the parts without looking at the emotional dynamic of their inter-relationship, the overall Gestalt of the complex system and its relational functioning.

## The fractal self: holistic and integral perspectives

The same point could be made in relation to the different modalities of the Body Psychotherapist (Orbach and Carrol, Chapter 5 in this volume): sensing, moving, emotion, feeling, imaging, thought, self-reflexive awareness. It is important to explicitly work with the whole spectrum of expressive and communicative 'channels' and to have different techniques for getting involved with all of them – that is one of the benefits of a holistic perspective. All of these modalities are avenues of experiencing and expressing self as process, for the client and for the system of the therapeutic relationship. It is important that therapists can expand their range of relating across the whole body/mind spectrum and all of these modalities. But as important is the *relationship between the modalities* that's where we can become aware of the re-enactment. As long as I switch modalities in pick 'n mix fashion, I can remain oblivious of the relational dynamic *between them*. For me, this is the essential difference between – what l would call – a holistic-integrative framework and an integral-relational one, a qualitative quantum leap similar to the established difference between eclectic and integrative perspectives. Although psychotherapy as we know is still a long way away from such a bodymind perspective, what I am proposing goes beyond a holistic framework which simply grafts the body onto established theory and practice, as an additional avenue. Beyond an holistic appreciation of the diversity and multiplicitiy of the many levels and dimensions of human existence, an integral perspective attends to the relationships between the parts, i.e. the meshworks and splits, the integrating and dis-integrating organising dynamics which weave the parts into a whole.

Paying attention to the parallel processes between psyche and soma, between psychology and biology, between brain and body, between memory and perception takes us into a holographic universe where past and present external relationship is reflected internally in the dynamic processes occurring in the body/mind matrix on the various levels and between the various levels. This is a two-way process: internal relationships are in turn reflected externally, and manifested interpersonally through enactment. Internal and internalised relationships, whether on a biochemical, neurological, muscular or emotional level, get constellated and acted out in external relationships (i.e. transference). In this way, uncontained internal conflict, if we think of it in its body/mind totality, gets relationally (re-)externalised to find containment in the other. This integral view where parallel processes weave the tapestry both of our inner and outer worlds and knit them together in a complex mystery, is implied in, what I call the notion of the 'fractal self'. A body psychotherapy perspective which transcends its traditional medical model bias, and embraces both the relational and the paradoxical implications of countertransference and re-enactment, can make a profound contribution to a 21st century bodymind 'fractal self' psychotherapy.

## Acknowledgements

I want to thank my colleagues at Chiron, who have struggled with me over the years and provided the support and context for me to formulate these ideas, and my wife, Morit Heitzler, without whose help and feedback this chapter would not have come together.

## Note

1  I have changed the name and all identifying features to ensure the client I describe remains anonymous since I have been unable to contact him for permission.

## References

Albery, N. (1985) *How to Feel Reborn*, London: Regeneration.
Buber, M. (1923 / 1970) *I and Thou*, Edinburgh: Clark.

Jackins, H. (1982) *The Human Side of Human Beings: The Theory of Re-Evaluation Counseling*, Seattle, WA: Rational Island.

Johnson, S. (1994) *Character Styles*, New York: W.W. Norton.

Kalsched, D. (1996) *The Inner World of Trauma*, London: Routledge.

Keleman, S. (1975) *The Human Ground: Sexuality, Self and Survival*, Berkeley, CA: Center Press.

Pert, C. (1997) *Molecules of Emotion*, London: Simon and Schuster.

Reich, W. (1972) *Character Analysis*, trans. V.R. Carfagno, 3rd edn, New York: Simon & Schuster.

——(1983) *The Function of the Orgasm*, first UK edn, London: Souvenir Press.

Rosenberg, J. (1985) *Body, Self and Soul: Sustaining Integration*, Atlanta, NJ: Humanics.

Samuels, A. (1993) *The Political Psyche*, London: Routledge.

Soth, M. (2005) 'Embodied countertransference', in N. Tolton (ed.) *New Dimensions in Body Psychotherapy*, Maidenhead: Open University Press.

Staunton, T. (2002) *Body Psychotherapy*, London: Brunner-Routledge.

Totton, N. (2003) *Body Psychotherapy: An Introduction*, Maidenhead: Open University Press.

Wilber, K. (1979) *No Boundary*, Boston: Shambala.

——(2000) *Integral Psychology*, Boston, MA: Shambala.

Winnicott, D.W. (1987) *The Child, the Family, and the Outside World*, Reading, MA: Addison-Wesley.

# 9

# HOW I DEVELOPED BIODYNAMIC PSYCHOTHERAPY

*Gerda Boyesen*

*Edited with a commentary by Clover Southwell[1]*

It has been a long journey: I originally trained in Norway, many years ago. Then I worked there, in hospitals and also in private practice. In 1968 I came to London. I have been based in England ever since, but have also worked abroad a lot, giving workshops and lectures and therapy in Germany, France, Spain and Australia, and so on. That has been good because until I came to London I had never taken an aeroplane. By then I was almost 50 years old, so I was quite hungry to travel, going everywhere.

I trained as a psychoanalytic-orientated psychotherapist in Oslo, and also as a Reichian. My training analysis was with Ola Raknes, the renowned Norwegian colleague of Wilhelm Reich. In order to become a Reichian psychotherapist, on top of going to university for psychology and on top of my psychotherapy training, I also went to physiotherapy school. After my basic physiotherapy training I went to Adel Bulow-Hansen's clinic to study her special method of neuro-muscular massage, because it was so extraordinarily effective with psychiatric patients (Boyesen G. 1987). In the two years I worked in Bulow-Hansen's clinic I learned two very important things. One was about the diaphragm, and the other was about listening.

## The diaphragm is the gateway to the unconscious

Everyone speaks about the psychological block, the emotional block, the muscular block, the energy block – all these blocks. I started to think about the diaphragm block. People speak about 'the breathing' just in general. I looked specifically at the diaphragm. I reflected on what Freud said: 'Repression [is] one of the devices serving to protect the mental personality. . . [But] the repression has been a failure. The repressed wishful impulse continues to exist in the unconscious' (Freud 1909: 49–52). When the repression fails, people become psychotic, or nervous, neurotic. In my view, to repress feelings and memories we have to use the body, and the diaphragm is the main muscle making the repression. I saw that when massage had made a patient's diaphragm freer, the repression was no longer so strong.

As long as the diaphragm was inflexible, the psychotherapy was more superficial. But when the diaphragm began to be free to move spontaneously, then the work went deeper. With some clients we have to work directly with the body to begin to loosen the diaphragm (Boyesen G. 1970). Repressed material then begins to become conscious so it can be worked with. I call the diaphragm the 'gateway to the unconscious.' The surfacing of the repressed material I call the 'dynamic updrift'. Emotions 'on top of the diaphragm' are superficial. Emotions from 'under the diaphragm' I call 'dynamic'. When we reach the dynamic process, the psycho-therapy can really work deep.

*CS: The Bulow-Hansen massage aimed specifically at posture change. The dia-phragm was worked indirectly, not directly. With the release of some chronic pos-tural tension in the body, there came a corresponding release in the diaphragm, and the patient would spontaneously take a deeper breath. Gerda Boyesen said it was only when the Bulow-Hansen massage had freed her diaphragm that she was able to connect with her deepest nature. She felt that her analysis had been largely 'above the diaphragm', i.e. with this crucial 'gateway to the unconscious' not yet fully open (Boyesen G. 1970).*

Once the diaphragm is free, simply relaxing can be enough to open the dynamic process. I call that 'dynamic relaxation' (Boyesen G. 1970). For some people even relaxation is too provocative. It is not just memories that may come up, but a vague or confused emotional pressure. This may not yet be recognisable as an emotion, but it can make people agitated or depressed (Boyesen M-L. 1974b).

## Neurosis and the vegetative system

At the Bulow-Hansen clinic, I realized that the patients who made the best psychological recovery were those who had vegetative reactions after the massage sessions, such as brief diarrhoea or flu-like symptoms (Boyesen M-L., 1974a). My massage, working on the chronic tension of the postural muscles, was so success-ful in freeing the diaphragm that sometimes it provoked too much. Some people could take it but some people got ill and had pains. I thought 'What shall I do?' I wanted to find how I could work with everyone.

The solution came as I discovered more about the vegetative system, and how I could work with that to moderate the effects of the massage. I read that two German researchers had investigated the bodies of some psychotic patients who had died and had found excess fluid in their muscle membranes. I thought, 'Is it this fluid that makes people ill'?

I got interested in the fluid and decided, 'With the more vulnerable patients I will work not with the muscle, because that provokes too much, but on the membranes between the muscle and the skin' (the connective tissue) . Sometimes I could feel the fluid in the membranes under my fingers, and could feel it emptying out of the membranes as I massaged (Boyesen G. 1979, 1987).

In Norway, when my psychotherapy patients expressed some insight that was really important for them, then after their simple statement I would hear their tummy rumbling. Just by chance I read in a Norwegian medical journal of some research about fluid in the intestinal walls. The researchers were interested in what goes out of the intestines through the walls, and also what goes into the intestinal tubes from the intestinal walls (Setekleiv 1964).

Then I started paying attention to my own tummy-rumblings. I got myself a stethoscope to put on my belly, so I could hear all the little sounds too. That started a whole new life! As I lay with the stethoscope on my belly, I would massage the membranes of my hands and arms. Then I would hear all sorts of watery sounds in the stethoscope – the sounds of the peristalsis of the intestines. It seemed that I was emptying fluid out of my membranes, and that this was connected with the sounds in the stethoscope on my belly (Boyesen M-L. 1974a).

So we come now to my theory of psycho-peristalsis. I concluded that the intestines have two tasks. One is to digest the food. The other is to digest emotional stress. My theory is that the peristaltic waves are not just helping the digestion of food. They also help take away the nervous stress. When there is too much fluid in the intestinal walls, the pressure makes people feel psychologically unwell. In the peristaltic wave, the intestinal wall contracts, squeezing out fluid, and so reducing this pressure (Boyesen M-L. 1974a).

I then began to use the stethoscope when I massaged my patients. When I got the watery sounds, I worked more in that place. I emptied the fluid, the nervous fluid, or as Reich would have called it, the 'energetic fluid'. And then people felt so good! I could work with everyone, even people who could not take the pure Bulow-Hansen massage.

I found that neurosis sits in the vegetative system. This is our most primitive system, and we cannot control it. The unresolved emotions are sitting not just in the muscles but also in the intestines. I call the intestines the 'emotional canal'. What happens in the belly affects a person's state of mind (Boyesen G. 1979, 1987).

I was full of this, but I couldn't speak about it in the hospital where I worked. No one there was interested. The doctors did not want to know about the mind, and the psychologists did not want to know about the body. The only people who were interested were my children. They said, 'We can't understand that the doctors don't understand what you tell us!' But they were only 4 and 5 years old, you know!

Many years afterwards a lover of mine sent me a newspaper cutting about a world conference for psychiatrists. Someone had found that nervousness and psychosis are linked with fluid between the nerve endings and muscles. That made so much sense. If you want to hit out, your nerves send an impulse to your muscles, but then if you don't hit, the impulse stays sitting there in the nerve endings. The doctors used a drug to reduce the fluid and that took away most of the fear. The psychotic people got better, but it didn't last for long. My massage emptying the fluid under my fingers was another way of reducing the fluid which the researchers were studying, as well as reducing the fluid in the intestinal walls, which I could hear in the stethoscope (Boyesen M-L. 1974a).

## The importance of listening

Now I want to come back to my time at the Bulow-Hansen clinic. The other big thing I learned there was to listen. When I came to Adel Bulow-Hansen she told me, 'I don't like psychoanalytic psychologists. I don't like that you are married because then you have not time enough. I don't like that you are Reichian' (because Reich was called 'the orgasm king', and Bulow-Hansen wasn't married). I so much wanted to learn from her that I had to promise her not to 'psychologize' the patients at the clinic, only listen to them.

When I first came to London my English was not good, and I didn't always understand everything my patients were saying. So sometimes I asked them. And they got very irritated. 'Here you come, this famous Reichian psychotherapist – the first in London – and you can't even understand what I say.' So, when I didn't understand what a patient was saying, I made myself very comfortable, and was sitting more and more relaxed. I said just, 'Hmm-mm. Yes, hmm, continue . . .' and suddenly my patients spoke more than they had ever spoken before. I just listened. And before I knew it, the patients had reached deep emotions, deep regression, deep understanding. This deep listening in the psychotherapy went very well; I saw more and more clients and it was exciting work (Boyesen G. 1979).

## The tragic level and the trivial level

I discovered what I call the 'tragic' and the 'trivial' levels of speaking. Before I realized the difference, I would use a 'tragic' voice to greet people in passing on the stairs. Then people would stop me and tell me their whole life story. When I was travelling people told me their whole story, and in the clinic the students told me their whole story. I call this 'the Aunt Lilian effect'. Aunt Lilian was in my husband's family. I did not know her well, but often met her at the many big family parties. Once Aunt Lilian said to me, 'Gerda, I do not understand why everyone tells me their life stories, when I only want to say "How are you?"' I did not understand it either, but some hours later I realized I had suddenly told her my life story! I had told her, 'I have to divorce my husband, I cannot live with him'. I hadn't told this to anyone, nobody else, and she was my husband's aunt! So, what was happening? Well, when she meant just to say, 'How are you, Gerda?' she said, 'Ge-e-erda, how ARE you?' And as I answered, it all poured out! Gradually I learned not to speak in the 'tragic' voice all the time. I learned the different ways of speaking. When I didn't want to let people go into that level outside of psychotherapy, I could use a different voice. To the students in the clinic and to other people's clients I just said, 'Hello, how are you?' very lightly. When I want to work deeply with people then I am in the tragic-positive, and I use my voice in the 'tragic' way.

CS: *Gerda Boyesen made fine distinctions also between the fluctuating levels of the client's consciousness and awareness within a session, and she developed ways of addressing people on the appropriate level by using carefully nuanced language, as well as by consciously using different qualities of voice.*

## The therapeutic presence

There was a patient who taught me a lot. He said, 'I have sexual difficulties and I have come all the way from America to have a Reichian treatment.' I gave him a Bulow-Hansen massage. And he came back. He said he was so tired. So he was sitting quiet, and I was sitting. I was just waiting to start to massage him. But he stayed quietly sitting. And then I went into a semi-sleep where I was afraid my head should fall down, so I sat with my head on my hand. I had my eyes half open so I could see when he was ready to start. But he didn't. And I started to feel wonderful 'streaming' sensations in my body. After fifty minutes I said, 'Now we have to end it'. And he left.

Next time he said it had been the most wonderful treatment, and since then sex had been good. So he sat down again, and I sat, and after fifty minutes I said, 'We have to end it'. Again he came back, very happy. And I thought, 'This is strange, I don't do anything. He comes here for Reichian treatment and I don't do anything'. And it went on like this four or five more times. I felt so fantastic each time afterwards, I thought, 'Is it fair that he pays me and I feel so wonderful!' So in our next session I held back my streamings. After that session he came back and said, 'I have had no orgasm, no good sex, nothing; what have you done?' He wanted the other treatment again.

So that made me ask myself, 'What was it? What did I do that made the difference?' I realized it was the atmosphere, it was the energy from me when I felt so good, that did it.

CS: *Gerda Boyesen took great care to cultivate in her students this therapeutic presence. It is based on the therapist being in touch with her own deep energy, and trusting the deep wisdom in the client (Boyesen G. 1970).*

## Working with regression

I'm not always the nice listener, sitting quiet like that. When a person comes into a regression, and wants, for instance, to protest to his father that he treated him unfairly, I'll tell him, 'Say it again! Say it again!' And there I use my force, I make my voice different, demanding. It doesn't help if I just say, softly, 'Say it again'. So we see it is important to use the voice intentionally in these different ways.

I call it 'Freud' when our repression fails and the painful material comes up, I call it 'Reich' for working with the body to help the psychotherapy, and I call it 'Jung' when people reach something beautiful and become more spiritual. I want to help people to come through the 'Freud', the painful memories, and reach the 'Jung', the happy ending. That is the word – you may think – we shouldn't use. A happy ending in psychotherapy means, people think, that you are not working really deeply. No! For me, the happy ending means we have left behind the bad feelings and touched the natural sweetness of being alive.

*CS: In the temporary regression of a biodynamic vegetotherapy session, a client can fully experience a primal scene with all its conflicts and frustrations. Gerda Boyesen then encouraged the client to express their inner impulse in that scenario directly to the people involved. This expression may come in words, cries, or gestures such as reaching out, hitting out, cringing away. With the therapist's support and acceptance, the client can find his own truth and reach a place of satisfaction, and so can move on. This happy ending does not mean fudging the painful history. It means completing the old emotional cycle (Boyesen M-L. 1975).*

*Biodynamic theory sees emotional arousal as the first, upgoing part of a natural cycle, involving physiological movement. As the emotions subside, we can complete the cycle if we can accept what has happened and come to terms with it. Then the upheaval in the body subsides and we return to harmony, and our energy is free to circulate, giving a feeling of satisfaction. The emotional cycle runs on three levels: our conscious awareness, our musculature and our vegetative system, including the psycho-peristalsis. Psycho-peristalsis functions only when the parasympathetic branch of the autonomic nervous system is active. It cannot function when we are tense or anxious, as then the sympathetic branch is active. Gerda Boyesen saw our innate and most fundamental form of self-regulation as our natural capacity to complete the emotional cycle physiologically, as well as mentally. Neurosis arises as this natural capacity gets obstructed.*

## The spiritual canal and the happy ending

I felt that there must be different canals for the energy in the body, one for the upgoing energy, the Freudian updrift of all the horrible things that you have repressed which are now rising up. And another canal for the 'Jung', the downgoing stream that makes us feel so happy.

And then by chance I understood it, in the way acupuncture works with the energy in the body. I went for acupuncture, first to Professor Worseley, who did wonderfully. Then he went to the United States and his assistant who stood in for him made me feel terrible. So I stopped. Later I spoke with another acupuncturist who said: 'He must have set the needles too deep. He set them in the emotional canal, instead of the spiritual'. So, when I massaged I started to work on the spiritual canal. When I worked at that level there came psycho-peristalsis and the patient always got the happy ending.

> One woman had so much fear, and she went into a regression in the session. She remembered when she was 1 year old. Her mother had her in the bathtub. Then the telephone rang, and her mother went to answer it. The little one slipped down in the bath and almost drowned. As our psychotherapy session was nearing the end, she was still full of fear. So, what should I do? I wanted to have the psycho-peristalsis dissolve the fear. I tried working on the eyes, I tried working on the mouth, but heard almost no sounds in the stethoscope. I tried everything except

137

the nose. Then I thought, 'Of course! If you drown, water comes into the nose.' I didn't want to put my finger in her nose, so I worked in her aura over the nose. Then at last I heard the psycho-peristalsis dissolving her fear and tension.

That was a happy ending. When someone goes into very deep work, as in regression, I try to bring them round to the 'Jung' in good time before the end of the session. I don't do the deep work right ten minutes before the end.

If I don't like a client, I have to work with that, and I have to get the client to come out with any anger towards me so we can work with that too. I love all my clients. Maybe I don't love them outside the therapy room, but when they come into my therapy room, I love them so much, that there are no criticisms. I don't care even if they lie because they will surely see the truth afterwards. So, there, that is important.

## Note

1 Gerda Boyesen gave a talk to the UKCP conference in September 2004, but was too unwell to prepare it for publication. Her colleague Clover Southwell completed the preparation, which was finished after Gerda's death on 29 December 2005. The editors are grateful to Clover Southwell for her work on this chapter, enabling readers to have a final opportunity to read Gerda Boyesen's words. Additional comments made by Clover Southwell, to elucidate where needed, have been included in the main body of the chapter and are set in italics to distinguish them from Gerda Boyesen's words.

## References

Boyesen, G. (1970) 'Experiences with dynamic relaxation', *Energy and Character* 1(1): 11–20, reprinted 1980 in *The Collected Papers of Biodynamic Psychology Vol. 1,* London: Biodynamic Psychology Publications.

—— (1979) *Entre psyche et soma,* Paris: Payot.

—— (1987) *Uber den Körper die Seele,* Munich: Kosel.

Boyesen, M-L. (1974a) 'Psycho-peristalsis Part I', *Energy and Character* 4(2): 35–57, reprinted 1980 in *The Collected Papers of Biodynamic Psychology Vol. 1*, London: Biodynamic Psychology Publications.

—— (1974b) 'Psycho-peristalsis Part II', *Energy and Character* 5 (1): 20–33.

—— (1975) 'Psycho-peristalsis Part V', *Energy and Character* 6 (1): 29–40; reprinted 1980, in *The Collected Papers of Biodynamic Psychology Vol. 1*, London: Biodynamic Psychology Publications.

Freud, S. (1909) 'Five lectures on psycho-analysis', reprinted 1960, in *Two Short Accounts of Psycho-analysis*, Harmondsworth: Pelican.

Setekleiv, J. (1964) 'Spontaneous rhythmic activity in smooth muscles', unpublished manuscript, Nevrofysiologisk Laboratorium, Anatomisk Institut, University of Oslo.

Southwell, C. (1988) 'The Gerda Boyesen Method', in J. Rowan and W. Dryden (eds) *Innovative Therapy in Britain*, Milton Keynes: Open University Press.

# 10

# HEALING FROM COMPLEX TRAUMA

## An integrative 3-systems' approach

*Claudia Herbert*

## Introduction

Facilitating client recovery from complex trauma is frequently perceived as a major challenge by therapists, who may feel overwhelmed by their clients' apparent fragility and vulnerability, the severity and complexity of their clients' problems, their difficulties to engage in a therapeutic relationship and, with this, the series of abandoned attempts at therapy in their clients' history. Further, traditional therapeutic frameworks, relying predominantly on language-based approaches and, less commonly, on body-centred methods alone, may only partially be able to meet this client population's multiple needs.

Recent advances in the fields of developmental neuroscience, trauma and memory research, cognitive science and information processing have enhanced our understanding of some of the underlying mechanisms that seem to be required for the development of a healthily functioning Self (Schore 1994, 1996, 2003; Siegel 1996a, 1996b, 1999, 2002; Steele et al. 2001; Gerhardt 2004). At the same time they point to the potential deficits which may arise, including complex trauma, when these requirements may not or may only partially seem to have been met. The implications of these findings suggest the need for the development of a therapeutic framework which incorporates the use of a whole spectrum of techniques (Herbert 2002, 2003, 2004a, 2005a, 2005b) that require new therapist competencies (Herbert 2004b, 2005a), which move beyond the limits of more narrowly focussed, traditional therapeutic orientations. Further, they require ways of working within a 3-systems' approach, which facilitates the recovery, processing and subsequent integration of traumatic material on all levels of human functioning.

This chapter will outline the rationale for the move towards an integrative 3-systems' approach to working with complex trauma and within this briefly introduce the therapeutic spectrum for trauma work (Herbert 2002, 2005a, 2005b) and explore the implications for working in this area. The chapter is based on the author's extensive clinical experience (Collard 2003) of working with trauma clients, her training in a variety of areas, such as clinical psychology, Cognitive Behavioural Therapy (CBT), schema therapy, Eye Movement Desensitization and Reprocessing (EMDR), as well as some experience of psychodynamic, Gestalt therapy and body-centred approaches, and her interest in energy psychology and holistic healing methods from Eastern and Western cultures, including meditation, yoga and mindfulness. Reference to some of the underlying theoretical findings will be made as appropriate.

First, a conceptualization of trauma will be provided and, second, the theoretical context of complex trauma will be outlined. Third, some of the limitations of traditional therapeutic approaches and the need for expansion of these will be explored. Fourth, the need for the move toward an integrative 3-systems' CBT approach will be proposed, a therapeutic spectrum for trauma work will be introduced and some implications for working successfully with complex trauma clients will be explored.

## Conceptualization of trauma

Current psychiatric classifications of trauma as defined by DSM-IV-TR (American Psychiatric Association 2000) or ICD-10 (World Health Organization 1993, 1997) in their diagnostic criteria for post traumatic stress disorder do not sufficiently capture the complexity of the problems trauma clients may be struggling with. One of the greatest areas of confusion from the perspective of a practising clinician is probably that currently no distinction is made between the psychological effects of a single or multiple isolated traumatic event and long-term, enduring trauma occurring during early childhood and critical stages of development.

A single trauma, or multiple isolated traumatic events, can have a major impact on people's psychological wellbeing (Herbert 1996, 2002; Herbert and Wetmore 1999). It can shatter their pre-existing sense of safety and trust within themselves, towards others and the world they live in (Janoff-Bulman 1992). This implies that they have had experiences which, prior to their trauma, would have enabled them to feel sufficiently integrated to build some sense of safety. This has now become threatened as a result of trauma. Rothschild (2000, 2003), expanding on an earlier definition by Terr (1994), has defined these types of traumas as Type I trauma for single traumatic events and Type IIA trauma for multiple, isolated traumatic events. Graphically, a Type I trauma could be presented by Figure 10.1.

Here, the middle line represents a person's lifeline, starting from the moment of conception or birth into this world (depending on the degree of past history a particular therapist chooses to work with) and continuing through the present to some time in the future. The oval shape around the lifeline functions like a looking glass, focusing mostly on the present and radiating back into the past and towards the future. This is based on the understanding that in order to live in an integrated and connected manner, our predominant focus of energy has to be in the here-and-now (Gendlin 1978, 1981, 1996; Kabat-Zinn 1994).

Events above the lifeline represent positively remembered experiences and below the lifeline, negatively perceived experiences in a person's life. All humans will have experienced a mixture of positive and negative life events, on a continuum of differing perceived strengths. If past negative life events have been sufficiently

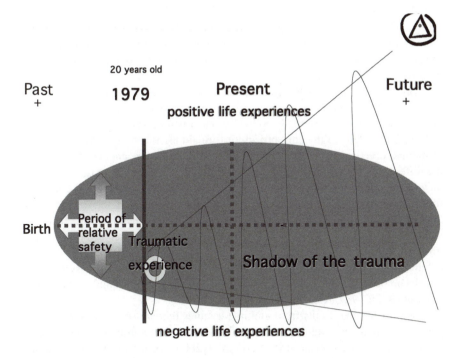

*Figure 10.1:* Type I and IIA trauma
*Source:* Herbert and Jarisch 1998

contained for a person, and if resources were available to process these so that they mostly did not have a lasting overwhelming effect, the person will have been able to establish an internal sense of safety and trust in themselves, others and the world.

Therefore when such people enter therapy, the single trauma (Type I) or the series of multiple, isolated traumatic events (Type IIA), which they have experienced, may be perceived as 'the worst experience they have ever had in their life'. To these clients it frequently feels that at the time of the trauma 'a shutter goes down' (represented in Figure 10.1 as the solid, vertical line at the time of trauma), which makes them feel disconnected from any sense of safety in their body, although they know rationally that they used to be able to feel safe prior to the trauma. From there on a client's energy system is disrupted, with the main focus of energy being absorbed by the client's preoccupation with the trauma and the further consequences of this. This is what has been referred to as 'living in the shadow of the trauma' (Herbert and Wetmore 1999) and is presented in Figure 10.1 as projecting from the time of the trauma out into the future.

Effective therapy for Type I and Type IIA traumas needs to focus on helping these clients work through and process the disturbing memories (in all their sensory dimensions, including body memories) associated with their trauma/s in order to help them integrate their experiences. Clients can then derive a new inner sense of safety and trust centred in the present moment, which incorporates the reality of their traumatic experience/s. This enables clients to redistribute their main focus of energy into the here-and-now and lifts the shadow of the trauma, transforming it into a new light.

Work with Type I and IIA trauma can be quite effectively achieved following, for example, the recommendations made for effective trauma treatment in the UK NICE guidelines for PTSD (National Institute for Clinical Excellence (NICE) 2005). Due to the current lack of formal classification of different types of trauma, practising clinicians may not be aware of, or pay enough attention to, the differences between the Type I and IIA traumas and the traumas, which will now be described as complex traumas. In clinical practice, at best this can have the effect of making clients feel unsafe and unable to engage in the form of brief therapy offered to them, and therefore feel unwilling to attend therapy. At worst, however, this lack of distinction and inappropriate treatment can lead to client re-traumatization, a total breaking down of their coping strategies (defences) and a deterioration in their condition, leading to flashbacks or dissociative symptoms, which can be misdiagnosed as a form of psychosis as it can resemble some of the features (Kluft 1987; Kluft and Fine 1993).

Complex trauma results from multiple traumas that are so overwhelming that people are unable to hold on to their resilience and cannot in their mind separate one traumatic event from the other. Rothschild (2000, 2003) refers to these traumas as Type IIB traumas. She has distinguished between a Type IIB (R) trauma, where the R stands for remembered, and a Type IIB (nR) trauma, where the nR stands for not remembered. Type IIB (R) traumas would include prolonged instances of overwhelming human suffering, such as instances of torture, Holocaust experiences, or prolonged, severe domestic violence. People experiencing Type IIB (R) trauma may have had a stable background and feelings of safety in the past, but their traumatic experiences would have been so devastating that they could not maintain their resilience. The other type of complex trauma, which is the predominant focus of the current chapter, refers to Type IIB (nR) trauma. In this case, there is no defined index trauma but rather a series of traumatic experiences, usually originating in early childhood and infancy. Traumatic material is often fragmented or only very partially accessible and unravels in stages, often in the form of body memories (Rothschild 2000, 2003). Figure 10.2 gives a graphical illustration of Type IIB (nR) trauma.

Type IIB (nR) trauma clients would have experienced repeated traumatic experiences from birth or early childhood and, as illustrated in Figure 10.2, often have had very little or no sense of internal safety. For these clients, the shadow of trauma would have been present for much or all of their lives at the point they enter therapy and they will be unable to remember a period of time when they have ever felt different. They may never have established a healthily balanced energetic system due to the compounding impact of repeated trauma.

In order to understand complex trauma clients' therapeutic needs, which differ

positive life experiences

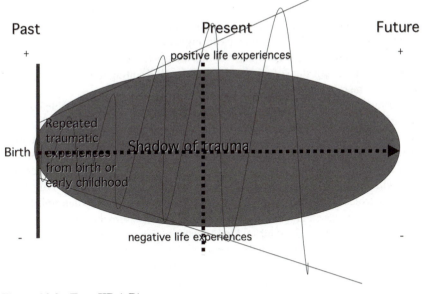

*Figure 10.2:* Type IIB (nR) trauma
*Source:* Herbert and Jarisch 1998

greatly from clients suffering from Type I or IIA trauma, and to arrive at a treatment model useful to Type IIB (nR) trauma, the theoretical context of complex trauma must be considered.

## Theoretical context of complex trauma

### *The significance of attachment*

Complex trauma sufferers often have little or no conscious access to a positive model of coping with life and they may never have known or experienced feelings of safety, love or esteem in their lives. Their current lives may be marred by feelings of underachievement and a stream of unhappy working or private relationships, physical or psychiatric problems, often accompanied by feelings of complete emptiness or severe pain inside. As babies, they may not have experienced a consistent and nurturing relationship with their primary caregiver or enduring feelings of unconditional love, valuing and safety. They may not have attained a sense of secure attachment (Bowlby 1969, 1988; Ainsworth et al. 1978; De Zulueta 1997; Brisch 2002) and subsequently may not have learned healthy affect regulation through the containing and reliable interactions with their caregiver (Schore 1994, 1996, 1997, 2003; Siegel 1996a, 1996b, 1999, 2002). Additionally, they

143

may have experienced their caregivers as a source of danger, which may lead to persistent anxiety states, affecting their brain development and functioning (Perry et al. 1995; Perry 1999), the hormonal mechanisms of their brain (Hofer 1994; Rothschild 2000, 2003; Gunnar and Donzella 2002; Gerhardt 2004), their healthy body development, functioning and structure and their formal educational achievements. Indeed, if they had experiences during which a freezing response occurred, their sympathetic nervous system (SNS) and their parasympathetic nervous system (PNS) might be in a state of chronic hyperarousal, resulting in extremely uncomfortable somatic symptoms.

Sufferers of complex trauma may not remember or have been able to work through and make sense of their experiences at the time. This would depend on their developmental age at the time of their trauma and the support system surrounding them. It is important that trauma in this context is understood as any experience, which to the young human organism at the time would have been registered as overwhelming, dangerous or harmful, possibly life threatening, and totally out of their control. Therefore the perception of what is traumatic will be determined by a person's developmental age and both the internal and external resources available to them at the time. A 3-month-old baby may experience being left crying for an hour in an isolated room as totally overwhelming, dangerous and life threatening, while a 7–year-old child may feel very angry about being left alone in a room for an hour, but may not be traumatized by this experience.

### Neurobiological factors

Depending on whether an event has been perceived as traumatic, certain neuro-biological changes may have occurred at the time of the experience. For example, neuroscientific research seems to indicate that there may be suppression or arrest of higher order brain functions, such as the hippocampus and parts of the frontal lobes, during overwhelming traumatic experiences (van der Kolk and Fisler 1995; Nadel and Jacobs 1996; van der Kolk et al. 1997; Post et al. 1998). As a result the sensory somatic and emotional experiences at the time of the trauma may be stored in specific memory systems, such as in the Situationally Accessible Memory (SAM) system, proposed in Brewin's dual representation theory of memory (Brewin 2001; Brewin and Holmes 2003). However, due to the arrest or suppression of certain neurobiological functions, this information would not have been able to inte-grate into higher order memory systems, such as the Verbally Accessible Memory (VAM) system (Brewin 2001; Brewin and Holmes 2003). This prevents sufferers of complex trauma from making rational sense of and verbalizing the connection between earlier experienced traumatic situations and the stored sensory somatic and emotional experiences resulting from these, which they may be experiencing in their day-to-day life. Often these are experienced in the form of body memories, which they may express as somatization.

Lanius (2005) has stressed the importance of the hypothalamus as the primary sensory gateway for all information reaching the neocortex. All sensory information, except olfaction, is routed through the thalamus to the neocortex. This enables the resonance between lower brain structures (such as the reptilian brain complex and limbic system) and top brain structures (such as the neocortex), and integrates top-down and bottom-up processing. Recent research seems to indicate decreased hypothalamic activity in complex trauma sufferers (Liberzon et al. 1996/1997, 1999; Lanius et al. 2001, 2002). Lanius (2005) points to the possibility that dynamic state changes in the thalamic system may account for the fragmented nature of the memories and dissociation observed in sufferers of complex trauma, as they have been unable to integrate their traumatic experiences between the three brain systems. Indeed, frequently people suffering from complex trauma experience a disconnection from their body sensations and their emotions, frequently accompanied by feeling 'shut down', 'numb' or 'frozen' in responsiveness.

## The relevance of information processing theory

Our understanding of complex trauma clients becomes significantly enhanced when we consider their current apparently destructive or unhelpful behaviour within the context of information processing theory, and acknowledge the underlying adaptive, survival enhancing origin of such behaviour. In order to cope with their experiences, they usually have developed a number of strategies, which, within the context in which they arose, had an adaptive, survival enhancing function, but which now are unhelpful and hindering in their current day life (Perry et al. 1995; Perry, 1999).

Frequently, the apparent inappropriateness or dysfunctionality of such behaviour may lead to diagnoses of personality disorder of various kinds. However, labelling people as suffering from personality disorders, while frequently done, may in actual fact not be very helpful. First, it is rare for people to fit neatly into the various categories of currently specified personality disorders, more often meeting criteria for more than one. Second, such diagnoses may serve to create a greater distance between the sufferer and the clinician who placed the diagnosis, while providing little information as to the actual clinical interventions that might be helpful to the sufferer. Third, the diagnosis of personality disorders of various kinds concentrates on dysfunctionality and does not take into account the apparent functionality of client's behaviour within the context in which it first arose, therefore confirming and further reinforcing clients' already often very damning, negative beliefs about themselves. Yet, understanding the functionality of such behaviour within an information processing context, can be very illuminating to both client and therapist, as it not only validates the client, but also provides helpful guidance as to where and how changes could be made in order for the client to adapt best to everyday functioning.

Sufferers of complex trauma may, for example, have difficulties engaging in or maintaining healthy, intimate relationships due to avoidance of attachments altogether, to distant attachments to another person, or to ambivalent attachments, which are characterized by repeating cycles of approach and rejection. Within this

145

context, the rejection is frequently initiated or provoked by the complex trauma sufferer. While this may not seem to make any functional sense in the context in which it is practised, when viewed from the perspective of its original adaptive function such behaviour becomes entirely understandable. Complex trauma sufferers who may have experienced rejection by one or several of their caregivers in the past may have learned to initiate rejection before becoming the victim of such and therefore feeling utterly overwhelmed and out of control. Although initiating rejection would of course also inflict a wound and hurt, at least the process remains under the control of the complex trauma sufferer, making it less sudden and overwhelming. It is therefore less likely to re-trigger the pain of the original wound of rejection (during childhood, which remains unprocessed), the impact and strength of which might otherwise utterly overwhelm the complex trauma sufferer. Rejection and withdrawal from intimate attachment relationships therefore serve as protective strategies when understood within the context of their original adaptive function.

## *Displaced responsibility and shame*

Frequently, complex trauma sufferers are unable to attribute responsibility where it belongs, such as to their primary caregivers. The adaptive value of this would have been that it was far too dangerous to blame the caregivers for any of their actions, even if these actions were neglectful, abusive and damaging to the child. At the time the child was utterly dependent on those caregivers for meeting the needs for general care, feeding and some form of attention and protection. The existential fear and horror associated with a threatened or potential loss of this would have far outweighed the negative consequences of enduring the abuse. As a result, survivors of complex trauma may feel themselves responsible for the treatment they have experienced, leading to a poor self-image, feelings of shame and a low sense of self-worth. This sense of self-responsibility is sometimes further reinforced by the actual verbal messages, which sufferers received as children from those responsible for the trauma during their abuse. Sometimes this belief may feel so enduring because it is, in fact, an actual trauma memory. Complex trauma sufferers may carry the belief of self-responsibility so strongly within themselves, that they have developed their own internalized, 'critical' or 'punitive' adult, who now maintains this belief through negative, internal dialogue, which holds them accountable not only for the experiences of the past but also for incidents relating to their everyday life.

Depending on the complexity and severity of the past traumatic experiences, their negative self-appraisal can be so damaging that sufferers experience self-hatred and self-loathing, which may lead them to want to abuse, injure or damage themselves. Their internalized feelings of blame and shame, especially after sexual trauma, may feel so powerful and absolute that they perceive themselves as 'dirty', 'damaged', 'contaminated' or 'marred'. Frequently, they want to protect others from these feelings as if they were carrying a contagious disease, which then serves as another factor for keeping themselves detached from close relationships with other people, including their therapist. Through their behaviour, sufferers of complex trauma perpetuate and repeat the patterns of their past abuse and recreate trauma in their current life, thus further strengthening their own underlying, unhelpful belief system and maintaining their dysfunction.

Complex trauma sufferers may have learned to subjugate their own needs and feelings in order to meet the needs of significant others, resulting in an impaired capacity to self-nurture. While this also would have had an adaptive function at the time, it may have now left them feeling very disconnected from their bodily and emotional systems. They may never have learned to notice and recognize their own needs or how to nurture them. Subsequently, they may have quite an undeveloped, immature sense of emotional Self, as represented by a very needy and un-nurtured 'inner child'. This may be apparent from the way in which they function within their current life and engage in their day-to-day interactions with others.

The above-summarized theoretical context of complex trauma, the inherent adaptive origin and subsequently often unhelpful or damaging manner of many of the patterns of behaviour, become highly relevant when considering the therapeutic needs of complex trauma clients. To date, although complex trauma clients have been treated with various forms of psychotherapy ever since the development of psychotherapeutic interventions, therapeutic successes have been varied. This client group, which includes clients diagnosed with personality disorders, including Borderline Personality Disorder (BPD) and Dissociative Identity Disorder (DID), is often perceived as a major challenge to therapists. Therapists may hold their own internalized beliefs of helplessness and hopelessness in the face of the complexity and endurance of these clients' problems, the extent and severity of their suffering and pain and, frequently, the destructiveness of their behaviour toward themselves and others. They may believe that there are limited opportunities for recovery for these clients and may feel hampered by some of the constraints and limitations inherent in traditional models of psychotherapy, in their attempts to help these clients.

Some of the limitations of the traditional therapeutic approaches will now be examined. It will then be proposed, based on our current knowledge of the context of complex trauma as highlighted above, that in order to be helpful to this client group we have to move beyond the limits of the more narrowly focussed traditional psychotherapeutic approaches toward a new approach to trauma work, which includes consideration of various therapeutic factors and the development of new therapeutic frameworks that take account of these clients' special needs and can facilitate their healing and recovery.

## Limitations of traditional therapeutic approaches

Many of the traditional therapeutic approaches contain elements which do not take sufficient account of the nature of complex trauma clients' problems and may therefore be of only limited utility in their attempt to facilitate recovery from complex trauma. Indeed, complex trauma clients frequently report abandoned attempts at therapy during which their needs have not felt met. For the purpose of this chapter a few of these elements are now highlighted, concentrating especially on some of the constraints of the traditional Cognitive Behavioural Therapy (CBT) approach and on those of non-directive, talking psychotherapies, such as psychoanalytic, psychodynamic, person centred and humanistic approaches. I do not claim for this to be a comprehensive and encompassing analysis, which would move beyond the scope of this chapter. Instead this is a sharing of observations, which stem from recognizing certain limitations in my own and other colleagues' clinical practice with complex trauma clients when trying to adhere to traditional models. This by no means, however, takes away from other elements of these therapeutic models that are clearly very helpful to clients.

### *Some limitations of traditional Cognitive Behavioural Therapy*

Traditional CBT describes a relatively narrow focus on the here-and-now of symptom presentation. While this can be a helpful focus for many psychological problems, complex trauma clients usually suffer from a complexity of symptoms, some of which may be quite undefined or not easily described or verbalized, such as their fear of close relationships, their feelings of mistrust, shame and disgust, their sense of internal weakness, their sense of emotional shut-down and frozen-ness and a general lack of safety. Further, due to their often considerable feelings of mistrust, fear and lack of safety, complex trauma clients may have learned to cover up or hide their true feelings and may initially present as more coping than they actually internally feel and functionally are. Complex trauma clients' problems may therefore not be very easily accessible, especially during an initial assessment session, and clinicians who stay purely at the level of symptom presentation are likely to miss the complexity of their client's actual problems, leading to their clients feeling misunderstood and not, or only very partially, met in their needs by the therapy provided.

Closely related to the above, another potentially limiting element within traditional CBT is the application of protocols and strategies that enable clients to resolve problems in the here-and-now. While it can be helpful to some complex trauma clients during particular stages of their therapy to focus on certain of their problems, using some of these protocols, the sole focus on this will not meet the complexity of these clients' needs. Such a focus assumes the existence of internal coping mechanisms that clients can draw on to make changes. However, when clients have been suffering from complex trauma this may not be the case at all. For example, many in this client group have significant concentration problems because much of their energy is absorbed with keeping their disturbing internal thoughts and flashbacks at bay. They may struggle with the structure of the protocols and the idea of homework assignments. For some this may trigger direct memories of their often difficult school experiences.

With its predominant focus on the here-and-now, the traditional CBT approach may give little recognition to the effect of these clients' past childhood experiences on their present day functioning. However, the link between the past as a learning environment for the present is a very important one, as it enables clients to understand the initially adaptive nature of their functioning, which often has become rigidified and now leads to functional difficulties within their present day environment. While the idea of changing strategies in the here-and-now is an appealing and important one, for complex trauma clients the fear of changing may be so overwhelming because, in the past, the patterns of their acquired functioning occurred for survival reasons. Therefore, unless they understand, recognize and are enabled to value the originally adaptive functioning of their strategies, the attempt to help them change can feel like 'tilting at windmills', due to the understandable, inherent fear of changing something that seems life-saving.

Further, rather than moving away from the fear, therapy for complex trauma clients needs to be able to equip them sufficiently to be able to know the fear, face it and then move through it and let it go, so that it can clear and no longer remain a hindering factor. However, in order to be able to face the enormity of the fear, which is often internally held by complex trauma clients, it requires a very safe, nurturing and trusting therapeutic relationship. For complex trauma clients, this can take a very long time to establish. The traditional CBT approach stresses the need for a collaborative therapeutic relationship, but does not pay any attention to the fact that early attachment patterns and indeed transference and countertransference are re-enacted within the therapeutic relationship. While the concept of collaboration is a constructive one for this client group, many complex trauma clients have never experienced collaboration and they may not at all be able to relate to, trust and make use of such a relationship at first. Within the current constraints of many health service provisions, the time it may take to help complex trauma clients to establish a collaborative relationship may not be given. However, for complex trauma clients, such neglect could be detrimental, as there is a risk that early dysfunctional attachment patterns are re-enacted and further client traumatization is caused as a result.

Currently, within the traditional CBT approach and much of the cited CBT trauma research, no distinction is made between Type I and IIA trauma and the Type IIB (R) and (nR) traumas. This may mislead clinicians into treating all types of trauma in a similar manner and, in the case of complex trauma, it could lead to retraumatization if clients are guided to process their past traumatic experiences (or even touch on these by being asked to talk about them) before they are internally sufficiently equipped and strong enough to do so.

Finally, another limitation of the traditional CBT approach is that its main focus is on cognitive processes as causes for client symptoms. While cognitions and the way in which we construct ourselves and the world are of much importance, for complex trauma clients many of their problems are triggered by information confined to their sensory motor and limbic systems, which may be quite disconnected from their rational systems (also a feature of dissociation). Such clients will frequently say, 'I know rationally that what you are saying is true, but it doesn't feel like this in my body.' Therefore overly focussing on cognitive processes may neglect the role of the body and the interrelationship between the body, emotions and the mind.

## Some limitations of traditional, non-directive talking psychotherapies

So far, I have focused on some of the limitations of the traditional CBT approach. However, other non-directive talking psychotherapies have similar or other limitations. While running the risk of gross oversimplification, I will include under this category, psychoanalytic, psychodynamic, person centred and humanistic approaches. One of the limitations of these therapies can be that to a greater or lesser degree they rely on the client to generate the material to be worked on in the session. This can have two effects. First, for complex trauma clients who frequently have not had any experiences of safety or containment, it can feel terrifying to be given the space to generate material about themselves. These clients may not be able to protect themselves from generating material, which they are not ready to touch on. Without internal safety mechanisms or anchors in place there is a danger that they may move too readily into sensitive material, risking feeling exposed and retraumatized by these experiences. At worst, they may disintegrate and dissociate further rather than being helped by their therapy.

Some of the non-directive talking psychotherapies in their traditional approach may indeed aim to break down client defences in order for clients to reconnect to and become conscious of some of the dynamics apparent in their earlier life. However, for complex trauma clients this can be highly retraumatizing, even dangerous to themselves or others, if they are not sufficiently resourced and strengthened first.

Second, another and quite different effect can occur. The emphasis on the client to generate the material to be worked with assumes that the client has the ability to access their material in therapy. As the main traditional therapeutic modality in non-directive, talking psychotherapies is verbal interchange, the material to be worked with usually requires some form of client verbalization. As mentioned before, a sole emphasis on verbalization neglects pre-verbal experiences, experiences which have been stored as body memories or in other sensory modalities. This material may therefore not be directly accessible to clients, who will not be able to touch on it by the sole focus on verbalization. Traditionally, these therapies have not taken into account the interrelationship between the body, emotions and the mind, thus potentially limiting client recovery.

While the non-directive, talking psychotherapies place greater emphasis on the therapeutic relationship and take account of transference and countertransference issues, for complex trauma clients re-experiencing aspects of the quality of their earlier relationships can feel too uncontained or unsafe if they have not been able to acquire a repertoire of internal resources first (such as self-soothing strategies, grounding techniques or methods to help them better to control their affect regulation). A non-directive structure of therapy, with possibly too limited direct guidance by the therapist, could further reinforce these feelings. Non-directive talking psychotherapies in their traditional application may not place sufficient emphasis on providing complex trauma clients with practical strategies to enable improvement in their functioning in the here-and-now.

As trust and safety are very important factors, but ones very difficult for complex trauma clients to attain, the rigid adherence to a fifty-minute session time for some of the traditional non-directive talking psychotherapies may indeed be counter-therapeutic. On several occasions I have heard therapists working within the fifty-minute session time frame say that their clients: 'were resisting the session because they "dumped" all the important material just a few minutes before the session was finished, so that the material could therefore not be worked with'.

Likewise, I have heard trauma clients tell me that fifty minutes was too short for them to get any productive work done. It felt to them that they had just settled down into the session and they were starting to feel safer and ready to share some of the important material when the therapist reminded them that session time was up. For these clients this can be retraumatizing and highly unsettling. They would have just risked opening themselves up to exploring some potentially very painful material, only to have to then carry this material out of the session completely uncontained, feeling open and possibly in a high state of physiological arousal. At best, this may make them feel very raw and unsafe and may confirm pre-existing experiences, that it is unsafe to open up, to disclose and to trust. At worst, if they haven't got sufficient internal resources to cope with their potentially high level of distress, it could endanger them, leading to further disintegration or increased symptoms of dissociation. Certainly, while the fifty-minute session time framework may suit the therapist out of habit, it may not take into account and be suited to meet the needs of complex trauma clients. The fifty- or sixty-minute session framework has not emerged out of validated scientific research demonstrating best practice for the client.

Another potential limitation of traditional, non-directive talking psychotherapies is that therapists may not actively guide their clients to counteract their under-standable avoidance of traumatic material. For complex trauma this has to be done extremely carefully and only when a client is internally strong enough and has built sufficient resources and strategies they can draw on to face and process their traumatic experiences. However, due to the potentially very painful content of the traumatic memories, clients may avoid making that connection and may journey into the pain themselves. They may talk about some of the issues connected to their traumatic experiences, but they may not go into the emotional and sensory experiences of the pain and the hurt unless there is some very skilled, gentle but nevertheless directly focused guidance to enable them to do so.

### The need for expansion of traditional therapeutic frameworks

With the emergence of neuroscientific findings and our increasing understanding of the underlying neurobiological processes of trauma and those of attachment; with new formulations of the function of dissociation (Nijenhuis and van der Hart

1999; Nijenhuis et al., 2003) with focused inner child work (Herbert 2002, 2003, 2004b) and with therapies that enable the processing of body memories, such as Eye Movement Desensitization and Reprocessing (EMDR: Shapiro 1995, 2002), there seems to be a need for an expansion of some of the traditional frameworks of psychotherapy in order to better meet this client population's needs. My own experience as a trauma therapist has shaped me to modify my approach to work in a way that allows me to attune to complex trauma clients' needs in order to promote their healing process. This has led to my recognition that therapeutic work with complex trauma clients requires a different framework and the use of a whole spectrum of therapeutic techniques (Herbert 2002, 2005a, 2005b) that require new therapist competencies (Herbert 2004a, 2005a), which move beyond the limits of traditionally, relatively narrowly defined, therapeutic orientations. It also calls for a move away from the tradition of claiming that a particular therapeutic approach is superior and is the only effective one for working with complex trauma. I am encouraged to note that my thinking does not stand alone, as quite separately, Rothschild (2003) called for an integrated trauma therapy, stating that 'no one method is one-size-fits-all'. Complex trauma clients require the use of a whole spectrum of therapeutic techniques in order to heal from their early developmental wounds (Herbert 2002, 2005a, 2005b) that move beyond the modalities of singular therapeutic approaches.

## *The move towards an integrative 3-systems' approach in trauma work*

Therefore, rather than limiting effectiveness in trauma therapy by adhering to specific therapeutic approaches, a new and more constructive approach may be to define specific therapeutic factors (Herbert 2004a, 2005c) required for trauma work and a therapeutic spectrum for trauma work (Herbert 2002, 2005a, 2005b), which highlights the phases that are helpful for complex trauma clients to progress through in order to achieve recovery and healing from their trauma. Within the scope of this chapter it is not possible to provide a detailed account of the therapeutic factors, although some of these will be outlined. Attention will be focussed on exploring the need for the use of an integrative 3-systems' approach to working with trauma. Some of the therapeutic implications of this will be explored and a therapeutic spectrum for trauma work will be introduced.

## An integrative 3-systems' approach

Due to the recent advances in developmental neuroscience and our increasing understanding of the neurobiology of trauma, as outlined earlier in this chapter, effective trauma therapy can no longer ignore the role of the body. New approaches to trauma work must take into account the triune nature of the human brain system and how this responds to trauma. Figure 10.3 illustrates that in order for clients to function as an integrated whole they need to be able to feel and experience a balanced flow of communication between all three systems of the brain, namely the

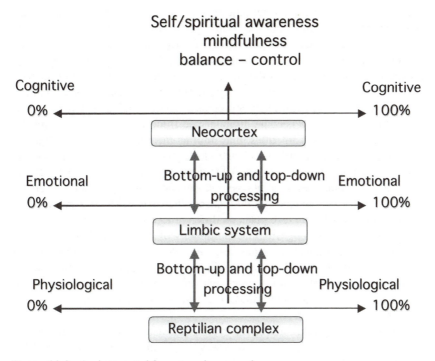

*Figure 10.3:* An integrated 3-systems' approach
*Source*: Herbert 2002, 2005b

cognitive, rational (involving neocortical brain functioning), the emotional (limbic system) and the bodily, sensory (reptilian brain) systems. Practices of meditation, mindfulness and spiritual awareness, for example, seek to help people establish such a balanced flow of energy between the three systems working to enhance human integration and consciousness.

In order to protect and increase a person's chances of survival from the emotional and/or physical pain of traumatic experiences, a split in consciousness takes place in a person, whereby the traumatic material becomes disconnected (dissociated) from active consciousness (disconnected from or only partially connected to certain neocortical structures of the brain). As outlined earlier in this chapter, memories of the traumatic experiences may get stored in the form of body or other sensory memories and may be largely unavailable to a person's rational, cognitive processes during their day-to-day life. This means that a person may be perfectly able to attend to daily functioning in life, may even by societal standards be functioning very highly, but this functioning can be upheld only through a disconnection between the person's cognitive, rational functioning (involving neocortical parts of the brain) and the emotional and bodily experiences (involving the limbic system and reptilian structures of the brain). Therefore the person lives life in a partially disconnected manner and with potentially quite restricted consciousness, which may have the effect that subsequent actions are not informed by the experiences of the person's emotional and bodily system but by their rational mind only.

While, on the surface, this may seem adaptive, the actual costs of this may be high for a person. For example, this would explain why people may engage in experiences or even set up their day-to-day patterns of functioning in ways which are physically or emotionally very painful, and yet be consciously unaware of their experiences of pain. Their conscious awareness and their rational, cognitive processes may have become disconnected from the language, and thus the needs, of their body and emotions, thus limiting them in their ability to function in a fully integrated and healthy manner. In Figure 10.3 this would be depicted by an over-dominant cognitive, rational system (high percentage activity) and an underactive disconnected or numbed emotional and bodily systems (low percentage activity). The consequences of the disconnection between these systems within human beings, which can take place on different levels of complexity depending on the onset, severity, longevity and multiplicity of the trauma, has far-reaching societal and even political consequences, the exploration of which moves beyond the scope of this chapter. This chapter will now briefly explore the consequences arising from this for the work with clients suffering from complex trauma and, within the context of this, will introduce a therapeutic spectrum for trauma work (Herbert 2002, 2005a, 2005b).

Frequently, complex trauma clients feel fragmented and are unable to perceive themselves as a unified Self. Sometimes, as would be the case in Dissociative Identity Disorder (DID), these fragmented parts can occupy distinct personality states, which sometimes have no conscious awareness of the existence of each other. More commonly, clients have some conscious awareness of separately functioning systems or parts within themselves.

The aim of work with complex trauma clients, regardless of the actual underlying therapeutic orientation of the therapist, is therefore to achieve gradual integration of the disconnected parts or systems into one unique Self. This entails therapeutic attention to two separate areas of work. The first focuses on work requiring attention to clients' here-and-now. This involves supporting clients with the acquisition of sufficient inner and outer resources and understanding, to help them increasingly to stop the cycle of recreating trauma in their current life, such as in their various relationships. This will help clients to feel stronger and more able to function in their day-to-day life, and it also prevents further fragmentation along the different subsystems of the brain.

The second area of therapeutic work involves revisiting clients' pasts. In order to achieve integration between separated parts of the Self, the therapist must help clients to gain access to the experiences held in their traumatic memory in order to process and work through the distressing emotional, sensory and somatic content of these experiences so that these can lose their impact on the client. However, in order to achieve access to the content of these traumatic memories, two important aspects need to be considered. The first is that due to the usually very distressing nature of the content of the traumatic memories, access will initially be blocked by

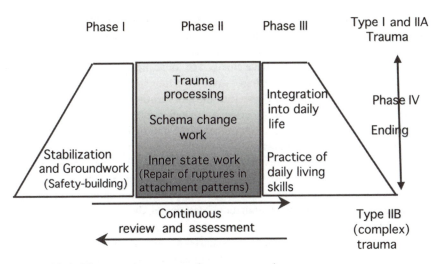

*Figure 10.4:* Therapeutic spectrum for trauma work
*Source*: Herbert 2002, 2005a, 2005b

the over-dominant cognitive rational system, which protects a client from feeling. This is an adaptive survival response from a system which, during past traumas, may have felt too weak to be able to tolerate and cope with the strong sensations generated. Therefore, in order for the therapist to enable the client now to gain access to the sensations, which have been stored from the past, they first need to be helped to feel stronger.

As outlined in Figure 10.4, which illustrates the therapeutic spectrum of trauma work (Herbert 2002, 2005a, 2005b), Phase I of trauma work needs to involve a period of safety-building (Herbert 2004c), stabilization and grounding. Figure 10.4 makes a distinction between therapeutic work for Type I or IIA and the more complex Type IIB (R) or (nR) traumas. In Type I and IIA trauma, Phase I may not require much time, as clients will have had a relatively safe and stable background, which trauma therapy can help them to reconnect to. In complex trauma, however, Phase I may require a considerable amount of time, as it includes helping clients to increase and strengthen their inner resources as well as their outer resources and to establish healthy boundaries. It also entails building a therapeutic relationship, which allows for a transitory period of active dependency (Bornstein 1995; Steele et al. 2001; Herbert 2004b, 2005a, 2005c) of the client on the therapist, and allows for the experience of interpersonal connection. In all trauma work, direct work with traumatic memories should not begin until the therapeutic relationship is secure and the therapeutic environment feels safe. Further, the client needs to have overcome any previously learned patterns of experiencing their dependency either as ridiculous, shameful, painful or denied, which as Steele et al. (2001) have outlined may be linked to the process of evaluative conditioning (Baeyens et al. 1993) as a result of complex trauma clients' own childhood experiences. Clients need additionally to be able to have learnt strategies, such as various 'self-nurturing' and 'self-soothing' techniques, to tolerate and regulate affect and emerging physical sensations to help them stay safe during trauma processing. Frequently, complex trauma clients will also need to have engaged in some 'Inner Child' work (Herbert 2003, 2004b) and/or 'schema-change' work (McGinn and Young 1996; Young et al. 2003), which form a part of Phase II of the therapeutic spectrum, as outlined in Figure 10.4, before any trauma processing can safely take place, and before their system will allow them to access the content of the traumatic memories. All along, as Figure 10.4 illustrates, clients are continually assessed and need to be encouraged with integrating their new learning and experiences into day-to-day life, as outlined in Phase III. Figure 10.4 also depicts differences in the length of preparation for the ending of therapy (Phase IV), whereby the more complex the trauma and the longer established the therapeutic relationship, the longer the preparation for the ending needs to be.

The actual content of the traumatic material should only be accessed in more depth and processed, once sufficient strength has been established within a client. Due to a potential hypothalamic dysregulation and a disconnection between neocortical substructures and those of the limbic and reptilian brain systems in complex trauma, as outlined earlier in this chapter, clients may hold no verbal or rational representation of certain past traumatic experiences. For these clients their experiences may literally be stored in the body without any conscious memory. Therapeutically, the question arises of how then to access the content of these memories. Traditionally, most forms of psychotherapy would have relied on some verbal account of clients' past traumas. They would have used some form of 'top-down' processing, starting with clients' verbal accounts of their past traumatic experiences and then helping them to access, process and integrate the emotional and sensory content of these memories. This is still an accepted form of trauma therapy. However, it will not work for clients who have no conscious access to, and therefore cannot verbally recall, their traumatic experiences.

These clients can, however, be helped by some form of 'bottom-up' processing. The latter requires the use of non-verbal methods of accessing the traumatic material. The material is accessed through focusing clients' awareness onto sensory, somatic or emotional stimuli within their body and encouraging clients to stay with and follow their respective sensations in order to notice where they lead to or what they may bring up for the client. This process can then facilitate connection to newly emerging images of experiences, which clients are then able to integrate into aspects of their conscious awareness. Neurophysiologically, bottom-up processing starts with accessing of traumatic material held in the limbic or reptilian substructures of the brain, in order to be able gradually to integrate this into a client's conscious processes, which requires the involvement of neocortical structures.

In my own therapeutic practice, I have found Eye Movement Desensitization and Reprocessing, which was developed by Shapiro in 1995, a very helpful method to facilitate bottom-up processing. However, for my work with complex trauma clients, I have adapted the standard EMDR protocol (Herbert 2002, 2005c) to suit these clients' therapeutic needs. I tend to carefully titrate the processing work and I use auditory bilateral stimulation (Grand 2001), a form of Dual Attention Stimulus (DAS), which enables greater client control and which therefore may be preferable to the use of actual eye movements for complex trauma clients. Other methods of bottom-up processing include the use of focusing (Gendlin 1978, 1981, 1996); other forms of sensory awareness techniques or body psychotherapy, such as Levine's SIBAM model (1992, 1997, 2005); Rothschild's somatic trauma therapy (2000, 2003); some forms of art therapy, such as sculpting, through which clients are encouraged to allow their hands to express what their body feels; and some forms of drama therapy, where clients are encouraged to follow and re-enact the emerging sensations or movements of their body within a safe, structured environment. Considering current findings, it becomes clear that whatever a therapist's therapeutic orientation, in order to facilitate the processing of non-verbal memories, which are held in emotional and sensory somatic representation only, therapists must have an understanding of the triune structure of the human brain and hold the skills to use some form of bottom-up as well as top-down processing.

## Conclusion

Complex trauma clients can be effectively helped to recover and heal from the effects of their past traumas. Therapeutic work needs to involve skilful interventions facilitating the gradual integration and communication between all systems of the triune brain. Such work needs to be tailored to each client's individual needs and pace, and it is a process which cannot be rushed or fitted into a generalized time framework. In this context it is helpful for clients to understand the role of the therapist as that of a facilitator of the client's own process of discovery, recovery and healing. The aim is for the client to learn to explore and develop an integrated healthy sense of Self so that eventually clients can live their lives in a functionally autonomous and emotionally mature manner. This is achieved through encouraging clients to take increased ownership of their new ways of thinking, perceiving and experiencing; increasingly to draw on their own newly built repertoire of coping strategies and inner resources; to make functionally healthy decisions, and in this way to develop an increased capacity for a healthy Self. It can be helpful to explain to clients that this is a process that is analogous to moving through the stages of childhood, adolescence and adulthood, during which they may re-experience various aspects of these developmental phases in therapy, without clients actually regressing to those states or deteriorating in their day-to-day functioning. For most complex trauma clients, the conditions of their actual childhood experiences would have been too distressing and unsupportive for them to develop their capacity for a healthy Self at that stage. However, in trauma therapy it is the role of the therapist to act as a resource that clients can draw on while they are moving through this process.

Successful therapy will involve an eventual separation between client and therapist and this will be a time of celebration for both. This may be likened to the process of adolescents or young adults leaving their parental home in order to establish their own place in this world. The therapist's role is to witness and facilitate the client's successful leaving of that home, after having nurtured, strengthened and encouraged the client's own inner resources so that the client can manage independent, successful and healthy functioning in this world.

The underlying emphasis of this work is on using an integrated 3-systems' approach (Herbert 2002, 2005b), aimed at balancing the body, emotions and the mind and thus enabling the emergence of an integrated sense of Self.

# References

Ainsworth, M.D.S., Blehar, M.C., Waters, E. and Wall, S. (1978) *Patterns of Attachment: A Psychological Study of the Strange Situation*, Hillsdale, NJ: Lawrence Erlbaum.

American Psychiatric Association (2000) *Diagnostic and Statistical Manual of Mental Disorders*, 4th edn, Text Revision, Washington, DC: APA.

Baeyens, F., Hermans, D. and Eelen, P. (1993) 'The role of CS-UCS contingency in human evaluative conditioning', *Behaviour Research and Therapy* 31: 731–7.

Bornstein, R.F. (1995) 'Active dependency', *Journal of Nervous and Mental Disease* 183: 64–77.

Bowlby, J. (1969) *Attachment and Loss: Vol. 1. Attachment*, New York: Basic Books.

——(1988) *A Secure Base: Parent-child Attachment and Healthy Human Development*, New York: Basic Books.

Brewin, C.R. (2001) 'A cognitive neuroscience account of posttraumatic stress disorder and its treatment', *Behaviour Research and Therapy* 39: 373–93.

Brewin, C.R. and Holmes, E.A. (2003) 'Psychological theories of posttraumatic stress disorder', *Clinical Psychology Review* 23: 339–76.

Brisch, K.H. (2002) *Treating Attachment Disorders: From Theory to Therapy*, New York: Guilford Press.

Collard, P. (2003) 'Interview with Dr Claudia Herbert', *Counselling Psychology Quarterly* 16(3): 187–93.

De Zulueta, F. (1997) *The Treatment of Trauma from the Psychobiological Perspective of Attachment Theory*, Proceedings of PTSD Conference, St George's Hospital, London.

Gendlin, E.T. (1978, 1981) *Focussing*, New York: Bantam.

——(1996) *Focussing Oriented Psychotherapy: A Manual of the Experiential Method*, New York: Guilford Press.

Gerhardt, S. (2004) *Why Love Matters: How Affection Shapes a Baby's Brain*, Hove and New York: Brunner-Routledge.

Grand, D. (2001) *The Power of EMDR: Emotional Healing at Warp Speed*, New York: Random House.

Gunnar, M. and Donzella, B. (2002) 'Social regulation of the cortisol levels in early human development', *Psychoneuroendocrinology* 27: 199–220.

Herbert, C. (1996) *Understanding your Reactions to Trauma: A Booklet for Survivors of Trauma and Their Families*, Witney, UK: Oxford Stress and Trauma Centre.

——(2002) 'A CBT-based therapeutic alternative to working with complex client problems', *European Journal of Psychotherapy, Counselling and Health* 5(2): 135–44.

——(2003) 'Healing the "Inner Child" – through the use of imagery re-scripting techniques', Symposium at Fourth EMDR European Association Congress, Rome.

——(2004a) 'Working with complex trauma – a 3-systems' CBT-based approach',

Workshop at the Ninth UKCP Professional Conference, Cambridge, UK.

——(2004b) 'Neither good nor bad – just perfect as you are! Establishing healthy affect control in clients diagnosed with personality disorders or complex trauma through the repair of early attachment problems', Workshop at the European Association for Behavioural and Cognitive Therapies (EABCT) Thirty-fourth Annual Congress, UMIST, Manchester, UK.

——(2004c) 'Installation of a Safe Place Protocol for use with clients who have no pre-existing concepts of safety', Clinical practice session presented at the Fifth EMDR European Congress, Stockholm, Sweden.

——(2005a) 'Towards new competencies in trauma work', – invited guest lecture at the Chester Trauma Conference, University College Chester, Chester, UK.

——(2005b) 'Healing from complex trauma – introduction to a CBT-based 3-Systems' approach' – Pre-conference Workshop at the Thirty-fifth Annual Congress of the European Association for Behavioural and Cognitive Therapies (EABCT), Thessaloniki, Greece.

——(2005c) 'Therapeutic factors in CBT with personality disorders and complex trauma' – In-conference workshop at the Thirty-fifth Annual Congress of the European Association for Behavioural and Cognitive Therapies (EABCT), Thessaloniki, Greece.

Herbert, C. and Jarisch, U. (1998) 'The use of energy distribution monitoring to affect schema-shifts in trauma', Presentation at Twenty-eighth Annual Conference of the European Association for Behavioural and Cognitive Therapies (EABCT), Cork, Ireland; also published in Herbert and Wetmore (1999).

Herbert, C. and Wetmore, A. (1999) *Overcoming Traumatic Stress: A Self-help Guide using Cognitive Behavioural Techniques*, London: Constable and Robinson.

Hofer, M.A. (1994) 'Hidden regulators in attachment, separation and loss', in N.A. Fox (ed.) 'The development of emotion-regulation: biological and behavioural considerations', *Monographs of the Society for Research in Child Development* 59 (2–3, Serial no. 240): 192–207.

Janoff-Bulman, R. (1992) *Shattered Assumptions: Towards a New Psychology of Trauma*, New York: Free Press.

Kabat-Zinn, J. (1994) *Wherever You Go There You Are*, New York: Hyperion.

Kluft, R.P. (1987) 'First-rank symptoms as diagnostic clue to multiple personality disorder', *American Journal of Psychiatry* 144: 293–8.

Kluft, R.P. and Fine, C.G. (1993) *Clinical Perspectives on Multiple Personality Disorder*, Washington, DC: American Psychiatric Association.

Lanius, R.A., Williamson, P.C., Densmore, M., Boksman, K., Gupta, M., Neufeld, R.W.J., Gati, J.S. and Menon, R.S. (2001) 'Neural correlates of traumatic memories in Post-traumatic Stress Disorder: a functional MRI investigation', *American Journal of Psychiatry* 158: 1.

Lanius, R.A., Williamson, P.C., Boksman, K., Densmore, M., Gupta, M., Neufeld, R.W.J., Gati, J.S. and Menon, R.S. (2002) 'Brain activation during script-driven imagery induced dissociative responses in PTSD: a functional MRI investigation', *Biological Psychiatry* 52: 305–11.

Lanius, U.F. (2005) 'Dissociative processes and EMDR – staying connected', One-day workshop at the Annual EMDR Conference UK and Ireland, Belfast, UK.

Levine, P. (1992) *The Body as Healer: Transforming Trauma and Anxiety*, Boulder, CO: Lyons.

——(1997) *Waking the Tiger*, Berkeley, CA: North Atlantic Books.

——(2005) *Healing Trauma: A Pioneering Program for Restoring the Wisdom of your*

*Body*, Boulder, CO: Sounds True.

Liberzon, I., Taylor, S.F., Fig, L.M. and Koeppe, R.A. (1996/1997) 'Alterations of corticothalamic perfusion ratios during a PTSD flashback', *Depression and Anxiety* 4: 146–50.

Liberzon, I., Taylor, S.F., Amdur, R., Jung, T.D., Chamberlain, K.R., Minoshima, S., Koeppe, R.A. and Fig, L.M. (1999) 'SPECT imaging in PTSD: activation studies', *Biological Psychiatry* 45(7): 817–26.

McGinn, L.K. and Young, J. (1996) 'Schema-focused therapy', in P.M. Salkovskis (ed.) *Frontiers of Cognitive Therapy*, New York: Guilford Press.

Nadel, L. and Jacobs, W.J. (1996) 'The role of the hippocampus in PTSD, panic and phobia', in N. Kato (ed.) *Hippocampus: Functions and Clinical Relevance*, Amsterdam: Elsevier.

National Institute for Clinical Excellence (NICE) (2005) 'Posttraumatic Stress Disorder: the management of PTSD in adults and children in primary and secondary care', *National Clinical Practice Guideline* no. 26, London: Gaskell and the British Psychological Society.

Nijenhuis, E.R.S. and van der Hart, O. (1999) 'Forgetting and reexperiencing trauma', in J. Goodwin and R. Attais (eds) *Splintered Reflections: Images of the Body in Treatment*, New York: Basic Books.

Nijenhuis, E.R.S., van der Hart, O. and Steele, K. (2003), 'Strukturale Dissociation der Persönlichkeit: Über ihre traumatischen Wurzeln und die phobischen Mechanismen die sie in Gang halten', in A. Hoffmann, L. Reddemann and U. Gast (eds) *Behandlung dissoziativer Störungen*, Stuttgart, Germany: Thieme Verlag.

Perry, B.D. (1999) 'The neuro-developmental impact of violence in childhood', a Special Child Trauma Academy website version, http//www.childtrauma.org (accessed 2 January 2006).

Perry, B.D., Pollard, R.A., Blakeley, T.L., Baker, W.L. and Vigilante, D. (1995) 'Childhood trauma, the neurobiology of adaptation and "use-dependent" development of the brain: how "states" become "traits"', *Infant Mental Health Journal* 16(4): 271–91.

Post, R.M., Weiss, S.R., Li, H., Smith, M.A., Zhang, L.X., Xing, G., Osuch, E.A. and McCann, U.D. (1998) 'Neural plasticity and emotional memory', *Development and Psychopathology* 10 (4): 829–55.

Rothschild, B. (2000) *The Body Remembers*, New York: Norton.

—— (2003) *The Body Remembers Casebook: Unifying Methods and Models in the Treatment of Trauma and PTSD*, New York: Norton.

Schore, A.N. (1994) *Affect Regulation and the Origins of Self*, Hillsdale, NJ: Lawrence Erlbaum.

—— (1996) 'The experience-dependent maturation of a regulatory system in the orbital prefrontal cortex and the origin of developmental psychopathology', *Development and Psychopathology* 8: 59–87.

—— (1997) 'Early organisation of the non-linear right brain and development of a predisposition to psychiatric disorders', *Development and Psychopathology* 9: 595–631.

—— (2003) *Affect Regulation and the Origin of the Self*, Hillsdale, NJ: Lawrence Erlbaum.

Shapiro, F. (1995) *Eye Movement Desensitization and Reprocessing: Basic Principles, Protocols, and Procedures*, New York: Guilford Press.

—— (2002) *EMDR as an Integrative Psychotherapy Approach: Experts of Diverse Orientations Explore the Paradigm Prism*, Washington, DC: American Psychological Association Press.

Siegel, D.J. (1996a) 'Cognition, memory and dissociation', *Child and Adolescent Psychiatric*

*Clinics of North America* 5: 509–36.

——(1996b) 'Dissociation, psychotherapy and the cognitive sciences', in J. Spira (ed.) *The Treatment of Dissociative Identity Disorder*, San Francisco, CA: Jossey-Bass.

——(1999) *The Developing Mind: Toward a Neurobiology of Interpersonal Experience*, New York: Guilford Press.

——(2002) 'An interpersonal neurobiology of psychotherapy: the developing mind and the resolution of trauma', in M. Solomon and D.J. Siegel (eds) *Healing Trauma*, New York: Norton.

Steele, K., van der Haart, O. and Nijenhuis, E.R.S. (2001) 'Dependency in the treatment of Complex Posttraumatic Stress Disorder and Dissociative Disorders', *Journal of Trauma and Dissociation* 2 (4): 79–116.

Terr, L. (1994) *Unchained Memories*, New York: Basic Books.

Van der Kolk, B. and Fisler, R. (1995) 'Dissociation and the fragmentary nature of traumatic memories: overview and exploratory study', *Journal of Traumatic Stress* 8 (4): 505–25

Van der Kolk, B.A., Burbridge, J.A. and Suzuki, J. (1997) 'The psychobiology of traumatic memory: clinical implications of neuroimaging studies', in R. Yehuda and A. C. McFarlane (eds) 'Psychobiology of Posttraumatic Stress Disorder', *Annals of the New York Academy of Sciences* 821: 99–113.

World Health Organization (1993) *The ICD-10 Classification of Mental and Behavioural Disorders: Diagnostic Research Criteria*, Geneva: WHO.

——(1997) *Composite International Diagnostic Interview (CIDI)*, Version 2.1, Geneva: WHO.

Young, J.E., Klosko, J.S. and Weishaar, M.E. (2003) *Schema Therapy*, New York: Guilford Press.

# 11

# THE BODY AS CONTAINER AND EXPRESSER

Authentic Movement groups in the development of wellbeing in our bodymindspirit

*Helen Payne*

### Introduction

This chapter examines a developing discipline named Authentic Movement (AM), which can be used to promote emotional wellbeing and health. It is one of many methods found in the practice of dance movement therapy (DMT) – soon to become a state registered profession alongside the other three arts therapies (art, drama and music). I will begin with an overview of Authentic Movement, its history, why it is used and with whom, and will follow this with sections describing Authentic Movement groups from both a practical and a theoretical basis together with examples. In brief, Authentic Movement as described here aims to increase connections between body, mind and spirit in the context of a group approach to health and healing, embodiment and wellbeing through movement.

AM is a powerful way of developing personal wellbeing using a unique form of free association in movement to bring mindfulness through kinetic meditation (in other words, contemplation of our internal world through movement of the body). The participant can learn to engage with a direct experience of themselves, of the group and of the transpersonal; an experience often beyond words and concepts. AM can assist, for example, in developing emotional literacy (intrapersonal intelligence), interpersonal skills and processes, body awareness, somatic intelligence, leading to body–mind–spirit connections. By gaining access and giving creative expression to inner worlds the invisible becomes visible or 'authentic,' claims Californian founder Mary Starkes Whitehouse (1979), although the term 'authentic' in DMT is found prior to this in Dosamantes-Alperson (1974).

The concept of authentic might appear confusing in this practice. However we could liken it to 'congruence' in the person centred approach (Rogers 1961, 1970; Payne 2004) which emphasizes the need for the feeling state in the therapist, as provoked by the client, to be maintained as truthfully as possible, whether or not this is disclosed to the client. It is sometimes difficult to know what is or is not congruent or authentic from any perspective, whether inner or outer. Congruence is experienced though, as a felt-sense of truth. Authenticity encompasses both polarities; what we might poetically call the darkness as well as the light: respecting the shadow while learning to hold the tension between these opposites in ourselves is part of the process in Authentic Movement.

Originally termed 'Movement-in-Depth' by Whitehouse in the 1970s, the method grew from its roots in dance, in Jungian thought, in mystical practice and in the pioneering work in dance movement therapy (Frantz 1972). Mary Starkes Whitehouse was a dancer, teacher and early movement therapist. She had a Jungian analysis and studied at the Jung Institute in Zurich. Her papers explore such issues as the role and experience of spontaneous and creative movement (Whitehouse 1958); the importance of following an inner impulse (Whitehouse 1970), the nature of embodiment in the process of change and transference (Whitehouse 1977) and the complexity of Jungian thought in relation to dance therapy (Whitehouse1979). Two of her students, Joan Chodorow (1991, 1997, 1999) and Janet Adler (1995, 1999, 2002), have each developed Authentic Movement further, incorporating understanding from analytical psychotherapy and the mystical disciplines respectively. AM in Europe has absorbed elements from other disciplines, for example from body work, DMT, Laban movement, psychotherapeutic group approaches, transpersonal development, research methodology, dance performance, and individual psychoanalytic psychotherapy (Penfield 2006).

Although more commonly a form of small group work with a teacher, AM may also be used as group psychotherapy with a facilitator. Authentic Movement practitioners work with adults in group or individual psychotherapy, working with those who seek wellbeing, and other outcomes, through embodiment in a body-based discipline. Most participants have had some personal development before. In one-to-one psychotherapy, AM will involve working more directly with the transference.

As with dance and DMT (and for that matter counselling and psychotherapy), men participate in AM far less often than women, which is a pity as more of a balance between male and female would nourish the masculine and feminine in each of us. Perhaps men are more likely to feel inhibited using movement in such a receptive way in the presence of other men and women. This phenomenon may connect to society's marginalization of the use of the body as an art form resulting in women, for whom cultural stereotypes may allow greater interest in dance and in connectivity, taking more of a lead in this discipline. The composition of AM groups is mostly middle class, similar to that of participants found both in group and individual psychotherapy and counselling, and in training programmes. Much more attention needs to be given to encouraging participation from others, including those from ethnic minorities, indeed anyone from any walk of life interested in learning from the body's wisdom.

AM has been used successfully with those with organic and non-organic medical conditions. Other ways in which AM groups are being used is to provide continuing professional development for dance movement therapists, counsellors, psychotherapists and psychoanalysts, dancers and artists. Those untrained in dance as an art form could be at an advantage over professionals who may first need to unlearn their dance technique.

## Authentic Movement groups

AM is entirely suited to group psychotherapy, where the holding capacity of the circle of external, conscious witnesses extends beyond that of any one therapist. Groups are self selecting, although the facilitator would normally interview participants to assess their suitability prior to starting in an ongoing group

AM groups are certainly suitable for anyone interested in wellbeing and spiritual growth, regardless of gender, ethnicity or class. However, in my view these groups would be unsuitable for those suffering from mental health problems such as clinical depression, psychosis, borderline conditions, or those needing ego strength building as AM group work demands so much self-direction.

When offered in a non-judgemental environment, or with 'unconditional positive regard' (Rogers 1957), AM provides a safe climate for moving in the presence of others. It is a good way to heal a trauma, to become your own person, to re-energize and to make timeless, deeper connections with others. It is the facilitator's task to prepare participants for the AM group as with any other group, for example by negotiating, clarifying and maintaining the ground-rules. It is also important in setting up an AM group to describe the nature of AM as a form including the different roles, the structures (such as time frames and group/spatial configurations), and the concept of moving from within. Therefore an educational role, particularly at first, is needed from the facilitator. My own style is to carefully design preparatory experiences and collaborate fully with the group for example, in setting ground-rules and time frames and in planning the sessions which might range from a couple of hours to ongoing/intensive weekends or residentials.

As with any personal development group, safety is essential (Payne 2001b). The participant in an AM group needs to be offered the 'good enough' relaxed environment of which Winnicott (1971) speaks, to be able to release into their movement impulses, thoughts, sensations, images. 'Reciprocal free association', so termed in Winnicott's Squiggle game of 'no rules' (Winnicott 1971: 16), where the therapist makes an impulsive mark on paper, then invites the client to turn it into something, after which the client takes a turn, simply cannot take place if the group members feel too much anxiety and too unsafe. This is of particular importance when starting in AM as the work is done in ways usually unfamiliar to the participants, such as moving with closed eyes, which may be difficult to do sometimes due to fear and anxiety. Changes in the structures or type of form used, new members joining and so on can threaten safety in the group from time to time as illustrated by the following participants' comments:[1]

> I would say difficulties revolved around adjusting to the changes in structures. Because [the] work is structured I feel safety in that, then when ways of using the form are changed or altered it can feel quite challenging yet also very important.

When new members join an established group [in an open group format] it is good, because it helps remind me of the ground form and makes me realize what I have understood and gained. However, it can feel unsafe when perhaps I have been at a different level in my own journey with authentic movement and again brings up issues of trust and safety.

## Roles taken in Authentic Movement groups

During an AM group, participants are invited to enter one of two distinct roles, and variations of these, as described by this group member:

Authentic movement groups enable the work to be broken up into component parts to explore, for example being the witness (silent, verbal or collective) and being mover. By exploring how the roles of witness and mover can be used by initially almost exaggerating separateness between them I am becoming skilled at experiencing them.

The primary form in AM is the 'dyad' (within which are the roles of the mover and her witness),[2] which is normally referred to as the 'ground form'. Each role is now described in turn.

### *Movers*

A person moving with eyes closed in the presence of another, the witness, is termed 'the mover'. In AM group work this role may be undertaken in a dyad in their own space, or in a circle formation where the movers move in the centre with one or many witnesses sitting in a circle around them. With their eyes closed, the mover is more able to attend to their inner world of thoughts, sensations, images, feelings and movement impulses. Sometimes group members resist closing their eyes, to begin with, as this participant recalls:

When I found out that the practice of Authentic Movement included moving with eyes closed I had an immediate negative reaction. To see is one of the main vehicles of communication between people (eye contact). I need to see, I need to look if I am looked at, and I need to look where I go and what I do. When I close my eyes I lose control of me, of others, of the environment. Now I know that when I move with my eyes closed in a trusted environment created by the facilitator, I go with my sight inside, and there I see more.

Movers endeavour to maintain an awareness of immediacy and to respond to inner experience with expressions such as stillness or non-directive movement. They are the first to be invited to speak about their experience, particularly any significant moment during it. They may or may not ask to hear from a witness, whether their own 'designated' witness or the 'free-floating' witnesses (see later) in the circle. The movers learn to track their movements and the inner accompanying experience. Movers learn to wait for the next movement impulse and in this process may, or may not, recognize truthful, or authentic, movement. In the presence of one (as in the dyad) or many witnesses (sitting on the edge of a circle format) movers begin this process by listening inwardly in stillness to find a movement arising from a deep, cellular impulse.

After their movement experience, which takes place within a previously agreed time frame, movers return to their witnesses. Movers are always invited to speak first. Each mover, in speaking of her story, recalls an embodied event or 'significant moment' or the whole experience, as remembered, may be shared. The mover may describe the movement together with associated feelings, sensations, images, body-felt senses, and thoughts.

At first the mover, when reflecting on her experience, may feel she did not know what she was doing, in a way similar to the experience of unconscious non-duality (Horrocks 2002). This dream state, like day dreaming, is a non-ego-controlled experience, in which the mind lets go of the separateness normally experienced between the self and other resulting in a third dimension, a non-duality. In the early stages of AM work (and sometimes later too), the mover's experience remains unconscious and thus unremembered when they recall their experience. I suggest this is pertinent to their development, this 'unremembered', in that by working solely with that which is remembered (even if that is nothing at all, not even the physical movements) the material emerging will be that which is ready to be processed at that time. It is crucial that both witness and mover trust in the mover remembering when the time is right. In the same way a person centred psychotherapist would only speak/reflect the material a client has brought to a session, rather than bringing in, for example, their own recall of her story from previous sessions, trusting the client will bring the material with which she is ready to work at that time. Consequently in this approach the therapist refrains from probing or questioning to uncover forgotten memories. Similarly a dreamer recalls a whole dream, or only parts of a dream, either of which is the only material with which the therapist can work.

Later on the moving experience may be more frequently like lucid dreaming where there is interplay between the dreamer and the dreamed. The creativity is in the interplay. It can also connect the mover to the numinous, the universal 'I' or 'big me' rarely found in everyday life. In this experience the freedom from, or loss of, ego or 'little i' (with attachments such as personal history, identity and so on) enables a greater connection with the collective body (Adler 1999) and a feeling of immense wellbeing.

## Witnesses

The term 'witness' refers to the role of the participant(s) who sits on the edge of the movement space (or circle) consciously attending, with eyes open, to the mover – the 'other'. The witness, the one who has chosen not to move, is not a watcher or an observer of the mover, but an empathic conscious and receptive participant. From this co-creation of reality, safety and a deep respect for each other ensues. The witness acts in the role of container for the mover's embodied immersion in the unconscious which unfolds whatever, and however it likes.

The witness endeavours to be present in the mover's movement and, while attending to her own thoughts, sensations, feelings, images and impulses, to allow these to be influenced by what she sees in the presence of the mover. She is in a state of being rather than doing although still active in tracking her inner attitude. This inner embodied tracking is similar to the phenomenon of the therapist's countertransference found in psychodynamic psychotherapy. The inner tracking, akin to mindfulness, is a state of acceptance and can include noticing all sorts of phenomena, for example hearing sounds in the environment, or being aware of bodily sensations, breath, images, feelings, kinaesthetic sensations or the need to move/act, thoughts and judgements.

The witness speaks only after the mover has spoken, and only if requested to by the mover. When the witness is asked to speak her witnessing, she does so non-judgementally, with unconditional positive regard and deep respect, honouring the mover's experience. Any judgements, interpretations or projections are owned by the witness. She is encouraged by the facilitator to speak only of those elements of her experience which link to aspects of the mover's already spoken journey or significant moment/event preferably spoken in the present tense to keep the experience in the here and now.

As the inner witness develops in the mover, so the mover too desires to be a witness, to track another's movements while she sits in stillness, being conscious of her own inner experiences of thoughts, sensations, images, feelings and movement impulses although refraining from enacting them. When we witness movers in this way it is as if we are moving inside ourselves in the way of the mover herself. Perhaps we inwardly mirror the mover's motor neurons at play. Rizzolatti et al. (1996) found that when a primate watched another perform an action that was within their own movement repertoire, the frontal cortex's mirror neurons fired up in a form of kinaesthetic empathy (Moore and Yamamoto 1988). Thus, while witnessing another move, we can often make an informed guess about what the mover is feeling, imagining or even thinking.

The concept of the 'wise observer/higher self' (Rowan 1993) in transpersonal psychotherapy is relevant here. For instance, by waiting for, and listening to, an inner prompt the mover (re)discovers a consciousness of the 'wise observer' termed the 'inner witness'. By clearly seeing this inner witness in herself the mover, as a witness, (re)gains a similar consciousness or presence to herself and the other, often resulting in compassion for self and others. This consciousness reminds me of a mother who sits with her child at play, aware but without intervening in the play. The child is making use of the 'potential space' or 'space between' which Winnicott (1971) discusses, that is the place where inner and outer reality are separate yet interrelated, the intermediate area of experience. I have discussed elsewhere (Payne 2001a) the process of witnessing in AM and how the use of the space between inner and outer reality links to the concept of the 'internal supervisor' as portrayed by Casement (1985, 1990) in clinical supervision.

## *Variations*

Other roles in the form are specified as: (a) the silent witness, that is the one who remains in the form as a witness but does not offer witnessing; (b) the designated witness, the one who has a named mover to witness for the whole time duration – naturally in the dyad the witness is always designated for their mover; (c) the free-floating witness, here the witness is drawn to witness a mover then another mover at any one moment within the circle formations; (d) the collective witness, the one who gives witnessing as an overview or theme/story relating to the whole group or configuration of movers; (e) the moving witness, where a mover offers witnessing from her inner witness, to another mover, although she was a mover at the time; and, finally (f) the meta-witness, this is a form of free-floating witnessing normally occupied by the facilitator.

Emerging phenomena have resulted in new roles being created in those groups of movers and witnesses I facilitate including: (a) the role of the 'non-witness – non-mover', that is, the one who is outside the form but remains in the group, sitting on the edge, outside the dyad or the circle of witnesses; and (b) the 'non-mover' role, for the one who elects not to move preferring to remain as a witness throughout the form. Consequently no role is marginalized – all are included. Roles can be requested by each participant prior to the start of the moving experience commencing.

## *Movers and witnesses*

I like Authentic Movement because it develops 'presence of the body', presence and attention to others and integration between body/emotion and awareness.

(A participant)

By using movement in a group setting as the vehicle for developing presence a unique integration can occur. The concept of presence is a familiar one to most forms of psychotherapy: the therapist aspires to being present for the client, who deserves this attending. In AM there is a desire in the witness to be present for their mover and a need in the mover to have a fully present witness. Yet this presence is not always perfect, movers may see the lack of it in their witness and are disappointed and witnesses notice they are sometimes far from being present. This desire and shortcoming in both mover and witness needs to be processed in the group. The facilitator is required to be fully present at all times which may be difficult to achieve. However, in my experience the more practised one becomes in the discipline, the easier is the mindfulness and therefore the lighter the presence offered.

In exploring the relationship between a mover and a witness (desiring to be seen, being seen or not seen, fearing being seen, and seeing/not seeing), the hidden becomes clearer as different people's perspectives intersect. Here, a participant acknowledges that the two roles entered into in turn can help to clarify processes: 'Experimenting with witness and mover roles, as and when uncertainties arise, is useful'.

The intersubjective experience between a witness and a mover can be immensely empathic. Sometimes, as the internal witness within each evolves, there is a meeting-moment between them which is termed a 'unitive experience' (Adler 1999). This is a moment when the 'witness consciously knows the experience of the mover because it is her experience at the same moment' (Adler 2002: 89). It is not a moment of merging but of a presence in both their internal witnesses, each of them is both separate and together at the same time. In this moment the mover's witness is completely aware of what the mover is doing and of her inner response to it. 'Her boundaries are porous as she consciously experiences her mover and herself as the same' (Adler 2002: 89), that is, experiencing this unity in a non-duality state of wholeness. Both the mover and the witness may later speak of being in a unitive state – a clear way of knowing, which includes intuition.

After repeatedly being seen clearly by a witness (at first this is mainly by the group facilitator) the mover begins to see herself with the result that her own inner witness develops further. Then when in the role of witness, after seeing another, the mover discovers a new ability to see herself. From these experiences, group members learn both self-witnessing and ways of being in relationship, in the here and now. In my approach the learning is supported by fully engaging organically, at different times, with both the roles of mover and witness.

The witness engages in a process of somatic-indwelling or waiting (Musicant 1994), containing her projections and her impulse to move, so that she may, without preconceived ideas, feel what it may be like for that mover. She also has to contain her desire to speak her experience when offering witnessing since the mover may not have mentioned that particular movement event/aspect of which the witness very much wants to speak. In this way her inner witness and capacity for containment and presence develops resulting in an empathic, authentic, non-judgemental connection with the self and another akin to findings from the humanistic therapies. For example, Rogers (1957) stressed the role of empathy, congruence (Payne 2004) and unconditional positive regard as three of the six necessary and sufficient conditions for therapeutic change.

As the mover's own internal witness develops, the mover often returns after the 'dream state' to recall, in the presence of a witness, a significant event in the movement. This is a conscious experience, as it is consciously brought to mind. It could be called a conscious non-duality. Non-dual experiences normally occur where a constellation of the opposites results in a third element in which a union or synthesis occurs. The opposite or counterparts within us are in contrast to the known (conscious) aspects of our personality. This unknown 'other' (similar to Jung's concept of the Shadow) is extremely fearful of consciousness and is therefore difficult to access in normal life. For example, the corresponding vice to the positive character-istic of compassion would not voluntarily present itself to the conscious mind. Yet without its counterpart the victory of compassion over the negative, or vice, would be unreal. This exerts a necessary psychic tension. The threat from this opposite is mediated by complementary processes in the unconscious. AM work aims to help each participant's consciousness to produce a uniting experience, and, through processing and working with this in movement, to own the menacing 'other' by recalling and verbalizing it. Once the 'other' has been embodied it can be recalled and expressed verbally resulting in integration and an increased sense of well-being. Outcomes from this process in AM work have included increases in emo-tional wellbeing, inner confidence and self-reliance, together with the capability both to separate self from other and to join with another.

The non-dual experience, uniting conscious and unconscious material, is both subjective and objective at the same time; involving both knowing and not know-ing; doing and not doing. Although the emphasis in AM group work is on the here and now, it is also true that recalling in the spoken word an event from the movement experience can add another dimension when shared with witnesses, especially if spoken of in the present tense. If, when asked by a mover, witnesses respond that they see the event described, the mover may then request they offer her the experiences they had when witnessing her movement. As an example I give below one of my experiences, as a witness, of a symbolic uniting of opposites (above and below):

> I see a windmill, its sails turning in a wind. The base is firmly in the ground and held in place by a root or chain or some sort. I feel I am a mediator between the sky and the earth, a connector.

By giving this witnessing to the mover, an increased sense of wellbeing was reported by her as her material become more fully integrated.

Witnesses, by learning to own which of their experiences are their own projec-tions, interpretations and judgements, can give the opportunity to the mover to accept or reject their perceptions. Here, a mover speaks of her difficulty when a witness fails to manage this:

> I find it particularly difficult when being witnessed by someone when interpretations are made and the content of the language not owned. Maybe this is difficult for me because in authentic movement as a mover I am inviting myself to become potentially more open than I otherwise would be.

> (A participant)

In other words it is experienced as unhelpful when the witness does project or interpret rather than owning their own story in their witnessing.

Issues concerned with attachment (Fonagy 2001) can become evident from the relationship between witness and mover, or participant and facilitator. Within the AM form the prominence of reflexivity, the capacity for verbal narratives from recalled direct experience of the self, together with the possibility of clear seeing from a witness, all held within a secure environment, gives the opportunity for healing insecure or anxious/avoidant attachments.

## The collective body

The term 'collective body' in AM describes the group as a whole (Adler 2002). An experience which movers or witnesses may have which reflects a collective theme in the group is spoken of by a collective witness. A desire arises in the group members to participate in the gestalt experience, to explore ways of relating to the many rather than the one without losing consciousness of the self. The phrase 'collective body' contains an implicit reference to Jung's term 'the collective unconscious': here I mean the experience that arises from the group's embodiment of unconscious material. For example, participants may experience powerful relationships, meetings and synchronicities within a group movement, for example two movers doing the same gesture, despite having eyes closed. These go beyond the individual, and encompass a greater sense of belonging. This concerns the collective desire for consciousness – the conscious body – which Adler conceives of as mysticism (Adler 2002). Indeed, one form of this state can be a greater awareness of the spiritual. Part of the facilitator's role here is to guide the conscious development of relationships such as those between the individual body, the collective body and a higher spiritual expansion. Moving, witnessing and sharing can enable connections between the individual, the collective and/or the universal body (the latter as a transpersonal experience). For example, archetypal figures (such as Magician, Priestess, King, Grim Reaper, Trickster, Jester, Warrior or Shaman) or myths are played out as movers embody archetypes experienced as living again in the mover and/or witness. They can provide a link from the personal to the collective body, giving images from which to give meaning to individual lives and communities. Jung reminds us that: 'fantasies guided by unconscious regulators coincide with the records of man's mental activity as known to us from tradition and ethnological research' (Jung 1947: 402).

He wrote of a 'dark impulse' which is the 'arbiter of the pattern created when the foot makes a dance step or the hand guides the crayon' (Jung 1947: 402). At the moment we feel vulnerable to chance, we do not know that someone else's consciousness is being shown the way by the very same impulse. From these and other reflections Jung surmised that there are certain collective unconscious conditions which 'behave like the motive forces of dreams' and 'act as regulators and stimulators of creative fantasy-activity and call forth corresponding formations by availing themselves of existing conscious material' (Jung 1947: 403). Jung based his theory of the impersonal collective unconscious on these unconscious regulators, which he saw as a synthesis of passive conscious material and of unconscious influences, resulting in a spontaneous amplification of the archetypes.

The stimuli in our environment (including movers' chance encounters with others in the container of the group, or movers' hearing for example, the birds' singing outside) can have a deep presence inside the mover/witness and become incorporated into their experience. Participants can then feel in direct contact with aspects in their imagination and in the real environment of consensus real-time. Movers can feel unity in suffering, compassion, joy or love for example when personal themes connect to universal themes in the collective body of experience revealed by that which is spoken of within the group. This experience of unity with others and/or a higher spiritual authority in an altered reality may increase a participant's sense of wellbeing, their understanding of personal themes and their felt-sense of 'universality'– the relief they are not unique in their suffering (Yalom 1985: 8).

## Authentic Movement structures

I became interested in Authentic Movement because by comparison to other body-oriented therapy groups it has a strong, complex and flexible structure. The structure of Authentic Movement provides rules about time, organization of different kinds and boundaries. In this way safety, respect, holding are ensured to support the individual and the group process.

(A participant)

Specific and carefully designed structures or rituals are crucial to the practice of AM, including the specific language adopted. The dyadic ground form, which may take place both in the early and later stages of the group, might be considered to emphasize individual self-awareness rather than the group process. However this format is usually preceded and followed by the facilitator acting in the role of free-floating witness or 'meta-witness' for the whole group as they physically move in the space. This meta-witnessing offered from the facilitator to each of those movers who request it provides the basis for their experience of being seen by the one who holds the overall role of container/parent for the group. In my experience it is vital to the development of the group that the facilitator acts as a free-floating meta-witness and contributes in this way, as well as through her normal facilitator's role.

In the ground form where one witness and mover work together for an agreed time period, changing roles after their sharing dialogue, the facilitator may at first offer coaching in the use of language to dyads. Or she may act as a silent witness to all dyads at once. This might be followed with triads (the dyad with an additional 'silent' witness – the one who does not offer witnessing at all – or with two witnesses perhaps), thereafter working in the basic circle format in which each mover has a designated witness. At all times, in all these structures of the AM form, the facilitator holds the time frame and the role of a free-floating meta-witness for all.

To further help participants to develop their capabilities as witnesses a circle of free-floating witnesses, as opposed to designated witnesses, is formed in which all who witnessed a mover inside the circle, can offer witnessing if asked to by a mover. The psychic elements are contained within the circle, the witness's attention is drawn towards a mover, and an opportunity is given for all the varying aspects of the individual body (participant) and the collective body (group), to be witnessed. A comparison can be drawn here with psychodrama whereby different parts of one protagonist are played out by several individuals in the group. The facilitator would again be a meta-witness throughout, sitting on the edge of the circle with the other witnesses, offering witnessing in response to a mover's request and at times offering collective witnessing. This role could be seen as synonymous with Rogers' (1970) view of the facilitator being less directive and interpretive in the development of the group process.

To continue with delineating the form of an AM group, the stage after the mover moves and before inviting witnessing is that of 'transition time'. This is a pre-scribed time period when movers and witnesses are usually invited to be alone in the group space to allow them, if they wish, to begin to process their experience. In my approach this is not a time for participants to leave the room. During this transitional phase, the facilitator may provide opportunities for art work, writing, poetry and clay work. Participants often create written, symbolic and other expressions of connections from the moving or witnessing experience. Sometimes participants offer these symbols or writings, as movers or witnesses, when they feel there is a direct relationship between their own experience and the mover's spoken story. Drawing and creative journal writing may bring further form and meaning to experiences, as expressed by this participant:

> The facilitator encouraging the use of image-making, writing and other creative media is helpful to me as well her clarifying the language used and continually acting as collective witness.

The facilitator, by creating a safe space, also enables the group to generate their own archetypes. For example, a mover returned to her place at the edge of the circle to ask if any witness saw a particular frozen moment of stillness as she sat on the floor with a turned head. One of the witnesses responded by reading from her journal about seeing a Medusa, who had turned her (the mover) into stone and wrote a story in her journal about this moment of 'turning into stone' which could be heard as 'collective witnessing'. She told the group that, at that very moment at which she was watching the mover, she saw another mover who appeared to be embodying a Medusa's head, flailing, with hissing and squirming snakes. She wrote of her fear and of a chill going down her spine. The mover was relieved to have heard this witnessing as she too had felt and heard a terrifying presence in the room and was petrified by it. Later another mover spoke of one of her significant moments where she had feelings of rage and power as she stood tall, hissing and spitting venom at the world. A connection was made in the group to the experience of terrifying rage, the Medusa and being turned to stone by fear.

In another example, following another mover's story, two witnesses commented on how they saw the very young baby this mover had described herself as being. Both witnesses saw the baby enjoying suckling and making noises with her lips. Another mover spoke as a moving witness. She had heard the sounds and sensed a baby nearby, happily gurgling, and had painted this in her journal. Yet another witness said she had felt motherly towards this baby, wanting to cuddle her. She felt warmed by the infant. Later in that same group experience a mover described a particular moment in which her struggle to attain something precious was just too difficult. She requested witnessing. I (as a witness) recalled seeing a figure struggling to reach something high up. She was quite close to me at the edge of the circle. I had written in my journal during transition:

> I looked up, and to my right to catch sight of a woman's face emerging from behind hands (I had drawn this image). She appeared distressed. I felt sad. On hearing the bell to bring the group experience to an end [the time period was finished] her eyes opened and, at that precise moment, seeing me seeing her, I felt seen in my sadness.

In the mover's reflections later in the group she told of how frustrated and disappointed she had been, unable to successfully resolve her desire for a baby. She said she had felt seen in her sadness by her witness (myself) and that being seen at that moment meant a great deal to her. It was then that I spoke from my journal (written and drawn in during the transition phase) of my experience in her presence. This illustrates the importance, in the way I work, of the procedure that the witness speaks only after the mover has spoken and then only on issues the mover has herself mentioned.

For some participants the creativity experienced in the movement process is another pathway to spirituality. In AM groups, spiritual matters, as well as group dynamics, may be explored. For example, during the 'breathing circle' or 'long circle' (group structures which begin by all witnessing the empty space) if all movers leave the space within the circle to return to the circle of witnesses the space becomes empty once again until the prescribed time has ended. Contemplation of this empty space can bring up, for example, human concerns such as loss and enrichment, but also of mortality, birth and rebirth. These may be articulated and processed in the large group, or in two separate groups of movers and witnesses.

## Authentic Movement and play

AM is not a set of exercises, nor is it the same as creative movement (Payne 1990) or dance movement therapy (Payne 1992, 2006), although it may contribute to the latter (Musicant 1994, 2001). Like DMT it fosters a participant's spontaneous movement although with a witness who is not always the therapist. The way the movement is spoken about in AM is normally different from DMT. In AM there is usually no intention to plan or organize the movement around a theme (as perhaps in improvisation for choreography) for example, and indeed the mover often ceases thinking in the usual way. AM is a completely self-directed approach in which participants may discover a movement pathway that offers a bridge between the conscious and the unconscious and between the group, the individual and the universal. It can be called the movement form of 'active imagination' (Chodorow 1991). It is particularly powerful because one moves before one knows it, for instance without conscious choice.

AM (and dance movement therapy) draws, to some extent, from the same spontaneous and creative well as is enacted in play. AM fosters personal growth by building upon our natural, dynamic, creative, spontaneous and self-expressive capabilities in an interplay of inner and outer worlds. Like play, AM permits the participants to express themselves, be themselves, accept themselves and be accepted by others without an outer task to perform. The process of play is one without an extrinsic goal conscious to the player at the time (Garvey 1986). The same could be said for AM.

In play therapy, children are encouraged to 'play out' problems, events, feelings and attitudes (Axline 1969). In this approach the cathartic element is emphasized whereby the child symbolizes a traumatic experience (such as sexual abuse) using dolls or other objects. By revisiting it with all the accompanying feeling states in the presence of a therapist, the child may move to a better integration of the experience. AM draws upon the same powerful capacities of play and self expression, again enacted in the presence of another, and witnessed by another. It similarly enables experiences to be enacted, often through the use of metaphor, even when they cannot be verbalized explicitly. The embodiment of a creative metaphor may enable regression and an integration and capacity to be oneself which was previously not possible. Winnicott (1971) suggests that: 'It is only in play that the individual is able to be creative and to use the whole personality, and it is only in being creative that the individual discovers the self' (Winnicott 1971: 54).

## Authentic Movement and Jung

Building on creativity and play and on Jung's method of active imagination (Jung 1968), AM uses symbolic meaning, seen in physical expression as another road to a descent into the unknown. The process of the mover (who cannot see the witness or facilitator) might be likened to Jung's concept of 'trancing' in an 'active fantasy' (Chodorow 1997: 3). Jung (1935) states in his Tavistock lectures:

[the patient] can see their [archetypal images produced by active imagination techniques] real meaning only when they are not just a queer subjective experience with no external connections, but a typical, ever-recurring expression of the objective facts and processes of the human psyche. By objectifying his impersonal images, and understanding their inherent ideas, the patient is able to work out all the values of his archetypal material. That is he can really see it and his unconscious becomes understandable to him.

(Jung, cited in Chodorow 1997: 146)

Here, Jung uses the term archetype to describe images from the collective unconscious (as opposed to the first layer of the personal unconscious) that have existed in human life from the remotest of times. Archaic, primordial images charged with psychic energy (the numinous) he thought were a 'piece of life itself', connected with the living individual by the bridge of emotion. The archetypal experience consists of imagery and affect (instinct/somatic and psychic). Jung emphasized the universal character of the collective unconscious, and thought that instincts (inborn, unlearned tendencies) and mythological motifs were already laid down in our brain in their pre-conscious form as 'invisible ground plans', inherited from our ancestors. These then interact with our consciousness which has available to it all the history of rituals, symbols, stories and so on from our own cultural sources.

Movement arising from the collective unconscious may have a foreign, chaotic quality in a form outside recognizable human culture. Some images witnessed in AM do seem to emerge from the primitive depths of life itself as though the mover is possessed, for example, by terror (the one who is shaking holds onto another for comfort), anguish (the never-ending sobbing and wailing of a woman) or rage (the monstrous one kicking and biting, nostrils flared, fingers like claws ready to scratch). This cathartic expression is held by the imaginative movement process inside the mover and by the witness outside. At other times the movement has parallels with the characteristics of nature, animals or mythological creatures (such as huge dragons breathing fire) and are less chaotic but equally trance-like. It is as though these life forms are 'being danced' (Chodorow 1999) or metamorphosed as in the shape shifting of the Shaman, for example. It is the facilitator and/or witness who offer the necessary symbols (as above) to the mover, as a context for the individual and/or collective images experienced.

## Authentic Movement and group process

The AM group process has some similarity to group analysis in the way the conductor (facilitator/witness) waits without overt action, participation or direction, empathically facilitating verbal communication to the group or to individual participants, and containing by her presence. In this approach it is crucial that participants bring back to the group any communications which have arisen between them outside the group experience in order to contain the group energy, which could be affected by any leakage of material or extra-group pairings (Bion 1961). In my experience this wider element of containment is also beneficial to the work of AM groups.

AM groups are normally open or slow-open (Yalom 1985), allowing for new members to join and others to leave, which requires time for processing in the group. The balance between action and non-action enables participants to experience the group from different perspectives. The relationship between participants, including the facilitator, is made clear and patterns begin to emerge. The relationships of movers with other movers, witnesses with witnesses, and movers with witnesses as well as participants with the facilitator, all provide opportunities for raising awareness of group-held issues and differing aspects of the group. In this way individuals can come face to face with their projections.

Verbal groups sometimes develop a breakdown in communication. However, AM groups, by using an approach which focuses on the content of the movement expression, rather than directly on the person or group, can enrich mutual communication, each one understanding the other from the other's point of view. The greater the authenticity in the mover's experience, awareness and expression, the more likely it is that the witness will see it clearly thus fostering clearer communication. This element links strongly with Carl Rogers' approach to group work:

> If the cues from speech, tone and gesture are unified because they spring
> from a place of congruence and unity, then there is much less likelihood
> that these cues will have an ambiguous or unclear meaning.
>
> (Rogers 1961: 342)

Similarly if the expressed movement (or sound) arising in the mover stems from a place where the feeling/sensation/image and so on are truly connected to the self then the movement (or contact etc.) is authentic and consequently is clearer to the witness. This unity or congruence brings about clarity of presence in the witness and in the mover's expression. Presence entails a here and now indivisible relationship to the self, another and the divine, and is the source from which grows all that it means to be human. The practice of AM enables access to the present moment, to our authenticity and to enhanced presence.

Rogers (1970) refers to a fifteen process model of group work which offers another way of describing some of the experiences in the AM group. The formative stages in AM groups may well consist of difficulties such as participants not being able to close their eyes, take the role of witness, or of a mover. Despite several hours of educational work during which the basic whole group movement and/ or dyadic structure of the mover and witness roles are experienced, participants may continue to feel they do not know what to do, in movement for example. This together with the reluctance, even shyness, is commensurate with Rogers' stages of 'milling around' and 'resistance to personal exploration'. Fears usually revolve around an assumption there will be a critical judge. An exercise to bring out the critic and acknowledge the power it has, is normally helpful at this point. The participants are encouraged by the facilitator to express negative feelings or thoughts in movement and words (similar to Rogers' identified trend of expressing negative feelings). A more meaningful trend usually follows, whereby participants are willing to take the risk of exploring personal and interpersonal material within the group, and tolerate the 'not knowing' in their movement process. Both movers and witnesses then start to show a greater openness and receptivity. The ability to respond to immediate feelings, thoughts, images and sensations becomes the norm.

Safety has been established by the facilitator holding the group through the first two stages, and this, together with a clearer understanding of the ground-rules, boundaries, language-use and structures in the AM form, usually lead, in Rogers' term to 'the cracking of facades' (Rogers 1970: 33). Here participants reveal congruence (or authenticity) in reclaiming their projections. In this way the need for defensiveness and a safe persona is dropped and a more real, honest, accepting process is engaged with, leading to greater empathic connection and presence between participants.

At times the facilitator might be confronted by a negative transference as the group develops. After processing, the group and sometimes the form itself may evolve. A growing acceptance of each other, built on a deep respect that each is doing the best they can, is demonstrated by a caring and sharing inside the group and an increasing awareness of each person's inner witness. The group process continues to move in and out of different patterns, depending on the levels of felt-safety. Some of this clearly connects with the model described by Rogers contrasting to the linear one proposed by Tuckman (1965) where all groups follow a number of predictable, orderly stages (norming, storming, forming, performing). Regression to previously experienced trends is noticeable just as in the individual client–therapist process. This may echo relationship phases between group members and/or intrapsychic processes. Authentic movement enables a deep regression at a personal level resulting in a truly embodied integration which leads to an increase in the felt-sense of wellbeing.

Normally I tend not to interpret or probe into what is perhaps behind a mover's expression (whether verbal or non-verbal). If interpretations or judgements (positive and negative expressions) are made, they need to be recognized and owned, so that each participant is encouraged to move towards a fuller acceptance of their total being (Rogers 1970). As participants start to feel less threatened, defensive and resistant in the group, they learn to hear and see each other and themselves more clearly. This greater capacity to witness results in increased learning from themselves and each other, as this comment illuminates:

> Having time to talk about experiences with group members makes links and meaning in the work for me, as does having space to integrate personal meanings to make sense of the work, such as keeping a personal journal, circle reflection time, and relating to more universal stories and concepts.
>
> (A participant)

Communication is thereby enhanced and the desire for creative expression deepened rather than resisted or inhibited. Participants develop the capacity to offer witnessing in a congruent, healing and empathic manner. The facilitator encourages both story making and story breaking whereby participants learn to tell a story coherently. This also allows for the story to be told in a different way by engaging the participant in a dialogue in the light of a new experience.

Participating in an Authentic Movement group can be a compelling and awe-inspiring experience. It draws participants from a range of backgrounds including the arts, the caring professions and from psychotherapy, those who are willing to open up to the power of the unconscious as contained, expressed and experienced in the body through stillness and movement.

## Notes

1 The participants concerned have given their permission for the use of their quotations in this chapter.
2 Please note the terms she/her/herself have been used while recognising that participants are of both genders.

## References

Adler, J. (1995) *Arching Backward*, Rochester, VT: Inner Traditions.
——(1999) 'The collective body', in P. Pallaro (ed.) *Authentic Movement: Essays by Mary Starkes Whitehouse, Janet Adler and Joan Chodorow*, London: Jessica Kingsley.
——(2002) *Offering from the Conscious Body*, Rochester, VT: Inner Traditions.
Axline, V. (1969) *Play Therapy*, New York: Ballantine.
Bion, W.R. (1961) *Experiences in Groups*, London: Tavistock.
Casement, P. (1985) *On Learning from the Patient*, London: Routledge.
——(1990) *On Further Learning from the Patient*, London: Routledge.
Chodorow, J. (1991) *Dance Therapy and Depth Psychology: The Moving Imagination*, London: Routledge.
——(1997) *Jung on Active Imagination*, Princeton, NJ: Princeton University Press.
——(1999) 'Her papers', in P. Pallaro (ed.) *Authentic Movement: Essays by Mary Starkes Whitehouse, Janet Adler and Joan Chodorow*, London: Jessica Kingsley.
Dosamantes-Alperson, I. (1974) 'Carrying experiencing forward through authentic body movement', *Psychotherapy: Theory, Research, and Practice* 11 (3): 211–14.
Fonagy, P. (2001) *Attachment Theory and Psychoanalysis*, New York: Other Press.
Frantz, R. (1972) 'An approach to the centre: an interview with Mary Whitehouse', *Psychological Perspectives* 3 (1): 23–34.
Garvey, C. (1986) *Play: The Developing Child*, London: Fontana.
Horrocks, R. (2002) 'Non-duality', *Self and Society*, 29 (6): 7–14.
Jung, C.G. (1935) *The Symbolic Life*, Tavistock Lectures, *Collected Works*, Vol. 18, Princeton, NJ: PrincetonUniversity Press.
——(1947) *The Structure and Dynamics of the Psyche*, *Collected Works*, vol. 8, Princeton, NJ: Princeton University Press.
——(1968) *Analytical Psychology: Its Theory and Practice*, New York: Random House.
Moore, C-L. and Yamamoto, K. (1988) *Beyond Words: Movement Observation and Analysis*, London: Gordon Breach.
Musicant, S. (1994) 'Authentic movement and dance therapy', *American Journal of Dance Therapy* 16 (2): 91–106.
——(2001) 'Authentic movement: clinical considerations', *American Journal of Dance Therapy*, 23 (1): 17–26.

Payne, H.L. (1990) *Creative Movement and Dance in Groupwork*, Bicester, UK: Winslow Press, reprinted 2003.

——(ed.) (1992) *Dance Movement Therapy: Theory and Practice*, London: Routledge, reprinted 2002.

——(2001a) 'E-motion: Authentic movement and supervision', *ADMT.UK Newsletter*, (13): 4.

——(2001b) 'Student experiences in a personal development group: the question of safety', *European Journal of Psychotherapy, Counselling and Health*, 4 (2): 267–92.

——(2004) 'Notes on authentic movement and congruence', unpublished paper prepared for Retreat in Authentic Movement, November 2004.

——(ed.) (2006) *Dance Movement Therapy: Theory, Research and Practice*, 2nd edition, London: Routledge.

Penfield, K. (2006) 'Another royal road to consciousness: the application of Freudian thought to Authentic Movement', in H.L. Payne (ed.) *Dance Movement Therapy: Theory, Research and Practice*, London: Routledge.

Rizzolatti, G., Fadiga, L., Gallese, V. and Fogassi, L. (1996) 'Premotor cortex and the recognition of motor actions', *Cognitive Brain Research*, 3: 131–3.

Rogers, C. (1957) 'The necessary and sufficient conditions for therapeutic personality change', *Journal of Consulting Psychology* 21 (2): 95–103.

——(1961) *A Therapist's view of Psychotherapy*, London: Constable.

——(1970) *Encounter Groups*, Harmondsworth: Pelican.

Rowan, J. (1993) *The Transpersonal: Psychotherapy and Counselling*, London: Routledge.

Tuckman, B.W. (1965) 'Developmental sequence in small groups', *Psychological Bulletin*, 63: 384–99.

Whitehouse, M.S. (1958) 'The Tao of the body', reprinted in D.H. Johnson (ed.) (1995) *Bone, Breath and Gesture: Practices of Embodiment*, Berkeley, CA: North Atlantic Books.

——(1970) 'Reflections on a metamorphosis', Impulse Publishing, reprinted in R. Head, R.E. Rothenberg and D. Wesley (eds) (1977) *A Well of Living Waters: Festschrift for Hilde Kirsch*, Los Angeles, CA: CG Jung Institute; reprinted in P. Pallero (ed.) (1999) *Authentic Movement: Essays by Mary Starkes Whitehouse, Janet Adler and Joan Chodorow*, London: Jessica Kingsley.

——(1977) 'The transference and dance therapy', *American Journal of Dance Therapy* 1 (1): 3–7.

——(1979) 'Jung and dance therapy: two major principles', in P. Bernstein (ed.) *Eight Theoretical Approaches to Dance Movement Therapy*, Dubuque, IA: Kendall/Hunt.

Winnicott, D.W. (1971) *Playing and Reality*, London: Tavistock.

Yalom, I.D. (1985) *The Theory and Practice of Group Psychotherapy*, 3rd edition, New York: Basic Books.

# 12

## TRANSFERENCE AND
## THE MEANING OF TOUCH

The body in psychotherapy with the client
who is facing death

*Joy Schaverien*

### Introduction

This chapter is intended to offer some thoughts regarding boundaries and the nature
and meaning of touch in psychotherapy. The boundaries of analytic psychotherapy
create an invisible frame that defines the borders of the symbolic and material
worlds. Abstinence from physical contact is a consequence of the understanding
of the emblematic nature of the transference. The interplay between transference
and countertransference might be seen as a dance between embodied experience
and psyche, desire and repulsion, impulse and restraint. When a patient faces a life-
threatening illness, embodied experience comes rapidly to the fore and the symbolic
aspects of the therapeutic relationship may come under extreme pressure. The limits of the psychotherapeutic frame may at times seem to be overwhelmed by the
very real impact of physical illness. There may be extreme pressure to collapse the
boundaries with regard to physical and external contact. It will be argued that the
most profound form of touch may emerge only when physical contact and meetings outside therapy are resisted. It is this abstinence that paradoxically facilitates
the individuation process to the end of life.

Psychotherapists in private practice are sometimes confronted with working
with those affected by cancers and HIV-related illnesses. Although there are many
common factors, this is different from working in an institution, such as a hospital
or hospice, where terminally ill people are the client group. When a therapeutic
relationship is already established, the onset of a life threatening illness may have a
profound effect on the psychotherapist. Confronted with common humanity in the
face of death, the psychotherapist may be led to question the analytic frame. Dying
does not merely pose a technical problem but it does bring technical issues to the
fore. It may create problems in maintaining the analysis.

This is evident when psychotherapists write about the experience. A number of
single case study books and articles have been published on psychotherapy with
the dying patient, for example Wheelwright (1981), Bosnak (1989), Ulanov (1994),

Lee (1996), Minerbo (1998), McDougall (2000) and Schaverien (2002). These writers address boundary issues and the challenge of maintaining the therapeutic relationship with someone who is seriously ill. While working with the distressing and very concrete reality of the immense losses facing the patient, adaptations to the analytic frame have to be made.

Perhaps this contributes to the 'special' status some such patients attain. Not all who face death involve the therapist in this way but certain people, who need to compensate for unlived aspects of their lives, draw the therapist into an intense and almost irresistible process. The psychotherapist is compelled to confront his or her own mortality and so his or her own individuation process may become involved. This may intensify identification with the patient and lead to anxiety about being a good enough therapist or to denial of the potential loss of the patient. In this situation, the patient journeys physically and psychologically to a place where, no matter what depth of analysis the psychotherapist has experienced, she or he has not yet travelled. This is accompanied by the certain knowledge that one day the therapist too will travel this path. This may be awe-inspiring and the power imbalance of the therapeutic relationship may subtly shift.

Moreover the bodily decline and associated vulnerability may engender a natural impulse to hold the patient physically – to offer actual comfort. However, to do so would concretize that which needs to remain symbolic. I hope to show how by resisting this impulse, at the same time as considering its meaning, a depth process is facilitated. Therefore touch is sacrificed in the interest of individuation.

## Transference and individuation

In the transference a particularly intense form of erotic engagement may constellate. It is as if the powerful archetypal state which death evokes, holds both therapist and patient in thrall, bringing awareness of the bodies of both into the consulting room. I suggest elsewhere that the gender of the dyad may influence this process (Schaverien 1995, 1996, 1997, 2002).

The erotic transference and countertransference is, as Jung makes clear, a very necessary and purposeful element in the work (Jung 1946). It is Eros transformed which leads to individuation. Individuation is described by Jung as 'a process of differentiation . . . having for its goal the development of the individual personality' (Jung 1913: para 757). This is achieved through the development of a symbolic attitude whereby split off and disowned aspects of the personality are differentiated and a conscious attitude attained. It may be that the threat of imminent death intensifies this process and makes it more urgent.

It is well known that Freud introduced the notion of transference (Freud 1912, 1915) in order to understand the intense forms of feeling, particularly love, which became manifest in analysis. Greenson (1967), following Freud, divides the analytic relationship into three parts: the real relationship, the therapeutic alliance and the transference. *The real relationship* is the real and genuine relationship between psychotherapist and client. When the client is terminally ill this 'real relationship' may increasingly come to the fore, as concerns regarding the physical deterioration of the patient demand attention. *The therapeutic alliance* is the alliance the patient makes with the psychotherapist whereby there is an agreement (not always stated) to work together to observe the transference. This alliance is based on trust, non-sexual liking, and mutual respect. *The transference* is unconscious and character-ized by both repetition and being inappropriate. To work with the transference the patient needs to be able to take a symbolic position in relation to her/his own mat-erial. Transference includes vestiges of all human relating including love and hate in their primitive forms. When the client is dying this too may be intensified.

## Countertransference

In the early days of psychoanalysis countertransference was considered undesirable because it indicated under-analysed elements in the analyst. It was the therapist's transference to the patient. Heimann (1949) and Little (1950) first suggested that the countertransference was a response to the whole analytic situation and there-fore a useful guide to understanding the transference. Racker (1974) developed this, considering transference and countertransference in terms of talion law. Like Jung, he considered that whatever is consciously expressed, its opposite is present but unconscious. For example if, in the transference, love is consciously expressed then hate will be present but unconscious. Conversely, if hate is conscious love will be unconscious. In Jungian terms this is the shadow of the conscious attitude. When death is the conscious element, its opposite, the life force, may be expressed through an initially unconscious erotic transference. When such powerful material as love and death are active the therapist may be drawn into an archetypally charged state where rational thinking is not easily maintained. Working with people who have not lived their lives to the full or those who are dying relatively young it is particularly distressing for the therapist. Further, when the client has no partner, like the patient I will describe, added pressures are placed on the therapist and the desire to act out may be difficult to resist. This raises questions regarding the nature of a therapeutic ending when the client is dying. Clearly there are no rules and each case has to be assessed at the time and in the full knowledge of the situation. It may be that in some cases to befriend the client is the most therapeutic solution. In others it may be appropriate for the therapist to withdraw when the work seems to be complete. However it may be in the interest of the client to continue analysis to the end.

## Henry

Henry was referred by his GP (general practitioner) for psychothera-py.[1] He felt so isolated and desperately lonely that suicide seemed the only option for him. At 46 years of age Henry was divorced and recently had been unable to function at work due to intense anxiety. He was employed at a senior level in a company where he was well respected.

Recently he had neglected a certain task and, fearing that his misman-agement would implicate the company in litigation, he had been unable to go to work. Seized with panic and psychologically paralysed he had taken to his bed and reverted to the depressed state which had haunted him intermittently for most of his adult life. He had returned to his parents' home where he had become totally isolated. He was unable or unwilling to communicate with them and he avoided approaches from family or work colleagues and so he spoke to no one.

At the time he was referred, no one knew that Henry was terminally ill, although the cancer, which was diagnosed three months later, must have already been active in him. It is of course evident that when we engage with someone in the analytic journey (McDougall 1995) we can never predict the direction that journey will take. Certainly neither he nor I could have predicted that Henry was to die two and a half years later.

The first contact was in December and my first impression of Henry was of a tall thin man with large glasses, wearing jeans, and looking somewhat unkempt. His accent gave the impression of a public school education, which belied his rather dishevelled appearance. At the end of the initial session he readily agreed to attend twice a week. He began the following week; he sat in the chair, ignored the couch, and without looking at me, he talked fast and his history poured out of him. By the time of my winter break, which was two weeks later, Henry had already engaged in analysis. His dependence was such that he was concerned about how he would manage in my absence. The countertransference reflected this and I too was worried about how he would survive. At this stage my concern was a response to his expressed suicidal thoughts. Later, especially as he became progressively more ill, this became a con-stant theme of the breaks in therapy. As time passed I was increasingly faced with the questions: would he survive? Would I see him again?

## Boarding school

Henry's anxiety about the breaks echoed his early history of repeated separations. He was the only son in a large family and the main trauma, as he presented it, was that he had been sent away to boarding school at the age of 8. The way this was communicated, it was clear that the wound was still fresh; it seemed as if he had been waiting to tell his story since that time. He recounted the excitement of the preparations, the packing and the journey. He was treated as special; as the only son in the family he was told he was chosen for this exciting event while his sisters were to stay at home. He was therefore unprepared for the appalling realization, on his arrival, of utter loneliness. He described feeling homesick and crying secretly under the bedclothes; there was no one to witness his distress, no one knew how unhappy he was. Bion (1982) gives a moving description of his own experience in this regard. From this time on in Henry's life, there was never anyone to mediate his experience. In the first months of therapy it seemed that he responded to this aspect of the relationship, to having a witness. He said: 'This is what I have been looking for all my life but I did not know what it was.' At last there was someone to understand and give words to the loneliness which had haunted him.

An example will give a sense of his despair and is relevant with regard to a later incident within the analysis. Soon after starting at prep school he ran a race; he was a very small boy and all the other boys were bigger than him, but with supreme effort and against all the odds he won. Having won he looked around and then realized that there was no one there to celebrate his victory. He desperately wanted his parents to have seen his triumph but they were not there. Immediately after the race he developed severe flu symptoms and was put to bed in the sanatorium of the school with a high temperature. His parents were contacted but told that it was not serious and so there was no need for them to come. As he recounted this he re-experienced the loneliness and despair he had felt and he became aware that, even at the time, he had realized that he was ill because he wanted his parents to come to him. When they did not come he felt truly abandoned and soon cut himself off from his feelings. Thus he learned not to cry.

His special role, as the only son in the family, was replaced by living as an insignificant boy in a vast male institution. A child in a boarding school is expected to conform to the collective values of the institution. Jung writes that:

> Individuation is a natural necessity . . . its prevention by levelling down to collective standards is injurious to the vital activity of the individual . . . any serious check to individuality, therefore is an artificial stunting.
>
> (Jung 1913: para 758)

This seems to encapsulate Henry's experience of boarding school; the child was no longer a special individual in a family, of girls, but a member of a collective – a group of boys and men. His emotional life was not valued and, at such an early developmental stage, this can, and did in this case, have catastrophic psychological consequences. Duffell (2000) and Schaverien (2002, 2004) provide further descriptions of this. When Henry returned home for vacations he was unable to communicate his suffering to his family and so he felt that no one really knew him.

The sense of betrayal and isolation, which began at this time, was to influence the rest of his life. He had never been able to communicate his distress at what he experienced as complete abandonment. This had left him with a deep yearning for his mother but also a vengeful anger. Very often boys who are sent to boarding school at an early age yearn for an idealized mother. The separation was a rupture, which came too early. Later, in adolescence, separation from the internalized mother is not possible because there has been too little actual closeness. From then on all women seem tantalizing, offering not only the hope of the idealized love object but also the constant threat of abandonment. This contributes to a pattern where women are idealized and then denigrated – loved and hated. This was replayed in the transference in which I was sometimes experienced as the yearned for home/mother/lover, alternating in quick succession with the boarding school/rejecting mother. Boarding school could be understood as an object of negative transference – loveless and cold.

## Homelessness

A sense of homelessness pervaded his life and yet he loved and hated the historic town house, where his parents lived, with equal intensity. It was his understanding that it was in preparation for his inheriting it that he was sent to boarding school. It therefore came as a great shock when he was 16 that his father, assuming his son not to be interested, made the house over to a trust and sold the associated business. The parents would live in the house for the duration of their lives but after that it would leave the family. Henry was devastated; he had lost the home to which he had planned to return and he was faced with having to consider earning his living for which he was totally unprepared. It seemed that his fury at this injustice had psychologically paralysed him and he had never stayed in a job, completed a course, nor lived in one place for any length of time since. It was possible to understand his depression as masking the fury he felt at these injustices.

This had produced a psychological pattern in Henry and he had never been able to find a place in the world. During the brief years of his marriage Henry had had a home but since his marriage had ended he had not had a significant relationship or a place of his own to live. He would stay with friends, and when this arrangement broke down he would resentfully return to stay with his parents. This paralleled his psychological state; when he was in a relationship he had been housed and when that broke down he was unable to house himself. He explained that once married he had been 'joined by the hip' to his wife. This indicates the level of regressed dependence he experienced within that relationship and it also gives some sense of the pattern which was to emerge in the transference. It was as if he 'fell into the therapeutic relationship'; it seemed to offer the promise of a psychological home.

## Transference

This was evident in one early session when he became very angry with me. I had given him my holiday dates in the previous session along with the bill. He shouted at me that he had always had doubts about psychotherapy; enraged he said, accusingly: 'I'm not coming back – I can do this myself – this is the most intimate relationship I have had in my life and you just sit there and tell me about holiday dates.' Thus the early dependence in psychotherapy replayed his history. He had described several relationships with women where he had invested everything and then withdrawn; he would unconsciously set himself up for rejection and then, when it happened, blame the other person. Now, when his anger had subsided and I had not retaliated, he was amazed and relieved. I was able to acknowledge his anger and how difficult it was for him when I told him I was going away. He agreed, relaxed and after this he seemed much relieved and a period of positive transference followed.

## Infantile and Oedipal transference

The transference immediately plunged him into associations with his early relationship with his mother. There had clearly been an emotional bond and he was moved to tears when he remembered a certain piece of music his mother had sung to him when he was very little. He said sadly that she no longer sang. After this session he talked with her about his early years. The memory had freed him a little; it was as if he had not felt held since this early time in his life but it was significant that there had been such a time. Thus it is that the work on the inner world produces outer world consequences.

The type of intensity with which Henry told his story and the evident dependence was immediately appealing. There were distinct but linked levels of interaction operating simultaneously. Henry's immediate transference was a regression to the early infantile relationship with his mother. This was evident when he stated that this was 'the most intimate relationship of his life'. When the infantile transference was active it seemed that I was experienced as a part object; a convenient breast or ear but not a person. This was evident when Henry talked rapidly and without looking at me and I felt as if I was in the presence of a ravenous infant. I recognized his tremendous need for nurturing and simultaneously his terror of me. An archetypal maternal environment constellated which was a response to the evident early deprivation.

However, this was not all: the transference was complex, evoking other early attachments and so the intense erotic atmosphere was not solely infantile. Searles (1959) writes of the Oedipal love experienced in the countertransference and it is clear that the Oedipal transference was activating a reciprocal countertransference. This affected the 'real relationship' and I was aware of Henry as a man and of a mutual sexual attraction evoked by the awareness of the irrefutable fact that we were both adults in an intimate situation. Thus, as well as the early infantile dependence in the transference, there was a sexual attraction, which was operating at both an Oedipal and a reality level. This was confirmed much later when he told me that, among his first impressions of me, was that I reminded him of his first serious girlfriend.

When such powerful material from different stages of development is activated, it would be inappropriate to respond to the unspoken appeal with physical contact. It would be confusing for the patient and difficult to distinguish the meaning of such touch. The therapist might offer a nurturing touch to the perceived infant but this might be mistaken for a sexual overture. The patient is vulnerable and this would concretize what needs to remain symbolic. It is this confusion on the part of the therapist that may lead to sexual abuse in psychotherapy (Springer 1995).

Thus disparate elements of the psyche, which had been invested in different women during Henry's life, now seemed to constellate in the transference and to evoke a positive attraction and sense of belonging. This was significant because it was soon to become almost unbearable for Henry to stay in therapy and this attachment generated the impulse to leave but, ultimately, it enabled him to stay.

I hope that I have conveyed the considerable erotic involvement that was present from the beginning. There was clearly a fit and the analysis started at depth. This attachment constituted a bond, which helped to sustain the relationship later, when it might otherwise have broken down. Furthermore the positive countertransference – the love I felt for him – came to serve an additional purpose once the terminal illness was diagnosed; it enabled me to accompany Henry with genuine concern. It is clear that physical contact would have been inappropriate in such an erotically charged situation.

### Diagnosis

We had been meeting twice a week for three months when Henry described physical symptoms which troubled him. He consulted his GP who sent him for tests; he was very quickly recalled and lung cancer was diagnosed within the week. His session was due immediately after the hospital appointment and he arrived having being told that he had cancer and that the prognosis was poor. This information had been delivered unceremoniously, by a junior hospital doctor. Henry arrived in my room reeling from the shock and unable to process the information. He was anxious about telling me and could not conceive of telling his family for fear of upsetting them. From that day until his death two years later he was rarely out of my mind.

He kept the diagnosis to himself that week. The following week, after some discussion and interpretation of his fear of contaminating others with his bad news, he decided to tell his eldest sister. Predictably she was upset and he found this almost overwhelming; he was barely able to contain his own feelings and those of other people terrified him. Eventually he was able to tell the rest of his family.

The full process of the next two years cannot be encapsulated in this chapter and so I will describe the main boundary issues that emerged. Henry's suicidal feelings were immediately forgotten in his desire to beat the odds and live. He gave up smoking from the day of diagnosis. A course of radiotherapy reduced the tumour in his lung. He often travelled the fifty miles to the hospital alone in a hospital car. On one occasion one of his sisters came from a distant town to keep him company but much of the time he went through the appointments and the treatment alone.

The boundaries of the analytic situation were now tested because he wanted me to go with him. There were times when he fantasized me accompanying him but he stated that he did not want me there as his psychotherapist. Therefore we had to work analytically with his desire for me as his ideal partner/mother, at the same time as acknowledging the very real loneliness of his situation. If I had travelled with him, and I did consider it, this would have broken the analytic frame and made future analysis impossible. I would have befriended him and, like his friends, he would have experienced me as unsafe.

I encouraged his moves to involve his parents and interpreted his destructive attitude towards them, but many of his attempts to make contact with them failed. He desperately needed someone with whom to share his hopes, fears, anxieties and the experience of the treatment, and that role fell to me. He discussed every facet of his worries about his body. On the days when he had to go to the hospital he was never far from my mind and, although I did not physically accompany him, I did so in spirit. When he was waiting for a particularly difficult appointment or going for tests, the outcome of which would have implications for his life expectancy, I gave him permission to phone me. If I was away from home I gave him a phone number so that he could contact me. He never abused this and phoned only when he was desperate or when he needed to share particularly good or bad news. On one occasion he phoned to say that the tumour had reduced as a result of the radiotherapy, on another that the doctors were unable to do any more for him. Thus the boundaries, while firm, were also adapted to accommodate the very real distress of the situation.

Henry spent a good deal of time in the library researching his particular form of cancer. He would discuss prognosis and possible outcomes. He made a decision not to accept chemotherapy, which he knew would make him feel very ill, after learning that it would not cure him. In some ways Henry feared death less than he feared life, and the illness gave his life a focus and a meaning that it had previously lacked. At one point when he was in remission he became aware of the problems he would have to confront without the illness. He realized he would have to find a job and somewhere to live and this threw him into a panic.

The analysis continued at depth. He became dependent and stated that if he became too ill to make decisions for himself, he would want me involved because I was the person who knew him best. This was a difficult situation because I did not want to foster this dependency. At every opportunity I encouraged him to turn to his family. They were there for him but they had their own lives in other parts of the country. Moreover Henry's old pattern of getting close and then rejecting people was often played out with his family and friends during the course of his illness. I was really the only person who was constant and who could mediate his anxiety and this was because, despite impulses to do otherwise, I held to the analytic frame. The contract to meet for fifty-minute sessions twice a week made me safe for Henry. It enabled me to observe and interpret his regular rejection of me. The fact that I remained in my chair and did not move physically towards him made it possible for him to accept this relationship. He began to risk confronting deeper and more disturbing material, which is an essential aspect of the individuation process.

## Sexuality and violence

Henry raged at me, he envied me because I was well and he was ill; this brought awareness of our respective bodies to the fore. He found his need of me humiliating. At times he was in despair and he could not bear the fact that I would not travel with him to hospital. He spat out what I offered him, telling me that there was no relationship between us and he attempted to abandon the therapy several times. On one of these occasions he became terrified of his sexual feelings. Henry unexpectedly missed several sessions. Each time I wrote acknowledging the missed session and confirming the next one. This happened for three sessions.

Eventually I decided that he needed some help to return and so I wrote interpreting his confusion and suggesting he could contact me by phone. He did so and, fortified with alcohol, admitted that he was unable to come because he had begun to experience sexual arousal accompanied by violent fantasies. It became clear that he was confused and frightened by the intensity of his feelings. After this conversation he was able to return and to confess that he feared he might attack or rape me; he became very aware that we were alone in the building. He said simply: 'What do you do if you fancy your therapist?' He felt first that this was inadmissible and second that it meant that he had to do something about it. He became acutely aware of the limits of the boundaries of the therapy room – would they hold? He desired, but also feared, that I would permit a sexual relationship with him or else that he would lose control and rape me. The idealization had broken down and the previously repressed sexuality and violence now emerged.

Once he began to speak of this, I was able to interpret the pre-Oedipal aspect of his feelings. This made sense to him and he linked it to his relationships with women where he would get close and then suddenly leave or withdraw emotionally. He said that he desired sexual intimacy with women but he had always felt, when he was in bed with them, that he needed something first, without understanding what it might be. As we explored the nature of his sexual fantasies it began to become evident that he desired maternal holding. He could not experience himself as sexual in relationship because his strongest desire was for holding.

Once he had admitted this he was able to contact his dependent, infantile erotic feelings. These were mixed up with sadistic, sexual and violent fantasies which dominated for a number of sessions. He told of his almost obsessive current interest in newspaper reports of men who had murdered their girlfriends. He worried about his potential to do the same, to murder me. During this phase he had dreams, which revealed his envious and murderous impulses. Gradually, as he expressed these feelings, they began to be less fearsome and overwhelming for him. He recognized them as merely one aspect of his inner world. As the violent feelings became more familiar, they dominated less and were gradually assimilated. Oedipal material emerged; he became interested in who lived in my house. The erotic transference now intensified and the relationship deepened. This is the purpose of the erotic connection; it deepens the patient's capacity for relatedness (Jung 1946).

Thus the symbolic nature of the transference, combined with the real relationship, permitted the experience to deepen. Within the frame of the therapy room I was, as time progressed, experienced by Henry as every woman (or aspect of woman) who had ever been important to him. Sometimes these were idealized and at others denigrated images of women. This was not easy especially as much of the time the connection between us was denied by him. He would not freely, nor openly, acknowledge that he was giving me anything of himself. Therefore I had to trust the countertransference as a means of understanding his communications. I made interpretations based in such experiences, which were usually confirmed by him at some later time. If I felt disconnected, it was usually because he was angry or encountering some other intense emotion and so cutting himself off from me. This was similar to his taking himself away from the therapy when he began to be sexually aroused but he became able to stay in the room and only cut off emotionally. Eventually he needed to do that less and would recognize it in himself and comment on it.

## Process

In the spring, a year after diagnosis, the radiotherapy had taken effect, the tumour was considerably reduced in size, and Henry felt physically much better. He was very positive and hopeful that this remission might last for a very long time. One day he brought photographs which he had taken of the spring flowers. They delighted him and he felt that the renewed growth of spring echoed his state; he was pleased to be alive and optimistic about the future. He was grateful and felt that the psychotherapy was helping and that life now held some hope of a positive future. It seemed that the cold of winter had turned to spring both literally and also metaphorically.

Reflecting on this one day he said sadly, 'I am a nice sort of a chap and all this is wasted [indicating himself]. You would think someone would have wanted it — and it will now go into the ground — to nothing'. I was profoundly moved; there were tears in my eyes and I spoke from the heart when I said, 'I think you are a nice sort of a chap'. He sat in silence and it was unclear to me what he was feeling for the rest of that session. After this intervention I questioned myself, feeling that I had broken some taboo — that I had lost the symbolic attitude. I feared that it had been seductive. However, when he returned for his next session he was able to tell me that this had had a profound effect on him. It was, he said, as if the ground had been swept from underneath him. He had been unable to speak because he was struggling with tears. He had realized that that was all he had needed someone to say to him when he was a little boy; he had always felt that he was seen as 'horrible'.

Thus my genuine affection for him communicated itself to him and enabled him to internalize an image of himself as lovable. The grief, which was fully present in that session, seemed to release him from the cycle of anger and depression. Such an intervention cannot be faked; at that moment I had been in touch with him. He had permitted himself to stay with the meeting in the moment and, instead of withdrawing or running away, Henry stayed with his grief. He permitted me to care. This was a profound form of touch, but without physical contact. Nor did he reject me in the next session, which would have been his usual pattern. Thus something positive emerged from this intuitive and genuine response to the immense sadness of the situation.

It seems that the erotic transference and countertransference, which was active in this therapeutic relationship prior to diagnosis, was now especially poignant and intensified. We both knew he was dying and, as time went by, it became increasingly unlikely that he would move from psychotherapy into making more positive connections in the world; there was so little time left. In the beginning of the chapter I suggested that the imminent death of the patient might intensify the erotic transference and this seemed to be the case now. Henry was coming to life in a new way within the transference. This included mourning all the losses that were imminent for him. It was this new-found psychological freedom which enabled him to relate and so deepened the feelings between us.

During this phase the impulse to reach out and touch Henry physically was very strong. However, I resisted it because the erotic transference was highly charged and such a breach of the analytic frame would have terrified him. It might have seemed to him seductive, promising more than just comfort in the moment. I think too that the impulse was partly a desire to repair what could not be repaired. Perhaps most importantly it would have stifled the emotion which was played out in between us at this time.

Henry found it almost impossible to cry and very often I found it almost impossible to restrain myself from crying. This was very powerful and not least as the relentless progress of the disease claimed more and more of his body. As the tumour in lung cancer spreads, it often puts pressure on the vocal cords. One day, two years after he first came to me, Henry's voice became hoarse; it was reduced to a whisper. He explained that the doctor had told him that it might not get better. It was a shocking realization followed by tremendous grief. We both experienced the sadness but when Henry saw that I was moved, he switched off his feelings. The feelings returned and then he asked: 'Will you miss me?' I nodded; I could have offered an interpretation. However the authentic answer was that I would miss him and it seemed to me that any other response would have been a betrayal; it would have been dishonest. Henry was never again able to speak out loud; from then on he could only whisper. Thus each stage in his deterioration brought additional considerations into play.

Henry hated to see emotion in me; it terrified him and he would run away, if not physically, by withdrawing emotionally. However, there were by now occasions like this one when he could sit quietly and experience the grief. I became able to differentiate my own grief from his projected feelings and to understand that, when he did not own his sadness, I would experience it as almost overwhelming. This eased when he had permitted himself to experience the depth of feeling associated with his potential losses. This profound form of emotional contact was facilitated by the fact that I resisted the impulse to touch him, to comfort him in his distress.

It was not long after this that he moved out of his parents' house and rented a house for himself. He began to contact friends he had not seen for years and to talk to his family. Thus it could be understood that the analysis was freeing him from old patterns of relating and he was beginning to make moves into the world.

## Hospital

As the body deteriorates, other professionals inevitably become involved. During admissions to hospital or hospices, analytic boundaries have to be adapted. In anticipation of this we discussed his wishes. I needed to be clear whether he would want me to visit him if he had to go into hospital. He said that he would want me to visit and that if decisions had to be made on his behalf regarding medication, he would want me to do this. I made it clear that if he wanted to maintain the analysis in this way he would have to make provision for it; he would have to prepare the space within the hospital for such eventualities. By now such outer world considerations had to be made alongside the interpretations of his dreams and understanding the transference.

It was nearly two years after the diagnosis that Henry phoned early one morning to tell me that he had called the doctor. He was living alone in his rented house and had awoken with difficulty breathing. The GP had immediately called an ambulance to take him to hospital. Henry phoned me as he waited for it to arrive; I sensed his anxiety and mediated it as best I could. An hour or two later he phoned and left a message for me to call him at the hospital. When I spoke to him he sounded faint and asked me to tell him where he was, that is what ward it was. Members of his family were going to visit him but he needed to speak to me; it was as if he needed to touch base. I was worried by his apparent confusion and concerned that if I left visiting him till I was free in the evening he might have died. (I phoned the ward sister to ask how he was and was reassured by her reply.) I reminded myself that his parents were with him and I had my other patients to see. It was important, because of his investment in the psychotherapy, to maintain my position as his psychotherapist and not rush to his side immediately. To do so would have been seductive; attempting to fulfil the role in which he tried to place me – as his partner. Thus a distinction was made in my mind, which maintained the analytic frame.

Later, when I was free, I went to the hospital and found him alone in a side ward, feeling better and able to breathe. He was sitting up in bed in his pyjamas. This was a strange situation for both of us; for months he had tried different ways to get me out of my room. This had been interpreted until it had become relatively easy to acknowledge the desire. The erotic element in the transference was by now a conscious feature of the relationship and there was a clear understanding that we would not go to bed together. The humour of the situation was not lost on Henry and he said, 'Don't tell me that I did this just to get you out of your room'. He was conscious of that possibility, as he noted that he had got me out of my room and I had 'finally got him lying down'. This was a reference to the couch – which he would never use. I stayed for the fifty minutes and then left. Later in the week, I visited him again, by arrangement. Henry was surrounded by flowers and cards from his family and friends, many of whom had responded to his hospitalization by travelling long distances to visit him. It was evident that when he permitted it they were there for him.

A week later he was discharged from hospital and returned to the pattern of living alone and coming to see me. His connection to me was changed by this hospital admission. In contrast to his previous life events he had experienced me as being there for him; when he phoned because he needed help I had responded. This established that I cared enough to be there when he really needed me; he could trust me. It could be said that this broke a therapeutic boundary but he was never misled; he knew that he needed me to maintain the boundaries of the relationship even in the hospital. Thus the analytic process changed and adapted to the reality of his life; the inner world and the outer world were coming closer together.

It was as if the individuation process was speeding up; there was urgency in the material. He was beginning to have a sense of agency in his life and this was reflected in the fact that he now had a place to live. Emotionally and also physically, he was 'housed'. Henry still became angry because I would not be all that he wanted me to be for him. He would still deny the connection between us but he would quickly recognize this denial.

### Hospice and home

The day my two week spring break began, he arranged to go into a hospice. His physical condition was deteriorating and he was less able to look after himself. I was away from home for one week and gave him permission to phone me, on my return, to make an appointment. When I visited him in the hospice he had told the nurses that I was his psychotherapist and arranged that we should not be disturbed during the fifty-minute session. Thus he ensured that the boundaries were maintained. He was feeling very weak and was convinced that he would never leave the hospice. He had dreamed he was making a bed; it was a huge white round bed, it was like polythene and, in the dream, he knew this was his death-bed. This dream was devastating in its simplicity; it seemed that he was becoming reconciled to the inevitability of his death.

This phase lasted a fortnight, and on one occasion when I visited he was feeling so ill that he was hardly able to speak. He had a fever and, after telling me how ill he felt, he lay down on his bed coughing and sweating profusely. I sat beside the bed in silence. He was wearing pyjamas and his feet were bare and he was apparently asleep. I had a strong sense that he was cold and so I got up from my chair and covered him up without apparently disturbing him. This could be seen as a form of touch but without overt physical contact. He continued sleeping but occasionally he would open an eye and look at me. This reminded me of the way a baby, who is apparently sleeping, opens one eye – just to check you are still there. After fifty minutes he awoke; it was as if he was conscious of the time and had used the session in this way. Later we were able to process this experience. He felt it was in some ways a repetition of the time when he had run his race at boarding school and then become ill and no one came. It was different this time because I had witnessed how ill he was and had sat with him. Later the same day, members of his family had done the same. He admitted that this was very important to him and considered the possibility that this had contributed to him being ill in this particular way.

Henry was offered medication that he was refusing. He asked me to speak to the hospice doctor on his behalf and I found her very concerned about him. He had been offered medication and counselling and had refused both. The refusal of counselling was not surprising, as he was already in analysis. However, it was something of a surprise to realize that the doctors were encountering him as a hostile, isolated and defended character. It seemed that the changes, which were taking place within him, had not extended to this situation. The transference here was to the boarding school; the hospice evoked regression to a dependent state within an institution.

The doctor thought that he could return home if he would accept the medication. I consulted an analyst colleague who was also a physician and she explained the potential positive effects of the medication he was being offered. On my next visit I was able to approach this topic from a practical as well as an inner world level. I explained how the medication might help him but I also interpreted his resistance to accepting help. I pointed out that he was replaying his recent experience of living in his parents' house and refusing their food. Furthermore, his resentment of being looked after by strangers was replaying the boarding school experience. A part of him did not want to leave the hospice; to die there would have been a bit like suicide, it would have punished those who cared for him. Thus my role was dual; on the one hand I was offering practical information and on the other using my therapeutic knowledge of him to reduce his resistance. After this session he agreed to take the medication and very soon he felt significantly better. One of his sisters offered to move in with him and look after him in his house; she could not bear for him to die in the hospice. Thus he was able to return home.

I offered to visit him at home but Henry was determined to maintain the analysis in the context of my room as long as possible. He continued to struggle to do so when he hardly had the strength to walk from his car to my room. We discussed what he would want me to do when he could no longer come to me; would he want me to visit him in his home? He said it would be time enough for me to do so when he could no longer get to me; thus he maintained the boundary. He continued to come to me until two weeks before he died.

Eventually he became too disabled to travel and I visited him. His body had deteriorated so there was little muscle tone and he could not move. He was given morphine to alleviate the pain. A week before he died he was bright and lively and he said that he felt 'more alive now than he had ever been'. He did not seem afraid to die and he knew that he had little time left. He found a renewed spiritual belief and turned to the God he had learned to trust when he had been a child. Many of his friends from the past came to visit him and he enjoyed their visits but he now found them exhausting. The last visit I made to him was a week later, when he was unable to speak and apparently unconscious. I sat with him for a while and then left. His family phoned me the next day to tell me that he had died three hours later.

## Conclusion

At the beginning of the chapter I suggested that abstinence from physical contact maintains the emblematic nature of the transference. I think that it has been evident in the case material that the interplay between transference and countertransference was like a dance between the elements I suggested in my introduction: embodied experience and psyche; desire and repulsion; impulse and restraint. The symbolic nature of the therapeutic relationship came under extreme pressure and, although it had to be adapted, the analytic frame held. Physical contact was resisted despite the desire. This evoked a profound form of emotional touch, enabling the individuation process to continue to the end.

## Acknowledgements

This chapter is developed from *The Dying Patient in Psychotherapy: Desire, Dreams and Individuation* (published by Palgrave Macmillan 2002), which includes the dreams and full story. An earlier version of this chapter was published in *the Journal of Analytical Psychology* 44 (1) (1999) entitled, 'The death of an analysand: transference, countertransference and desire'

## Note

1  In order to preserve confidentiality, Henry's name and the details of his life have been altered.

# References

Bion, W.R. (1982) *The Lost Weekend*, London: Karnac.

Bosnak, R. (1989) *Dreaming with an AIDS Patient*, Boston, MA and Shaftesbury, UK: Shambala.

Duffell, N. (2000) *The Making of Them: The British Attitude to Children and the Boarding School System*, London: Lone Arrow Press.

Freud, S. (1912) 'The dynamics of the transference', *Standard Edition*, ed. J. Strachey, Vol. 12, London: Hogarth Press.

——(1915) 'Observations on transference love', *Standard Edition*, ed. J. Strachey, Vol. 12, London: Hogarth Press.

Greenson, R. (1967) *The Technique and Practice of Psychoanalysis*, London: Hogarth Press.

Heimann, P. (1949) 'On countertransference', *International Journal of Psychoanalysis* 31: 81–4.

Jung, C.G. (1913) *Psychological Types*, *Collected Works*, Vol. 6, London: Routledge.

——(1935) *The Soul and Death*, *Collected Works*, Vol. 8, London: Routledge.

——(1946) *The Psychology of the Transference*, *Collected Works*, Vol. 16, London: Routledge.

——(1955) *Synchronicity: An Acausal Connecting Principle*, *Collected Works*, Vol. 18, London: Routledge.

Lee, C. (1996) *Music at the Edge: The Music Therapy Experiences of a Musician with AIDS*, London and New York: Routledge.

Little, M. (1950) 'The analyst's total response to his patient's needs', in M. Little (ed.) *Towards Basic Unity*, 1986 edition, London: Free Association Books.

McDougall, J. (1995) *The Many Faces of Eros: A Psychoanalytic Exploration of Human Sexuality*, London: Free Association Books.

——(2000) 'Theatres of the psyche', *Journal of Analytical Psychology* 45 (1): 45–64.

Minerbo, V. (1998) 'The patient without a couch', *International Journal of Psychoanalysis* 79 (1): 83–93.

Racker, H. (1974) *Transference and Countertransference*, London: Hogarth Press.

Schaverien, J. (1995) *Desire and the Female Therapist: Engendered Gazes in Psychotherapy and Art Therapy*, London and New York: Routledge.

——(1996) 'Desire and the female analyst', *Journal of Analytical Psychology* 41 (2): 261–87.

——(1997) 'Men who leave too soon', *British Journal of Psychotherapy* 14 (1): 3–16.

——(2002) *The Dying Patient in Psychotherapy: Desire, Dreams and Individuation*, Basingstoke: Palgrave Macmillan.

——(2004) 'Boarding school: the trauma of the privileged child', *Journal of Analytical Psychology* 49 (5): 683–707.

Searles, H. (1959) 'Oedipal love in the countertransference', in *Collected Papers on Schizophrenia and Related Subjects*, 1986 edition, London: Maresfield.

Springer, A. (1995) 'Paying homage to the power of love: exceeding the bounds of professional practice', *Journal of Analytical Psychology* 40: 41–61.

Ulanov, A.B. (1994) *The Wizard's Gate: Picturing Consciousness*, Einsiedeln, Switzerland: Daimon Verlag.

Wheelwright, J.H. (1981) *The Death of a Woman: How a Life Became Complete*, New York: St Martin's Press.

# 13

# 'IN THIS BODY, A FATHOM LONG. . .'

## Working with embodied mind and interbeing in psychotherapy

*Maura Sills*

*Co-authored with Judy Lown for publication*

### Introduction

Body psychotherapy is often associated with the application of touch and physical contact between psychotherapist and client. This approach has grown out of a long tradition of understanding the inseparable nature of body and psyche (Reich 1933; Sheldon 1940; Boyesen 1982; Boadella 1987; Keleman 1989; Rolf 1989; Kurtz 1990; Lowen 1994; Eiden 1999; Feldenkrais 2002). Those following this tradition have a deep understanding of the subtle energetic underpinnings of various defended forms of thought, emotion and somatization of personal history. These psychotherapists are frequently explicit in their use of touch. Their sensitivity and expertise have been central in supporting therapeutic inquiry through body as well as mind.

Equally, there are many psychotherapists who believe that touching a client might be intrusive and invoke inappropriate transferences, yet have sensed in the relationship with their clients energies which are indeed subtler than those of cognition, thought and emotion. There is, in the presence of their clients, a kind of 'knowing' of a wider implicate field.

I would like to suggest that, even without physical touch, an awareness of body and body-process, including sensations, feeling tones and body characteristics, can deeply inform psychotherapeutic work. This subtle realm has been described by Eugene Gendlin (1988) in terms of the 'felt sense'. This is an embodied territory characterized by kinaesthetic sensitivity suffused with feeling tone. Gendlin describes it as 'a special kind of internal bodily awareness'. In his words,

> A felt sense is not an emotion. We recognize emotions. We know when we are angry, or sad, or glad. A felt sense is something you do not at first recognize – it is vague and murky. It feels meaningful, but not known. It is a body-sense of meaning.
>
> (Gendlin 1988: 10)

MAURA SILLS

The 'felt sense' in many ways echoes, in an embodied form, what William James (1890) was pointing to when he referred to 'the vague'. This was, for him, the realm of dimly perceived relations and objects, referred to in terms of 'psychic overtones', 'suffusion' and 'fringe sensations'. He used the analogy of a river where 'every definite image in the mind is steeped and dyed in the free water that flows around it.' James suggested that it is important to 'pay attention to the vague'.

## Embodied field of consciousness

This subtle embodied field has also been identified and described from within the disciplines of science and ecology and within certain spiritual traditions. In biophysics, for example, Mae-Wan Ho has demonstrated how quantum-level fields seem to organize all life forms and respond to experience (Ho 1993). Her research with single cell and invertebrate animals shows that these organisms are organized within a stable quantum field of light. The field of light seems to order the anatomy of the organism and is intelligently responsive to the environment.

Other research shows that water is directly affected by thoughts and emotions and can hold the memory of experience. For example, Masaru Emoto (2004) has demonstrated how water that has been exposed to different kinds of thoughts and emotions will form different types of crystalline structures when it is frozen. Wholesome or positive emotions create beautiful crystalline structures while unwholesome or negative emotions cause the structures to break down or fragment. Moreover, water can be affected by extremely subtle influences in the immediate environmental field. Even the silent thoughts of the experimenters were sufficient to create different responses.

A third area of research which highlights the significance of field consciousness is that of Rupert Sheldrake who postulates that personal and ancestral memory is passed on through fields of energetic interconnection. He calls these 'morphogenetic fields' (Sheldrake 1982). Rejecting the idea that memory is stored in the brain and central nervous system, Sheldrake sees the brain more as a kind of receiver for tuning into the 'morphogenetic field'. This field is seen to hold the memory of all arising conditions, including all past events and all potential futures. It is available as a source of information and coherency to all human beings through resonance. In this way, all the conditions of the past, present and future are available to all of us in each moment of life if we are prepared to attune ourselves appropriately.

This recent Western research is yielding more and more evidence of interrelated fields of memory and intelligence suggestive of a consciousness at work at a very deep and primordial level of organization. Such findings are strikingly consistent with the much older tradition of Buddhist psychology and practice. In this tradition, mind is not seen to be separate from the body. There is one word, 'namarupa' (mindbody), to describe the nature of consciousness and human personality. As psychotherapists, we often talk of valuing and including mind, body and spirit in our work. Within a Buddhistic experiential understanding, there is a oneness of mind, body and spirit. They are interdependent and inseparable. Prevailing

Western thought tends to see the mind as generated by the brain or neural function. Following from this, it also tends to elevate cognitive understanding and conceptual awareness as constituting reality. In Buddhism, the mind is more like a field that includes the entire body. Furthermore, it expands, flows and interpenetrates the mindbodies of others. Intelligence and compassion are qualities of this seamless consciousness and not dependent upon cognition. The cognitive processes themselves are defined in terms of a sense organ, comparable to the other five senses of sight, smell, touch, taste and hearing, through which we experience the world.

So, in this tradition, not only is mind indivisible from body but also all phenomena are seen to mutually arise within a unified and ubiquitous field of interconnection. The Venerable Thich Nhat Hanh calls this 'interbeing' – all things are interdependent, mutually arise and interbe (Thich Nhat Hanh 1988). All of us are connected at this level of interbeing: one mind, many beings. From this perspective, everything is accessible through the vehicle of the body. As the Buddha famously put it:

> In this body, a fathom long, with its thoughts and emotions, I declare are the world, the origins of the world, the cessation of the world and the path leading to the cessation of the world.
>
> (Anguttara Nikaya, IV, 45)

## Non-cognitive nature of mind

If the mindbody is a whole field of experiencing, stretching way beyond the cognitive and the individual, psychotherapy becomes a process involving subtle layers of 'knowing' at all levels of our interbeing. In everyday life, as well as in therapeutic practice, there are times of 'knowing' without thinking. Usually this is experienced in that realm of 'the vague', in that territory of subtle sensation and feeling tones that are accessed through the 'felt sense' of the body rather than through cognitive activity. It often manifests as something that has meaning but no agenda or goal. It is mostly very fleeting and non-verbal. When we try to find words to describe it, it's gone, yet we know we have been changed by the experience. Again, this is usually at the level of a felt bodily shift, not through cognitive understanding.

This 'direct knowing' – or 'clear comprehension' as it is referred to in Buddhism – communicates meaning and relatedness. It works beneath the forms of emotion and prior to conceptual organization. It flows from below even the subtle energetic layers. It arises from the depths of the ground of emergence itself. When we experience this in therapy, we open to the profoundest levels of transformation.

In early Buddhism, the faculty of 'direct knowing' is seen as a function of what the Buddha called 'citta'. This term has many connotations and has been translated in a variety of ways. It is probably best described as a locus of awareness within the movement of personality. Rune Johansson, a Swedish psychologist and Buddhist scholar, defines it as 'not the same as "personality", rather a centre within personality, and a conscious centre of activity, meaning, continuity and emotionality' (Johansson 1985: 34).

In an early discourse (Anguttara Nikaya, I, 10), the Buddha states that 'citta' is unconditioned: it is inherently luminous and free. This freedom is obscured, however, by conditions that come from outside. Thus at the heart of human experience is a luminosity and openness that we rarely perceive because of the way our experiences condition us.

Much later, Western philosophers have referred to this process as an 'obscuration of being' (Heidegger 1962). In psychotherapeutic terms, it is the development of the personality and self-constructs that form these obscurations. Franklyn Sills' most recent work (Sills 2005, in preparation) describes how we all exist along a source–being–self axis.

## Source, being and self

Source could be described as that interconnected and open ground of emergence from which all phenomena, including ourselves, co-arise. As Sills puts it:

> In some forms of Buddhism, Source is considered to be an inherent emptiness manifesting in form as the radiance of pristine awareness, a naturally enlightened, open and centred ground state that connects and informs all beings.
>
> (Sills 2007, in preparation)

Other spiritual traditions use different terms, but all tend to point to a spiritual ground of meaning to life and to the possibility of exploring and engaging more fully in this realm of meaning.

'Being', says Sills, is 'a centre of sentience and awareness in the midst of self-constellations, the heart of "I-am"', which is naturally relationship-seeking and provides the necessary continuity and coherency for a centred and responsive sense of self. We are interconnected at a root level to all other beings. It is this basic interbeing that energizes object-relations-seeking. Early developmental experience, the infant–mother relational field and therapeutic process in general can all be understood in relation to this archetypal being-to-being interconnection. We seek other beings to know our own being. Being arises from source and source mediates being-to-being interconnection. Being is 'citta' and when 'citta' is freed, its source is known. 'Self', Sills continues, 'is the conditioned sense of who we are'. It is 'a constellation of psycho-emotional-physiological processes that we generally identify as "me" or "myself"' (Sills in preparation).

It is not a fixed entity but arises out of a dynamic and fluid process of exchanges with others and the world around us. It is formed through relationship and its purpose is to mediate being's relationship to the world and to maintain relationship in the midst of all conditions and relational processes. Importantly, 'self is not just a mental construct, but is a *tonal, embodied feeling-experience. I am what I sense myself to be*' (my emphasis).

According to this model, source is an ever-present and ever-available wellspring of inherent health and wellbeing which can be accessed through embodied being-to-being relationship. Self is like a wheel that spins in response to relational life. Being is the hub of that wheel and is a direct conduit to source, which gives meaning to it all. Much of the focus of psychotherapeutic work is concerned with the disruptions that can occur in this whole interconnected process.

These disruptions can happen at various stages of development. Frank Lake (1987) talks about how if the womb is not a welcoming and nourishing environment for the prenate there can be a dislocation at a cellular level of the baby's basic sense of being. Donald Winnicott (1965) describes how a lack of acceptance, recognition and warmth early in the life of the infant can rupture the continuity of being and lead to the construction of a 'false self'. We need to have been well-enough nurtured and nourished to sustain a being-nature that is intact enough to remain in touch with source. Very few of us have been fully recognized at a being level. It is often interruptions in our continuity of being that make us lose sight of source, that obscure it from our view.

## Embodied presence in psychotherapeutic practice

The extent to which the therapist can orientate towards a being-to-being relationship with the client is the extent to which the lifeline between source, being and self can be restored. The therapist needs to occupy a very wide empathic holding field to include both a maternal archetypal attunement with the developmental wounding and inner states of the client and an awareness of the ever-present possibility of connection to source. In this way, a holistic relational field is established which attends not just to the conditions arising but also to the nature of the universal and unconditioned ground of our being. If the therapist can embody the intentions of warmth, acceptance, nurturance, safety and recognition then, in the words of the philosopher, Husserl, being can naturally 'unconceal' itself (Kockelmans 1998) and access to source is reopened.

The body is the site in and through which all this is experienced and it is the client's capacity to attune to the subtle layers of bodily experience which often holds the key to therapeutic transformation. What Gendlin (1988) is describing in his depiction of the 'felt sense' is a kind of global perception of the whole of arising process in any one moment of emergent experience – a sense of 'all of it'. All those sensations, emotional tones, mental constructs, symbols and images that compose our self-constellations are directly experienced as an embodied and coherent whole. It expresses how we organize and maintain the meaning of our experiences. To access this is to access how we 'do ourselves'. It's like knowing the veils through which we view everything rather than looking through those veils.

For example, a client might be describing a recent experience of 'failure' – at work or in relationship. Her process might be gathering momentum and taking the form of 'I've always been a failure and always will be.' As the client deepens into the 'felt sense' layers of this in her body, she might begin to contact some cloudy, uncomfortable, constraining sensations. There might be physical tightness and restriction, a sense of not being able to breathe or move, accompanied by images of being crushed and squeezed. How these experiences originated is less important than how they are being experienced now and what kind of a 'handle' the client can find to express them. She might say a word like 'demolished' or 'annihilated'. She tries this out a couple more times to see if it fits her current experience and turns to her body for a response to the question, 'What is it about this that makes me feel so demolished/annihilated?' Her body loosens as it gives her the answer, which she does not need to put into words. She has 'got' it at a deep embodied level and she gains some space within the self-system that was erupting into a surge of reactions but now experiences a direct 'knowing' that this was not the truth of the matter. She has been able to explore the experience of suffering without becoming it all over again. She has been a witness to her own process rather than being lost in it.

To enable this to happen, the therapist in many ways has to undo the habits of a lifetime. In the West we are trained in the techniques of cognitive, conceptual and explicate inquiry. A wide and implicate field of inquiry needs to include the personal, the interpersonal, the transpersonal, the collective unconscious, the ancestral, and to acknowledge namarupa, the psychological, the spiritual, the whole being. To become available to the fullest extent of this field requires a shift in both intention and attention. We need to be able to move from a linear assumption of cause and effect into a subtle, sensing relational field where we can attend to whatever is arising moment to moment. This shift is like a resourced receptivity where we are content to attend to the moment through the experience of its effect.

We cannot grasp for information from this implicate field of consciousness. We become informed at all levels through our internal resonances, responses and reactions. As we continue to attend to them, these effects become more and more subtle and less personal. It is this quality of interested listening through our hearts and bodies, together with a willingness to be affected, that brings us in to a profound level of embodied presence imbued with the openness of awareness. As we develop our capacity to stay aware and to be co-present with the other and the field in which we sit, more and more will 'unconceal' itself.

## Inner practices of the psychotherapist

In a still and receptive relational field, both practitioner and client can meet in embodied presence that manifests a natural interconnection. This field provides a portal of relationship through which inherent intelligence and compassion can arise. It is a field which holds past, present and potential future. If the therapist is orienting towards a wide field awareness together with an awareness of body process, if she is sensitizing herself to the territory of the 'felt sense' and if her intentions are to meet at a being-to-being level then there is an invitation for 'direct knowing' to arise. This quality of 'direct knowing' is one that can be cultivated by psychotherapeutic practitioners. When we can touch this quality of being-ness within the therapeutic relationship it can help dissolve the barriers to being co-present and resonant with the other. The realization of our non-separateness occurs when the relational field between therapist and client is experienced as safe, empathic, interconnected and unified. In this conjoined field, there can be a clear comprehension of process and of the health underlying the process.

In the Buddhist tradition, awareness is the foundation of inquiry and awakening. Awakening need not be some grand extreme experience. It could be seen more in terms of sustaining, regenerating and resourcing our sense of being-nature in daily life so as to keep alive that vital connection between self, being and source. A central practice in supporting this intention has been described by the Buddhist scholar, Nyanaponika Thera, as 'Sustained Attention' (Nyanaponika Thera 1975: 30). This is a way of focusing and maintaining 'Bare Attention', which is 'the clear and single-minded awareness of what actually happens *to* us and *in* us, at the successive moments of perception' (Nyanaponika Thera 1975; 30, emphasis in original). With consistent practice, we notice the self-referential labelling that occurs with every act of perception: every object appears in the light of added subjective judgements.

Nyanaponika Thera (1975: 33) likens the practice to using 'sieves of increasingly finer meshes by which first the grosser and then ever subtler admixtures will be separated until the bare object remains'. This allows things to speak for themselves and

> Because Bare Attention sees things without the narrowing and levelling effect of habitual judgements, it sees them ever anew, as if for the first time; therefore it will happen with progressive frequency that things will have something new and worthwhile to reveal.
>
> (Nyanaponika Thera 1975: 35)

As an inner practice of the psychotherapist, this process endows the practitioner with a quality of light and sure attention so essential for meeting the sensitive, evasive and refractory nature of consciousness. Nyanaponika Thera points out that we cannot do this without 'slowing-down' (Nyanaponika Thera 1986: 74). Most of our mental and bodily movements, he says, are characterized by a rapidity and impatience that blunts our consciousness. This is fuelled, as well, by the technologically driven society we live in. The hurried rhythm of modern life means we are burdened by 'a vast amount of indistinct or fragmentary perceptions, stunted emotions and undigested ideas' (Nyanaponika Thera 1986: 76). Thoughts, feelings and perceptions rarely get a chance to complete the entire length of their natural lifetime. We mostly cut off the end phase of subtle vibrations and reverberations by rushing on to the next impression or next stage in a train of thought before the earlier ones have been fully comprehended.

This is similar territory to William James' 'free water' of 'the vague' where fringe sensations and thoughts and dimly perceived objects and relations float around. The premature cutting off of mental, emotional, physical and psychological processes stultifies our sensitivity on many levels and is one of the ways in which aspects of our consciousness become fragmented and disjointed.

A conscious 'slowing-down' of process and 'sustained attention' to whatever arises offers a means of recovering the fullness and clarity of consciousness. Nyanaponika Thera maintains that it does this in three main ways.

First, it tends to intensify consciousness. Whatever is arising in the field of consciousness gets an opportunity to exert a strong and long-lasting impact. We can stay with it and deepen into it, rather than rushing onto the next thing.

Second, it helps to clarify and to provide a fuller picture. Usually, the first impression we have is what captures our attention in the most striking way. But there might be less obvious or less subjectively interesting aspects other than those we initially notice. Or sometimes our first impression can be deceptive or misleading. Only if we maintain a continuity of light and non-judgemental awareness, beyond those first impressions, can further detail be revealed and a more complete picture emerge.

Third, it uncovers the relatedness and interconnection of our human condition. It does this by allowing an unfolding of relations, previously dimmed or obscured, to take place. Rather than seeing things in artificial isolation, connections can come into view which reveal not only patterns in our own experience and environment but also wider patterns of communality with the experiences of others. Furthermore, we can begin to perceive their conditioned and conditioning nature.

When psychotherapists adopt this intentional practice of slowing down the process of what is happening and sustaining a depth of attention, the client is held in a continuing field of presence and awareness in which the 'orphans of consciousness' (Sumedho 1990) can find their way home. As clear comprehension casts light on the client's processes and patterns, what she often discovers is that 'this is not all I am'. In addition, for both therapist and client, there is a strengthening and sharpening of the subliminal faculties of memory, intuition and subconscious organization. By practising a means of accessing the more subtle layers of our consciousness, it becomes possible to attune ourselves to those deep and primordial levels of interrelated fields of memory and intelligence. Nyanaponika Thera offers a lovely image for this of a mountain lake that 'is fed not only by the outside rains, but also by springs welling up from within its own depths' (Nyanaponika Thera 1986: 78).

It is widely recognized within modern psychotherapy that it is the quality of relationship between therapist and client that is far more important in effecting change than any particular theoretical orientation or technique. This suggests the primacy of inner practices for practitioners that support and nourish their capacity for depth of relationship. Although theory can inform us of the specific conditions of the territory a client might be experiencing, it is regular and sustained contemplative practice that can cultivate the ability to maintain a still presence in the midst of both personal and relational conditions.

There are many contemplative practices, both within and without the spiritual traditions, which support this intention. Within Buddhism, it is the practice of Mindfulness which is central. This is a wider application of the practice of 'Sustained Attention'. It is based on resensitizing the practitioner to the fullness of their human condition. Sitting and walking meditation practices, together with specific body-based awareness practices, support a form of inquiry which encourages the development of field awareness. As we sensitize ourselves to our own condition, we also become more sensitive to that of the client. In the therapeutic relationship, information can be communicated directly through subliminal field awareness. It is this field of presence that allows a distillation of meaning as the client's process impacts the practitioner.

## Three fields of attention

Mindfulness practice helps the therapist to orientate across three fields of attention. The first of these involves attention to our own inner weather. We need to be able to bring awareness to our own mindbody and to the sensations, feeling tones, mental states and mental contents which arise within this field. As Nyanaponika Thera points out, this 'sifting process' can become increasingly inclusive and refined until it becomes expansive and aware enough to hold all levels of mind, body and spirit (Nyanaponika Thera 1975: 33). This field of attention helps us to contact our energetic midline and establish a kind of 'vertical' connection with the earth below and the 'heavens' above. It is important to be able to attune to this field and to return to it time and again in order to sustain attention to the second field.

This is the 'horizontal' connection of being in that field of presence with another person. Here, we come into energetic relationship with another and the challenge is to orientate 'this embodied mind' towards 'that embodied mind'. We don't have to know what to say or do. The intention is to be present, allowing ourselves to be affected by the other and noticing how I am affecting the other, how the other is experiencing me. In this endeavour, the therapist needs to bring awareness to her own thoughts, feelings, emotions and sensations as much as to the client's. This is essentially a 'joint practice' where awareness is brought to whatever arrives through the gateway of relationship. It becomes largely irrelevant as to whose experience is whose in the light of the clarity which awareness brings. There is a recognition of mutuality in the human condition which allows attention to extend to the third field.

This could be described as that expansive and interconnected relational field which opens up when contact and connection deepen through relationship. In a being-to-being meeting, layers of experience 'unconceal' themselves from beneath the obscurations generated at the level of self-constructs. At these deeper levels, some of the strategies that have been adopted to protect the self loosen or fall away as we drop into more existential and spiritual aspects of our being. We are opened up to a depth of contact where meaning arises.

It is at these depths that we begin to reconnect to source, or to 'the Core' as it is called in Core Process Psychotherapy. When we start to let go of fixed senses of self we need something to let go into. As we experience ourselves more as a process than a permanent entity AND we are feeling met in relationship in that 'centre of sentience and awareness' then there is something much bigger for us to let ourselves into. We can allow ourselves to be held by that in us which is not separate from the non-separateness of others. We can make ourselves available to the inherent health and wellbeing at the heart of our existence.

## Re-sourcing unconditional contact

There is a long-established principle in Western psychotherapy of holding an attitude akin to the Rogerian 'unconditional positive regard' (Rogers 1951) towards clients. It is this that forms a fundamental basis for the facilitating environment of warmth, acceptance and recognition so necessary for therapeutic transformation to take place. It can be a huge challenge for the psychotherapist to actually embody this principle in a consistent and 'good enough' way. If the therapist is also intending to hold open an even wider implicate field, where there is a readiness to stay available to the unknown, the challenge can be even greater. Access to resources that maintain the therapist's orientation to source and nourish their capacity for interconnection is vital.

In Buddhism, there is a description of four interrelated unconditioned qualities that are characterized as boundless and limitless because they emerge from that 'naturally enlightened, open and centred ground state' that is the Core. These are loving kindness, compassion, sympathetic joy and equanimity. They are said to naturally arise when awareness is brought to the conditioned reactions that usually block their way. In a sentient existence where we are so affected by people, events, things, our own moods, thoughts, emotions, reactions and limitations, it can be very difficult to experience the natural empathy of the heart. Self-constructs and personality strategies, arising out of our own experience of wounding and impingement, often form obscurations to these deep innate qualities.

The Buddha defined these states by what they are not, by reference to the conditions of which they are absent (Sucitto 2003). Loving kindness arises in the absence of hatred and aversion, compassion in the absence of ill-will and indifference, sympathetic joy in the absence of jealousy and envy and equanimity in the absence of judgement and discrimination. They arise not from an act of will but from conscious attention to the blocks and obstacles which get in the way of uncramped openness to ourselves and others.

In everyday life, we sometimes experience such states during extreme crises or situations where there is a direct cutting through of the conditioned reactions. The death or serious illness of a close relative or friend, for example, can bring about a welling of love and compassion. When we do find ourselves responding in this way, it often comes from the place in us that is non-separate. This is a place that knows how it is to suffer even if we do not share exactly the same form of suffering, that knows what joy feels like even if it's a different kind of joy. We do not have to have had the same experiences as each other to know what it feels like to have those experiences and to resonate from that place in us. However, we cannot respond openly to one another if we ignore our conditioned reactions or if we simply try to pump up compassion and warmth. We can access these heart qualities only if we acknowledge and attend to our reactions.

Hence the importance of the therapist consciously attending to her own thoughts, feelings and sensations within the therapeutic relationship. In the therapeutic encounter, as in everyday life, the unconditional qualities of loving kindness, compassion, sympathetic joy and equanimity are constantly present even if they are obscured. When we bring awareness, say, to that feeling inside of dislike or repulsion or to that sensation of tightness and restriction or to that pang of jealousy and resentment, we give these conditions space to dissolve and make way for the possibility of the natural qualities of the heart to co-arise in the relational field. This is also where, clearly, an ongoing contemplative practice supports the ability of the therapist to bring awareness to these processes.

An openness to these qualities is a huge resource (and hugely re-sourcing) for therapists' intentions to be present and available for their clients. They are qualities that can be both energized and leaned into as a source of support. They also help the therapist to orientate towards the particular unmet needs and developmental territory the client might be experiencing at any time. Loving kindness helps to welcome and receive openly whatever arises in the therapeutic space and to offer appropriate nourishment. Compassion helps the therapist to stay with the client's experience, no matter what it is, to continue receiving and hosting the 'guest' who has been invited and welcomed in. It supports our intention to know the other's experience as closely to our own as possible.

Sympathetic joy enables us to resonate with the client's joyful experiences as well as their suffering. It's about sharing in the sense of wellbeing – a joy that one can truly enter into and savour inside oneself even when the 'origin' appears to be in another's experience. This quality is also very relevant to helping the client to end therapy – to rejoice in the client's growing independence and strength and to be able to let them go. It's like feeling and expressing a sense of 'I rejoice in you being yourself'.

Equanimity is an expansive quality, implying space for everything. It's the opposite of contraction, which is a familiar conditioned reaction. It can help us to have space for more and more experience and to be able to receive the impact of more and more experience. This is where we often have to give particular attention to our limitations and our tendencies to close off. It's about having a deep sense of caring for the other but knowing they have to find out for themselves whatever they need to find out. It's about holding the space and offering the space for the other to make their way in the world. In the Western psychotherapeutic tradition, Winnicott refers to very similar territory when he talks about 'the capacity to be alone' (Winnicott 1965), in describing what happens when a child has received enough love and nourishment to have developed an inner container for their expanding experience and growing independence. Ajahn Sucitto describes this process as 'love manifesting as trust' (Sucitto 2003). We all have to experience 'good' and 'bad', fears and joys, success and failure. This is about trusting our own capacity to be present with these passing conditions and trusting another's capacity to do likewise.

In those times when these qualities do arise, even if for a moment, we experience them in an embodied way. When we touch loving kindness, we feel the welling up of open-hearted warmth and love. In moments of compassion, we feel the vibration of the heart empathizing with another's experience. When we resonate with the other's good fortune, we feel the delight and lightness that enters our heart. When we expand to include more and more of the other's experience, no matter what it is, we feel the sense of spaciousness that arises. It is in the embodiment of these Core experiences that a depth of contact and meaning occurs.

## Conclusion

A consequence of much Western individualistic philosophy has been to split mind, body and spirit. Such a division is artificial and does not recognize the multilayered and interconnected nature of our existence in which all experiences are enfolded. From a holistic perspective, to talk 'about a body' is to acknowledge an embodied field of consciousness which encompasses conditioned self-constellations, our being-nature and an unconditioned Core state that is already open and free. It is to recognize not only that 'this body' is not separate from mind and spirit but also that 'all bodies' are interlinked and interbe at many levels. A body is the holding field of a variety of processes – mental, psychological, physiological, emotional and spiritual. These processes can be accessed through awareness. It is the inner practices of awareness that in and of themselves can open the possibility for an unfolding process of transformation to take place.

To include the spiritual is not to import some separate dimension of experience but to open to an integral aspect of our embodied human existence. Since it is this aspect which holds the deepest source of our wellbeing, it is essential to orientate towards it in any healing process. We need to include very centrally an orientation to this level of felt reality. In psychotherapeutic practice it is as important to hold an awareness of the presence of the Core state and its heart qualities as it is to hold the self-constructs and personality positions of the client. It is only when both the universal and the conditional come into balance that healing can truly begin. Jung pointed to this when he stated that it is the role of the therapist to hold both universal and conditional forces until balance is attained (Jung 1976). It is only then that the client can be freed from limiting conditions and restrictive and defended personality constructs.

To embody the intention and awareness of offering space for this in the therapeutic process does not require any religious belief or faith on the part of the therapist. Indeed, that can sometimes get in the way. It does help, though, if the therapist is motivated to explore the spiritual aspects of her own existence. Spiritual and psychotherapeutic explorations share in common a commitment to inner investigation. Undertaken as a practice of embodied awareness in relationship, the two converge and become one path of enquiry. Even without personal experience in this territory, keeping the possibility open can offer the client and the work a greater holding space. It can open client process to greater potential.

In Core Process Psychotherapy, we believe that healing occurs within embodied fields and states of spaciousness and coherency. As the therapist develops a relational field that is still, warm, empathic and resonant, implicate information is subliminally conveyed and known silently with clear comprehension. Within this kind of relational field, a client might truly hold their suffering in balance and open to an experience of their human beingness that is beyond words.

## Acknowledgement

Franklyn Sills, my husband, is the co-founder of the Karuna Institute. His ongoing enquiry into the nature of our existence and meaning has informed all my work.

## References

Anguttara Nikaya, I, 10, Pali Canon, trans. 1975, Kandy, Sri Lanka: Buddhist Publication Society.

Anguttara Nikaya, IV, 45, Rohitassa Sutta, Pali Canon, trans. 1975, Kandy, Sri Lanka: Buddhist Publication Society.

Boadella, D. (1987) *Lifestreams*, London: Routledge.

Boyesen, G. (1982) 'The primary personality', *Journal of Biodynamic Psychology* 3.

Eiden, B. (1999) 'Reich's Legacy', *Counselling News* 6 (January): 12–14.

Emoto, M. (2004) *Hidden Messages in Water*, Emeryville, CA: Beyond Words.

Feldenkrais, M. (2002) *The Potent Self: The Dynamics of the Body and the Mind*, Berkeley, CA: Frog.

Gendlin, E. (1988) *Focusing*, 2nd edition, New York: Bantam.

Heidegger, M. (1962) *Being and Time*, trans. J. Macquarrie and E. Robinson, Oxford: Blackwell.

Ho Mae-Wan (1993) *The Rainbow and the Worm: The Physics of Organisms*, Singapore: World Scientific Publishing.

James, W. (1890) *The Principles of Psychology*, Cambridge, MA.: Harvard University Press.

Johannson, R.E.A. (1985) *The Dynamic Psychology of Early Buddhism*, London and Malmo, Sweden: Curzon Press.

Jung, C.G. (1976) *The Practice of Psychotherapy*, 2nd edition, trans. R.F.C. Hull, London and Henley: Routledge and Kegan Paul.

Keleman, S. (1989), *Somatic Reality, Bodily Experience and Emotional Truth*, Berkeley, CA : Centre Publications.

Kockelmans, J.J. (1998) *Edmund Husserl's Phenomenology*, West Lafayette, IN: Purdue University Press.

Kurtz, R. (1990) *Body-Centred Psychotherapy: The Hakomi Method – The Integrated Use of Mindfulness, Nonviolence and the Body*, Mendocino, CA: LifeRhythm.

Lake, F. (1987) *Personal Identity: Its Origin*, Oxford: Clinical Theology Association.

Lowen, A. (1994) *Bioenergetics: The Revolutionary Therapy that uses the Language of the Body to Heal the Problems of the Mind*, Harmondsworth: Penguin.

Nyanaponika Thera (1975) *The Heart of Buddhist Meditation*, London: Rider.

——(1986) *The Vision of Dhamma*, London: Rider.

Reich, W. (1933) *Character Analysis*, New York: Noonday.

Rogers, C.R. (1951) *Client-centered Therapy: Its Current Practice, Implications and Theory*, Boston, MA: Houghton Mifflin.

Rolf, I.P. (1989) *Rolfing: Re-establishing the Natural Alignment and Structural Integration of the Human Body for Vitality and Well-being*, Rochester, VT: Healing Arts Press.

Sheldon, W.H. (with the collaboration of Stevens, S.S. and Tucker, W.B.) (1940) *The Varieties of Human Physique: An Introduction to Constitutional Psychology*, New York: Harper.

Sheldrake, R. (1982) *A New Science of Life*, New York: Tarcher.

Sills, F. (2007) 'Being and becoming', unpublished work in progress.

Sucitto, Ajahn (2003) 'Cultivating the Brahma Viharas', Sussex: Dhamma talk at Chithurst Monastery, July.

Sumedho, Ajahn (1990) *Teachings of a Buddhist Monk*, Sharpham, Devon: Buddhist Publishing Group, Amaravati Publications.

Thich Nhat Hanh (1988) *The Heart of Understanding*, Berkeley, CA: Parallax Press.

Winnicott, D. (1965) *The Maturational Processes and the Facilitating Environment*, London: Hogarth.

# WHEN PSYCHE MEETS SOMA

## The question of incarnation

*Beverley Zabriskie*

## The central question

The issue of the body is entangled in the mythic roots of psychoanalysis. Since Freud turned to the ancient tale of Oedipus, psychoanalytic inquiry has focused on two of Oedipus' three encounters: Oedipus' patricidal collision with his father, and his incestuous mating with his mother. But Oedipus' journey included another fateful episode. Between murdering his father and marrying his mother, Oedipus faced the Sphinx. The monstrous Sphinx asked the question learned from the Muses: 'What being, with only one voice, has sometimes two feet, sometimes three, sometimes four, and is weakest when it has the most?'

Oedipus' answer has echoed through the centuries: 'Man, because he crawls on all fours as an infant, stands firmly on his two feet in his youth, and leans upon a staff in his old age.' (Graves 1960: 372).

Psychoanalysis has focused on the parental dramas of Oedipus as afflicted son, rather than on the riddle's subject: the body. Despite the theoretical discourse about the body – should it be on a couch, or in a chair? – despite an emphasis on sexuality, the body has been present as an absence in many psychoanalytic traditions. In attending more directly to the realities of the body, current psychotherapies take up the response to the Sphinx and the existential riddle that locates the body at the centre of human concerns about time, mortality and the sequence of incarnated life.

## The imaginal Sphinx

The Sphinx is interested in how embodied man crawls, walks and hobbles. And yet, with her woman's head, lion's body, serpent's tail and eagle's wings, she herself springs from the human imagination, a faculty that moves freely through and beyond the body. Both monstrous and mythic, the Sphinx is a creature of nature and fantasy, a mixture born from human observation and caprice.

The riddle presumes much: that a human being is a creature of culture able to contemplate and reflect on itself as a creature of nature, and can give voice to its experience in language. It presumes the capacity for reflection, expression, imagination and invention.

Oedipus, meanwhile, was painfully attuned to the paces and needs of the body. Taken from his mother at his birth, his feet were twice wounded by his father, first in infancy and then as the young man on the road. With his early wounding and wounds, he knew the imperatives of crawling on all fours, of standing on his own two legs, and of seeking support.

The issue between Oedipus and the Sphinx brings the body to the fore as the vehicle and venue of human totality, rather than as an instrument driven toward perversion. The sweep of the riddle is more embracing and inclusive than whether men wish to kill their fathers and sleep with their mothers, and deeper than motifs of abandonment and revenge.

In the current and active discourse among the analytic traditions, the expressive analyses, body therapies and neurosciences, we are again confronting the Sphinx head on, so to speak, and pursuing the pivotal exchange between monster and man. In reframing the ancestral narrative of the psychotherapies to zoom in on that scene, we gather information from our natural existence on all fours and muse on the possible thirds that support limping humankind.

As members of the helping professions, we continue the exploration of human life as movement from the four and the two of nature, toward a third perspective: speculation, reflection, synthesis. We do not submit to our fates through the words of Oracles, but rather accept and engage our humanity as both physical and psychic. As psychological beings, we intervene in the givens, to move from sensations to feelings, from reactions to responses, from pain into suffering, from pleasure into joy, from existence into experience, from the meaningless to the meaningful.

Knowing the answer did not save the young Oedipus from the painful process of living out his crippling life to a lame and blind old age. Knowledge and consciousness, talking and understanding do not avert us from the progressions and consequences of the mortal life. But alertness to what Jung called 'the psychoid', the spectrum of felt and considered experience where the physical and the psychic meet, offers a point of reflection on which to lean as we proceed in both our lives and practices as creatures of body and psyche.

In the imaginal language and metaphor of embodied mind, we are summoning the Sphinx. Its weight gives perceptual and imaginal gravitas to the butterfly, the elusive and ephemeral creature whose Greek name is 'psyche'. While the 'therapoids' of the ancient Greek world were those in service to the psyche or soul, as modern therapoids, we pursue the riddle and reality that the butterfly cannot fly far from the Sphinx's preoccupation with the physical dimensions of humanity and human existence. As analysis of the conscious and unconscious spectrum of the psyche increasingly converges with the brain–body spectrum of the neurosciences and the mind–body range of body-oriented and expressive therapies, we are still finding new questions and answers about the domains and dimensions of the human enterprise.

## The question of the ages

From archaic ritual to the most current neurosciences, the lifespan of the body has occupied the human mind.

The body – as the carrier of life, and the vehicle for death – has been a focus since we first had the notion of mind – that is, the capacity to be both subject and object, the ability to reflect, observe, wonder, and so suffer. The body – its needs, its wants, its capacities and its limits – has been the stimulus and the source of most endeavours, from the most poetic imaginings, to artistic achievements, to experimental research –whether it be in the mummy embalming rooms of ancient Egyptian pyramids or the laboratories of the neurosciences.

While an emergent property of body, expansive mind's objection to the felt limits of mortal incarnation has also been the prime provocateur of human imagination. The body has been perceived as the vehicle of death and the means to the afterworld. Even our Neolithic ancestors arranged the bodies of their dead in a foetal position, facing east, so that they might participate in the rising of the sun.

Since ancient times, the body has both been celebrated as a temple of experience, and denigrated as the prison of perdition, requiring denial and flagellation. Our myths and religions have employed the hope for transcendence – framed as the life of the soul after the death of the body – to promote fantasies of heavenly compensations and warn of hellish consequences beyond the mortal edge. The different paths to these ends still inform the immense cultural and religious divides of our various systems of belief, still shape collective identities and struggles.

I was reminded of this while travelling recently in the Spanish Pyrenees. In a ceiling fresco of a Romanesque church in a small mountain town, on one side, angels beckon naked women and men happily popping out of their graves, their resurrected bodies carrying their tombstones as if they were light as feathers. On the opposite ceiling slope, devils seize the deemed sinners, and herd them into the fiery mouth of a devouring dragon. The faces of the damned and of the redeemed express opposite emotions of expected joy and dreaded doom.

Looking at the church ceiling, I recalled ancient Egyptian imagery suggesting a similar sensibility. In the moment of judgement at life's end, the person's heart would be put on one side of a scale, and a feather on the other. If the person had found inner truth and lived in right relation to the laws of the kingdom and the cycles of the earth and universe, one's heart would be light as a feather, and the person would proceed toward the after-life. If the heart was heavy, it would fall off the scale into the mouth of a devouring chimera.

Three days later, in the Bilbao Guggenheim Museum, I saw the compelling installations of a video artist entitled 'Bill Viola: Temporality and Transcendence'. Now in high tech form, here were angels again, huge audio-video images of mortality and transformation: *Five Angels for the Millennium*, which I had seen first at the Tate Modern; Viola's version of the Egyptian Book of the Dead, *Going Forth by Day*, *The Crossing* and *The Passing*.

On screens and with surround sound, there were extraordinary images of the body's descent and ascent, of annihilation by fire and water, of drowning and emerging from the waters. And there were frames from his series *Passions,* with modern faces showing timeless emotions from fear and astonishment, from anguish to joy.

These art works – the centuries old naive Christian iconography and the sound and imagery of a contemporary Zen video artist – address the same psychologically complex question. While moving along the chronological spectrum of our bodies' mortal lives, do we simultaneously experience psychic dying and deaths, renewals and resurgences, descents and ascents? If burned in suffering, or drowned in grief, do we rise to the occasions and re-enter the next cycle of life? Is life lived only on the mortal, material slope toward the dragon of death, or is human life to be engaged as a process, of sequential releases and renewals, within and yet not determined only by the physical passage of the body?

As psychotherapists, we frame these questions in psychological terms, not in the theologies of religious beliefs nor as artistic vision. For psychotherapy, these are the issues of the considered life and of identity: what is more than genetic in the individual? What is more than statistical in the personal? What is mind if not brain? What is psyche if not body?

To the truth of our senses, we add the explicit and implicit understanding that a person's life is not a string of facts, but rather a series of experiential occasions. As the individual psyche influences how one experiences and narrates the occasions of a life, it can modify, calibrate and reorient the creation and reception of experience.

The body as subject has been the ground of self-experience, the knower of pleasure, the carrier of relationship, the instrument of creation and procreation. Our bodies tie us to our past, allow us to be present in the present, and lead us toward our future. They take us both to life-affirming encounters and death in personal and collective collisions. The body is also the bearer of pain.

The body as object has evoked the desire to love and adore, excited the need to exercise control over oneself or another, and incited the sadistic obsession to possess, torture and destroy. It has also been a means of meditation about matter and mind, psyche and body.

My perspective emerges from my Jungian tradition, Jung's attention to bodily states, and his insistence on the importance of emotions. For confirmation, he often turned to historical symbolic systems as reservoirs for personal and collective speculation.

As Jung perceived mind and matter as two concepts for the same substance, he was drawn to the work of pre-enlightenment philosophers and experimenters who used the operations of alchemy as Rorschach tests. Thinkers and scientists, such as Cambridge's Isaac Newton, tested the correspondences between matters of the mind and the mind in matter by observing transmutations in their experimental materials while meditating on transformations in their inner states. Watching the interactions of salts, sulphurs and mercury, they formulated theories of intrapsychic dynamics among body and spirit and soul. The experimenter's integrity as a soul–spirit–body triad in an interactive relation with the world depended on careful calibration amidst lived experience, reflection, and meaning. This sensibility of inner and outer correspondences was split in two with the Cartesian dualism of 'I think, therefore I am'.

Just as Jung looked to pre-Enlightenment alchemistic philosophies to heal that split, the neuroscientist Antonio Damasio called his 1994 study *Descartes' Error* and in 2003 published *Looking for Spinoza*. In our various psychological approaches, in the physical sciences, and in the neurosciences, we are again placing the human being as a mind–body continuum in correspondence, context, and conjunction with the surrounding world.

## The psychoid emotions

The inquiry into how psyche uses body was central in the nineteenth century studies in Paris of hysteria and conversion syndromes by Charcot and Janet. Meanwhile, in the United States, William James was positing fields of experience, and fluid margins between mind and matter, conscious and unconscious, the invisible activities of depth psychology and the non-visible actions in subatomic physics.

Jung studied in Paris and read James while also working with inpatients at the Burghölzli clinic, a therapeutic community, where his chief, Ernst Bleuler, sought the chemical bases of schizophrenia. As a 29-year-old psychiatrist, in 1904, Jung further developed the word association experiment, demonstrating how psychogalvanic markers, anomalous timing and reactions point to a 'complex', a 'bundle' or quantum of emotionally laden psycho-physical energy which reacted reflexively. Taking this as body's evidence for the existence of an unconscious, Jung sent his results to Freud in 1907. Hence the body brought them together. As so often happens, this meeting around body did not guarantee a lasting relationship.

In his private practice, Jung pursued an interactive model which led to his theory of the 'psychoid', of psyche in its most embodied forms: the complex, the emotions, and the active imagination. Addressing clinicians (including Bion) at the Tavistock clinic in 1935, Jung spoke of 'a projection which happens between two individuals . . . of an emotional and compulsory nature' (Jung 1935: 138). Emotions 'of the projected content always forms a link, a sort of dynamic relationship between the subject and the object – and that is the transference' (Jung 1935: 138). As the 'emotions of patients . . . are very contagious when the contents which the patient projects into the analyst are identical with the analyst's own unconscious contents'; then they 'both fall into the same dark hole of unconsciousness and get into the condition of participation. This is the phenomenon which Freud described as countertransference' (Jung 1935: 140).

The psychotherapist, he continued, may become 'psychically infected'. While psychotherapists are thus 'apt to become a little queer', it remains the doctor's 'duty to accept the emotions of the patient and to mirror them' (Jung 1935: 139).

In *The Psychology of the Transference*, Jung's concept of countertransference alludes to historical precedents. He wrote that analysts are like

the old alchemists [who] were often doctors . . . they could collect information of a psychological nature, not only from their patients but also
from themselves, i.e., from the observation of their own unconscious
contents which had been activated by induction.

(Jung 1946: 201)

Such psychological induction 'inevitably causes the two parties to get involved in
the transformation of the third and to be themselves transformed in the process.
(Jung 1946: 199).

For Jung, emotions are 'not detachable like ideas or thoughts, because they are
identical with certain physical conditions and are thus deeply rooted in the heavy
matter of the body' (Jung 1946: 138). He extends the continuum from ideas and
body to psyche and matter: 'psyche and matter exist in one and the same world, and
each partakes of the other' (Jung 1951: 261).

In therapeutic interactions, projection creates the third realm of an activated
field of relational energy. The vibrations and oscillations of physical energy fields
registered and shared by two perceiving bodies and reflecting minds are more
noticeable in the intensified analytic transference field.

Contemporary neuroscience confirms this thesis. In *The Mind-Brain Reality*,
Regina Pally writes:

While most of psychoanalytic literature has focused on the unconscious
symbolic meaning of non-verbal communication, neuroscience emphasizes the unconscious influence that one person's non verbal communication has on another's biology, emotion, and verbal conversation . . .
[and] reveal that non-verbal communication of emotion, as is well illustrated by attachment, regulates minds and bodies between individuals
. . . carry information about bio-emotional states between individuals,
thus regulating the biological functioning of both people.

(Pally 2000: 95)

To function in this psychoid domain, all sorts and levels of affect, sensory awareness, association, and reverberation within and between the psyches of both patient
and analyst must be privileged and registered as sensations and affects arising from
a mutual field of commingled psycho-physical energies. Sometimes these emerge
through perceived anomalies, or confirmed correspondences between the patient
and the analyst, between inner states and outer occurrences. If the therapeutic space
is secure, these may be explored from a psychic perspective, and given internal and
relational relevance and meaning. If dismissed, they live in the bogs of our brains,
made soggy with murky suspicions that after all, life is fate determined by magic
rather than destiny guided by choice.

We all have many examples from practice of charged and synchronous communications between psyche and body. We often do not expose them, under the
illusion that to contribute to science, we must stress statistical results and quantified
research.

Our fear of being 'soft' has kept us from full description of our empirical experience. While scientists must submit to matter and measurement, they have not laboured under such internal restrictions.

The Nobel Laureate neuroscientist Gerald Edelman (1992: 114) discusses 'qualia', that is, phenomenal or felt properties, 'the collection of personal or subjective experiences, feelings, and sensations that accompany awareness'. They are

> phenomenal states – 'how things seem to us' as human beings . . . the actual sequence of qualia is highly individual, resting on a series of occasions in one's own personal history or immediate experience.
>
> (Edelman 1992: 114)

Edelman observes that we 'cannot construct a phenomenal psychology that can be shared in the same way as a physics can be shared.' (Edelman 1992:114) Yet, he concludes: 'It is our ability to report and correlate while individually experiencing qualia that opens up the possibility of a scientific investigation of consciousness' (Edelman 1992: 115).

Pally writes that

> perceptual processing contains both ubiquitous, species-wide elements and personal, individual elements. Neuroscience offers psychoanalysis the opportunity for a deeper understanding of how our perceptions are shaped by the past, by our emotions, and by influences of which we are unaware.
>
> (Pally 2000: 20)

The neuroscientific observations of brain offers weighty proofs for the anecdotal observations of the psychotherapies. Often, its findings foster a humanization of mental illnesses, freeing them from unconscious fundamentalist and often gendered judgements about the sources and causes of psychic and emotional disturbance.

Conversely, the human moments from therapeutic practice give flesh to skeletal scans and statistics. They offer the incarnated context of therapist and patient working not only to recognize the circuits of the brain but also to unpack the embodied wisdom of the mind.

## Information through imagery

Jung also followed Theodore Flournoy in his emphasis on imagery as a form of communication in the therapeutic process. He once remarked 'every word of wisdom is the truth of the instincts – it simply reveals the image which is buried behind the instincts. Instinct is the dynamic side of the images' (Jung 1997: 684). He also described images as 'the instinct's perceptions of itself':

> The richness of the human psyche and its essential character are probably determined by this reflective instinct. Reflection re-enacts the process of excitation and carries the stimulus over into a series of images which are

reproduced in some form of expression. This may take place directly in speech, abstract thought, dramatic representation, or ethical conduct, or again, in a scientific achievement or a work of art.

(Jung 1947: 117)

For physicist David Bohm, images are 'a key bridge between the older emotional brain and the more intellectual neocortex' (Bohm 1988: 26). The neuroscientist Rudolfo Llinas and his colleagues suggest a neurological basis for an internal, image-creating process. They speak of 'endogenesis', the generation of survival-enhancing images by intrinsic, continuing processes of the brain rather than sensory experience through incoming signals from the world (Llinas and Church-land 1997).

In analytic practice, there are frequent synchronous communications through shared imagery. The therapist notes that an image comes unbidden, as if up from body into mind, and some time later in the session, a patient tells a dream with precisely that image: a turtle, a waterfall, a blackbird. Like the vibration – oscilla-tions of physical energy fields – the shared imagery of two perceiving bodies and reflecting minds are more easily noted in the intensified analytic field, informed by the notion that on the continuums of body–mind, and mind–brain, body's internal and external perceptions are metabolized by mind as imagery.

What is the matrix by which images are non-verbally communicated among and between persons? Contemporary astrophysics theorizes an 'anthropic principle' which contends that as animate beings made up of the same combinations as the elements of the universe in which we exist, we can finally understand its deep structures. Mathematicians theorize that 'the human brain, as part of nature, obeys nature's laws, and thus may have evolved to detect the patterns that are 'really present' (Stewart and Golubitsky 1993: 259). In other words, symbols which emerge from imagination and the psyche may be effective and communicable because we exist in a continuum of a macrocosmic network to which our micro-cosmic minds are kin.

## Body in practice

In my practice, I have observed an especially moving and shaking genre of unconscious imagery in dreams of patients who are dealing, knowingly or unknow-ingly, with injury, disease and death. There have been dreams of going beyond the crossroads into a land of grey fog, or of going into the surf and not returning.

As instinct and imagery, as psyche and body reflect each other, images in patients' dreams offer comment on physical disease and impending deaths. When therapists engage with patients' illnesses and terminal states, we must differentiate between the ego–body and psyche–body relationship. With obvious exceptions, the ego cannot be held responsible for an illness, while the psyche has many ways of responding.

In one clinical instance, an older woman was corrosively angry at her-self for smoking and subsequent lung cancer. She could not find peace.

220

I then reminded her that after she suffered sexual abuse as a child, the only medication available to her in that time and place was nicotine. Her smoking habit formed in the attempt to treat the depression and anxiety of trauma and post traumatic stress.

I have often heard the axiom that a patient can defer or dispel illness by finding its meaning. This ascribes magical meaning to the disease and fosters an anti-therapeutic tendency to blame the patient if there is no cure. This mistakenly locates meaning in illness itself, rather than in the depth dimensions of human responses to injury and illness.

In the interactions of body and psyche, and the intrapsychic domains of conscious and unconscious knowing, the dream is often the mediating third. At times of crisis and illness, life and death conflict, Jung observed archetypal images.

Some time ago, a celibate brother in a religious order came into treatment. Then 55, he had not spoken to a woman other than his mother since he entered the order at 16 years old. I was impressed at the rapid openness with which he revealed himself. After a few months, on a Tuesday before Christmas, he dreamt:

I hear an explosion in the attic of my house. I rush to the telephone to call for help. As I pick up the receiver, I look into a mirror. On the other side of the glass, a woman sits surrounded by a circle of men. She beckons to me. Transfixed, I hang up before the call goes through. I step into the mirror to join her. She says: 'By June, you will be dead.'

On hearing this dream, I recalled Jean Cocteau's film scene of Orpheus entering the underworld through a mirror. Four days after his dream, during his annual family Christmas visit, this man had a cerebral haemorrhage – an explosion in the attic of his body. He died with his head in his mother's lap. By Juno – the archaic great mother figure – he was dead.

Sometimes a dream may contain an image of healing. Often these dreams also have an archetypal valence. I have written elsewhere (Zabriskie 2000) of an analysis of an elderly man with hepatitis B, which had eaten at his liver. Then a liver tumour was found. As he prepared for his medical treatment, he dreamt:

I am sitting in my analyst's office alone. She comes through a door – not the door to the waiting room but its twin door, which leads to the back hall, unknown and unseen. As she enters, she lifts her skirts, revealing her private parts. I am astounded, perplexed, and amazed.'

The figure of the female revealing herself is, in many cultures, a typical ritual gesture and an act of regeneration and restoration at times of need, grief and crisis.

In one myth, the crone Baubo shows her genitals to make the mourning Demeter, in grief for her lost daughter Persephone, laugh. The Egyptian goddess Hathor, who personifies the energy which conceives, creates, brings forth, rears, encourages, maintains, and celebrates, plays a similar part in her quintessential myth. When the old sun god Ra was sulkily retreated from his battles, as 'mother to her father', Hathor came and bared her private parts. Ra, roused to laughter, arose and went forth again.

> The physical implication of the dream and this figure became apparent when the patient later received his medical report. Chemotherapy killed the tumour which was hanging from the bottom of his liver. 'Complete Necrosis'. But the effects of hepatic disease block the flow of blood through the liver toward the heart, so waste products are not processed. This man's life was preserved because his 'peri umbilical collateral vessels' reawakened. In other words, the dormant umbilical system from his time in the womb was reactivated from the pressure of his blood, which then bypassed the diseased liver. 'The image is the instinct's perception of itself.' His dream announced the presence of regenerative process before the MRI recorded it.

In dreams, the body is often depicted as a powerful, instinctive animal. Before a serious illness, Jung had a dream in which his illness and recovery were suggested through the image of an undomesticated beast:

> The primeval boar, a gigantic mythological beast, has finally been hunted down and killed. It has been skinned, its head cut off, the body is divided lengthwise like a slaughtered pig, the two halves only just hanging together at the neck. We are occupied with the task of bringing the huge mass of meat to our tribe. The task is difficult. Once the meat fell into a roaring torrent that swept it into the sea. We had to fetch it back again. Finally we reach the tribe. A great ritual feast is going to be celebrated.
> (Jung 1975: 606–7)

The body is the locus of individuality and personal definition, the source of emotion, imagery, and also empathy. The body is also the common ground we share with all humans, as well as our means of relationship and communication.

Our bodies link us to all other sentient beings in our own time and era, and to all who have ever been embodied. They provide us with the vehicle through which the psyche expresses itself as we crawl, walk, and limp through the many phases of our incarnated lives, and give voice to the experience of being human.

# References

Bohm, D. (1988) 'Beyond relativity and quantum theory', *Psychological Perspectives* 2 (spring/summer): 25–43.

Edelman, G. (1992) *Bright Air, Brilliant Fire: On the Matter of the Mind*, New York: Basic Books.

Graves, R. (1960) *The Greek Myths*, New York: Penguin.

Jung, C.G. (1935) Lecture V, Tavistock Lectures, *Collected Works*, Vol. 18, Princeton, NJ: Princeton University Press.

——(1946) *The Psychology of the Transference*, *Collected Works*, Vol. 16, Princeton, NJ: Princeton University Press.

——(1947) *On the Nature of the Psyche*, *Collected Works*, Vol. 8, Princeton, NJ: Princeton University Press.

——(1951) 'Researches into the phenomenology of the self', *Collected Works*, Vol. 9(ii), Princeton, NJ: Princeton University Press.

——(1975) *Letters*, Vol. 2, in G. Adler (ed.) Princeton, NJ: Princeton University Press.

——(1997) *Visions*, Princeton, NJ: Princeton University Press.

Llinas, R. and Churchland, P. (1997) *The Mind-Brain Continuum*, New York: Carfax.

Pally, R. (2000) *The Mind-Brain Reality*, London: Karnac.

Stewart, I. and Golubitsky, M. (1993) *Fearful Symmetry: Is God a Geometer?* London: Penguin.

Zabriskie, B. (2000) 'Transference and dream in illness: waxing psyche, waning body', *Journal of Analytical Psychology* 45 (1): 93–107.

# INDEX

Page entries for main headings which have subheadings represent general aspects of that topic.
Page entries for tables are denoted in **bold**
Page entries for figures are denoted in *italic*